TRUTH AND INDIGNATION

TRUTH AND INDIGNATION

Canada's Truth and Reconciliation Commission
on Indian Residential Schools

Second Edition

Ronald Niezen

Teaching Culture: UTP Ethnographies for the Classroom

UNIVERSITY OF TORONTO PRESS

Copyright © University of Toronto Press 2017
Higher Education Division

www.utorontopress.com

Library and Archives Canada Cataloguing in Publication

Niezen, Ronald, author

      Truth and indignation : Canada's Truth and Reconciliation Commission on Indian residential schools / Ronald Niezen. — Second edition.

(Teaching culture : UTP ethnographies for the classroom)
Includes bibliographical references and index.

Issued in print and electronic formats.

ISBN 978-1-4875-9438-1 (softcover).—ISBN 978-1-4875-9440-4 (PDF).— ISBN 978-1-4875-9439-8 (EPUB)

      1. Truth and Reconciliation Commission of Canada. 2. Native peoples—Canada—Residential schools. 3. Truth commissions—Social aspects—Canada. 4. Ethnological jurisprudence—Canada. I. Title. II. Series: Teaching culture

E96.5.N54 2017   371.829'97071   C2017-903405-7   C2017-903406-5

We welcome comments and suggestions regarding any aspect of our publications—please feel free to contact us at news@utphighereducation.com or visit our Internet site at www.utorontopress.com.

North America	UK, Ireland, and continental Europe
5201 Dufferin Street	NBN International
North York, Ontario, Canada, M3H 5T8	Estover Road, Plymouth, PL6 7PY, UK
	ORDERS PHONE: 44 (0) 1752 202301
2250 Military Road	ORDERS FAX: 44 (0) 1752 202333
Tonawanda, New York, USA, 14150	ORDERS E-MAIL: enquiries@nbninternational.com

ORDERS PHONE: 1-800-565-9523
ORDERS FAX: 1-800-221-9985
ORDERS E-MAIL: utpbooks@utpress.utoronto.ca

The University of Toronto Press acknowledges the financial support for its publishing activities of the Government of Canada through the Canada Book Fund.

Printed in Canada

CONTENTS

ABBREVIATIONS

AFN	Assembly of First Nations
AHF	Aboriginal Healing Foundation
CBC	Canadian Broadcasting Corporation
CEP	Common Experience Payment
FPIC	free, prior, and informed consent
IAP	Independent Assessment Process
IRS	Indian residential school(s)
IRSSA	Indian Residential School Settlement Agreement
NABS	Native American Boarding School Healing Coalition
POI	Person(s) of Interest
PTSD	post-traumatic stress disorder
RCAP	Royal Commission on Aboriginal Peoples
RCMP	Royal Canadian Mounted Police
RHSW	Resolution Health Support Worker
TRC	Truth and Reconciliation Commission of Canada

FIGURES

PREFACE TO THE
SECOND EDITION

This second edition of *Truth and Indignation* was planned from the beginning. When the project began, the Truth and Reconciliation Commission (TRC) on Indian Residential Schools had not yet started its hearings and I did not know quite what to expect. Once things were under way, however, it did not take long to see how the Commission had chosen to approach statement gathering, to make ritual and symbolic forms of expression a central part of its activities, and in particular how it was limited by its mandate to what I now call "survivor centric" or (comparatively) "victim centric" forms of inquiry from certain individuals and not others. Under these circumstances, it seemed a good idea to produce a book while the Commission was still engaged in its work. This rationale was also connected to a commitment to "truth" or to the procedural logic of scholarly inquiry. In an institutional process of limited duration like the TRC, it is impossible for observations and conclusions to be checked against reality after the fact. By coming out with the book a year before the Commission was to submit its final report (two years, as it happened), the intention was to allow critics to check my observations against subsequent events of the Commission as it continued its work. Of course, there was always the risk that the Commission would change course and start doing something different, or that audiences in the remaining events would respond differently. As it turned out, the Commission remained remarkably consistent, despite the diversity of the indigenous peoples in Canada whose legacies of residential school experiences it was intended to address. The conditions were there for a contribution to productive critical engagement in the scholarship on the Truth and Reconciliation Commission.

That this did not happen—and more precisely *how* this did not happen—was to me the most surprising result of this book's early appearance. When I gave public talks, objections to the content of the first edition of this book focused on its presentation of narratives from the priests, brothers, and nuns who had been involved one way or another in the operation of the schools. One statement from an audience member, who identified herself as a residential school survivor, in the question period of a talk I gave at the Faculty of Law at McGill University has stood out in my memory as expressing the sentiment behind these objections particularly well: "The priests have had the dominant discourse for more than 150 years. Now it's our turn." (I honestly cannot remember how I replied.) This statement succinctly expresses a view of truth and history that is very important, and that in some ways defines the times. There is an argument here for privileging the voices of the once dominated. Truth has an inverse relationship to power. There is an "us" and "them" quality to legitimate knowledge, implying an element of political resurgence. All of this ran squarely against my (perhaps naive) intuition that the sense of offence and exclusion toward the work of the Commission by many of the people who ran the schools was something that needed to be written about and better understood.

This second edition is therefore centrally concerned with a problem of knowledge, the emergence of regimes of truth through public inquiry, and the production of history in the context of political mobilization and the quest for social justice. In taking on this topic, I have chosen to leave the text of the book largely unchanged, with only minor additions, updates, and corrections, leaving the substance of new work in an epilogue. Here my intention is first to bring the reader up to date with the work of the Commission and the public and institutional responses to the submission of its final report in December 2015. To this I have added some further reflections on the TRC and the problem of knowledge, presented in a wider context that considers "victim centrism" as an emerging aspect of the global project of transitional justice.

RONALD NIEZEN
Montreal, April 2017

PREFACE

The subject of Indian residential schools doesn't easily let go once it has gotten hold. It has all the markings of a cause that provokes a kind of persistent, nagging, sympathetic sense of wrong: the desecration of children's innocence by those with spiritual and institutional authority over them, the political harm inherent in policies of state-sanctioned assimilation, and government and church avoidance and obstruction of the work of the Commission, recalling their characterization by a peer reviewer of this book as unrepentant, "morally tainted perpetrator institutions." But I was also motivated to write this book by an additional perspective. An important incentive was provided by the opportunity to include the remembrances of residential schools and efforts to overcome their legacy by former educators—above all Oblate priests, brothers, and nuns, some of whom had worked in the schools and some who had not. This came about in 2009 when my research assistant, Marie-Pierre Gadoua, pursuing her doctoral project on Thule and Inuit artefacts in the collections of the Oblate's Deschâtelets residence in Ottawa, became aware of the priests' unusual (from the perspective of dominant public discourse) views concerning the history of these schools and the (then) recently implemented regimes of compensation and the Truth and Reconciliation Commission. In response to this information, I initiated a series of interviews at the Deschâtelets residence, which Marie-Pierre and I did singly or together, and which soon developed into what might be described as a national-scale campaign (international if one includes an interview done by Marie-Pierre in Rome) to follow through on the willingness of the Catholic clergy to put on record their views about the history of the schools and about the impact on their lives of the Independent Assessment Process (discussed in chapter 3) and the Truth and Reconciliation Commission (TRC) on Indian Residential Schools. I also initiated a wider study of the TRC once it was underway, broadening the scope of the inquiry to include local, regional, and national events, as well as interviews with organizers and participants.

Through the inclusion of the narratives of those who once worked in the schools or administered them, the topic became more multidimensional: it included the perspectives of the "accused," *their* sense of injustice emerging out of public moral rejection. More substantively, the project became about the production of knowledge and the construction of belonging as it broadened to include the way that knowledge is channelled along particular conduits of opinion that foreclose entire realms of experience. The topic became something more than a description of a truth and reconciliation commission in action; it became a potential source of insight into the creation of new narratives of suffering within contested narratives of power—in other words, a good place to spend some time investigating things in detail, just to see where the topic would go.

The publication of this material had its start with a chapter in *Public Justice and the Anthropology of Law*, where the subject of Canada's TRC serves as an illustration of the way that public audiences are able to influence legal process, and of the way that legal process, in turn, can be a source of social membership and identity. The context of this publication made it clear to me that the topic had more going for it than the exposure of controversy—not that appeal to readers' sense of wrong was in short supply. For those drawn to accounts of misguided policy and institutional harm, there is plenty here to make one indignant. But controversy alone is not a secure foundation for knowledge of social process. Public attentions are fickle, institutions adapt, and expectations are met or disappointed (it often doesn't matter which) as people move on to the next cause; meanwhile conditions of suffering might endure, but in new circumstances of invisibility and absence. The socially formative responses to controversy, it seems to me, are in some ways more significant than the causes themselves. The collective sense of indignation has a different, broader meaning than the particular causes that provoke it. Expressed as succinctly as possible, I am struggling to come to terms with a situation in which appeal to a universal humanity becomes a way to particularize the self. Or, to put it another way, this book has as much to do with the socially constructive power of rights as with the destructive power of wrongs.

Some readers will note (perhaps disapprovingly) that I am bringing this book to press while the Commission is still doing its work. In doing so, I am making an effort to use the long duration of the Commission to achieve an unusual exercise in scholarly accountability. In the brief window between the appearance of this book and the end of the mandate of the Commission, there may be an opportunity for readers to make their own observations, to do their own "event ethnography," and to compare what they find with what I have presented here. There could well be pedagogical and/or scholarly advantages to this that I will leave them to discover.

My research assistants were, each of them, more than trainees; they were active collaborators and motivators in this project, and without them it would not have even started. They include Amy Binning, Talia Bornstein, Gregory Brass, Gabriella Djerrahian, Doris Farget, Adam Fleischmann, Ian Kalman, Alexandra Olshefsky, and Abra Wenzel. I am saving for special acknowledgement (I'm sure the others won't mind) the contribution made by Marie-Pierre Gadoua, who first introduced me to the priests at the Maison Deschâtelets in Ottawa, thereby setting the whole thing in motion, and who contributed to the project throughout as an organizer, translator, bookkeeper, and researcher.

The employment of research assistants, travel to Commission events, and many other aspects of the study were enabled by generous funding from the Canada Research Chairs program and by an Insight Grant from the Social Sciences and Humanities Research Council. The manuscript benefited a great deal from the extensive and insightful remarks and suggestions made by three anonymous peer reviewers. It also benefited from a variety of conference, seminar, and workshop presentations. I am grateful for the insights and encouragement derived from participants of the Law and Society Association meeting in Honolulu; the American Anthropological Association meeting in San Francisco; a lecture and workshop at the Leibniz Institute for Regional Geography in Leipzig; a workshop on "Customary Law and Legal Pluralism" hosted by the Intellectual Property Issues in Cultural Heritage Project at York University, Toronto; a "Friday seminar" sponsored by the Centre for Society, Technology and Development (STANDD) at McGill University, Montreal; a workshop on "Indigenous Peoples, Truth and Reconciliation: Comparative and Critical Perspectives" hosted by the Centre for Human Rights and Legal Pluralism at McGill University; a workshop entitled "Rethinking Historical Trauma in North American Aboriginal Contexts" sponsored by the National Network for Aboriginal Mental Health Research; a workshop entitled "Native Residential Schools: Legacies for Research" sponsored by the Université de Montréal; and a panel at the 2013 meeting of the Association francophone pour le savoir (Acfas), "Les représentations mémorielles: entre traces, archives et reminiscences," hosted by the Université Laval, Quebec. Some of those who spoke with me on the subject matter of this book, at these meetings and outside of them, had particular influences on my knowledge and the direction I took with it (with no personal responsibility for either): Brieg Capitaine, Gabriella Coleman, Rosemary Coombe, Doris Farget, Mark Goodale, Robert Hitchcock, Laurence Kirmayer, Roderick Macdonald, Jane McMillan, Genevieve Painter, Tobias Rees, Alberto Sanchez, Maria Sapignoli, Colleen Sheppard, Karine Vanthuyne, Richard Wilson, and Allan Young.

Several aboriginal organizations were especially helpful in providing me access to the views and experiences of aboriginal people: the Onkwata'karitáhtshera Health and Social Services Research Council, Kahnawake, the Outreach Residential School Atlantic Committee (ORSAC), and Chief and Council of Chisasibi, Quebec. (The latter made consent available to me to conduct research at the TRC community event in Chisasibi, which I was unfortunately unable to attend. Karine Vanthuyne later kindly provided me with recordings from this event.)

I owe special gratitude to all those who were willing to participate in interviews (or, given the open-ended method that I used, perhaps I should say those who engaged in conversation), sometimes recorded and sometimes not. This included the priests, brothers, and nuns whom I have just acknowledged, but equally those who participated in the work of the Commission: survivors who gave statements in Commission hearings, health support workers who made efforts to make them feel safe and to comfort them, and organizers who worked tirelessly to make it all happen. Whatever other content or qualities this book might have, their voices are essential to its outcome.

RONALD NIEZEN
Montreal

Chapter 1

THE SENSE OF INJUSTICE

AFTER JUDGMENT

Many of us have become used to hearing about corporations being sued for a few million here and a billion or two there, so much so that the amounts involved have ceased to be "staggering" and are often of no more than passing interest. This might explain why the largest restitution award in Canadian history did not garner much attention. The cost to the Government of Canada and to the churches that are signatory to the Indian Residential School Settlement Agreement (IRSSA) has not been finally determined because compensation is still being awarded to individuals on a case-by-case basis, but it will certainly be in the billions. And it is somehow right and proper that the billions involved should fail to capture our interest because there are other things happening around this event that are more compelling, or at least that deserve to be so.

The settlement's cost stems from the national-historical nature of the harm at its origin. Spanning a period of approximately 100 years, from the late nineteenth century to the late twentieth century, the federal government of Canada put into effect a policy of Indian education through residential schools, based largely on an already established US model of Indian boarding schools. The main distinguishing quality of Canada's residential school program was that it involved collaboration between the federal government and a variety of Christian churches: Anglican, Catholic (especially the Oblates of Mary Immaculate, responsible for some 60 per cent of the schools across Canada), Presbyterian, and United. At the time of Canadian Confederation in 1867, there were two schools in operation. By the time the last schools closed in the mid-1990s, approximately 140 Indian residential schools (IRS) housing 150,000 children had been in operation. There are some 86,000 people alive today who once spent time as a child in an Indian residential school. And (as I discuss further in chapter 2) it is their removal from their families and their frequent experience of abuse in the schools that was at the origin of the lawsuits in the early 2000s that resulted in a Settlement Agreement and one of the most costly regimes of compensation ever awarded as an outcome of litigation.

Interesting as this might be, the main subject matter of this book concerns what happens on the other side of the courtroom and the out-of-court negotiations, in the period after judgment—the remedial processes sometimes referred to as "transitional justice"—in which truth and reconciliation commissions have recently become key institutions. The harms committed through the residential school policy were cumulatively recognized as a serious, systemic human rights violation. This calls for more than jail time for perpetrators of the worst abuses and a financial penalty for the institutions involved. It calls for the state to be more fully brought to account; it calls for the consequences of state action to be narrated and publicly recognized; and, through such recognition, it calls for assurance that the same kind of harms will not be repeated. In the interest of recognizing harms and avoiding their recurrence, truth and reconciliation commissions have become the remedy of choice in the aftermaths of many serious human rights violations.[1] In *Unspeakable Truths*, Priscilla Hayner provides a detailed survey of forty truth commissions that have taken place over the past forty years. The chronology starts inauspiciously with the 1974 Commission of Inquiry into the Disappearance of People in Uganda, which worked under and made recommendations to the government of Idi Amin; through the highly influential 1995–2002 Truth and Reconciliation Commission of South Africa; and up to the current or just-completed commissions that began their work in 2009, including that of Canada. The central insight brought by Hayner's survey is that there is no single answer to the problems of organization, allocation and use of judicial power, and how to manage (if at all) the human impact of painful memories and national self-examination.

We can illustrate the varying solutions to common problems found by truth commissions worldwide with reference to the issue they all face of "naming names." How does one balance judicial principles of due process with popular demands of perpetrator identification and retribution? South Africa dealt with this issue in part through its carefully constructed regime of conditional amnesty, essentially encouraging perpetrators to name themselves by giving testimony about their involvement in political crimes, with amnesty being conditional upon their truthfulness; meanwhile, the names of the accused were regularly broadcast in media coverage of the public hearings.[2] Argentina's truth commission, established in the aftermath of the disappearances and torture that took place in the anti-communist "dirty war," received testimony from over 600 survivors of detention camps and faced a difficult decision about whether to publish the names of those identified as abusers, ultimately opting to include some names in passages of testimony cited in its report. And Chile's commission, investigating state-sponsored violence under the Pinochet regime, made the decision not to publish the names of perpetrators in its report, citing a mandate that prevented it from taking a position on the legal responsibility of individuals. The list of names of those accused of torture and murder compiled by the Chilean commission has consequently never appeared in public.[3] Due to the unique circumstances of litigation at its origin, Canada's TRC was the only truth commission to have so thoroughly extinguished the identities of possible perpetrators from its proceedings, preventing their names from even entering the record through survivor narratives, and maintaining their invisibility and anonymity all the way through the Commission's activities. As I will soon discuss further, Canada's TRC to a unique degree gave preference to information-gathering and dissemination over judicial process.

Anyone who has seriously considered the acts of bearing witness in truth commissions will recognize that they can be simultaneously replete with possibilities of insight and ambiguity. Some might be initially drawn almost against their wills to the horrors that are the subjects of testimony, not the seemingly mundane act of *giving* testimony. The images and information we pay attention to first usually turn out to be less compelling than the perplexing fact that we are compelled by them. I am more interested in the things that are in the background of a survivor being in front of a microphone and saying what they have to say. They are there because of something horrible that happened in the past, something that was done to them or that they did, something for which the state was ultimately responsible. The past tense here is important: it *happened*. This is where the truly significant issues begin. What stands between experience and narration? What is the motivational connection between the events of the past and the later telling of it? What makes it important or even necessary to tell one's story, to narrate personal pain publicly in the context of collective victimization? Not everyone does. Something between the violence and the telling of it provided an incentive for the witness to speak.

There are four unique qualities of Canada's Truth and Reconciliation Commission on Indian Residential Schools that make the connections between event, memory, and narration especially problematic. First, Canada's was the only TRC to have been initiated as an outcome of civil litigation. It was not conceived in the aftermath of a brutal war, there were no journalists who died on the front lines, and because of this it did not have the kind of national and international attention that feeds into a broad public will to overcome a legacy of state-sponsored harm. Truth and reconciliation commissions are usually associated with regime change (hence the term "transitional justice") and come from a general awareness of (if not direct experience with) the harms of the state. When TRCs are held, the interruption of the trajectory of the state is considered to have already occurred. The Commission has been given a mandate intended to overcome a legacy of harm and to mark a transition to a new, more just, equitable, and human-rights-compliant state.

But the judgments that took place in the background of Canada's Truth and Reconciliation Commission were those of the courts, outcomes of litigation, not of history. This unique circumstance has several consequences that are important to consider. Foremost, the Commission began its work with the understanding that there was little public awareness and acknowledgement of the history of the human rights abuses in question, certainly less than has been the case in other truth commissions. This included a relative lack of awareness of the existence of the Commission itself. And following from this, it meant that the Commission was actively engaged in promoting this public awareness, even as it gathered testimony. Ultimately, it meant that the testimony presented to the Commission was oriented more toward the persuasion of others concerning its basic premises, leaving more room for doubt and contestation over institutional responsibility and the essential truths of history. To an unusual degree among truth commissions, its organizers saw themselves as facing the challenge of persuasion, of convincing public audiences that, taken together, the realities depicted in the lead-up to trials and negotiations have a historic dimension that calls for reform of the dominant narrative of the state.

The second unique feature of Canada's Truth and Reconciliation Commission (closely related to the first) has to do with the extent to which its terms of reference separated it from judicial proceedings or powers. The mandate of the TRC was constructed through the negotiations of the Settlement Agreement, and it took on a number of qualities that bear the imprint of this fact. Under the terms of the Agreement, the TRC was prevented from holding formal hearings, acting as a public inquiry, or conducting any kind of legal process. It was, in other words, designed as an information-gathering rather than a judicial body. An out-of-court process of compensation, the Independent Assessment Process (discussed further in chapter 3), was established through the Settlement Agreement as a separate regime from the TRC, and it was in the Independent Assessment Process's private hearings where accused perpetrators were sometimes named and given the opportunity to respond. But the a-judicial qualities of the Commission went further than its partition from compensation regimes. It did not have subpoena powers, and it had no other mechanism to compel attendance or participation in any of its events or activities. As mentioned, it was prevented from "naming names," from identifying any person in any of its activities or reports without the consent of that individual, unless the identity of that person had already been established through legal proceedings (i.e., by being convicted of the alleged wrongdoing). There was no dilemma at the conclusion of the Commission concerning what to do with the identities of possible perpetrators, because there was never a list of names; the Commission was prevented by its terms of reference from receiving them into the record in the first place. Nor was it permitted to make reference in its reports or recommendations to any possible civil or criminal liability of any person or organization. That is to say, in contrast to those truth commissions that prioritize prosecution (such as that of East Timor, with its Special Panels for Serious Crimes), Canada's TRC was prevented from acting on any possible extension of "truth-telling" into judicial procedure.[4] In comparative terms, it can be situated squarely among "victim-centred" truth commissions, such as those in Rwanda and Nigeria, established in the aftermath of ethnically based violence.[5] It was from the outset released into a limited enclosure, with no range of authority that might lead to some sort of reckoning for the responsible or extend the information it received beyond a focus on victim narratives.[6]

The third unique quality of Canada's TRC is that it was the only truth commission with a primary focus on the victimization of children. Other commissions, of course, have included harm done to children within their range of inquiry, and a few, such as the second Ugandan commission of 1986–95 and the Sierra Leone commission of 2002–4,[7] considered in depth the harm done to children who were recruited as sexual slaves and soldiers. But in Canada's TRC the victimization of children was the single, central, unwavering focus. This means that the distance in time between the violence and narration of it was unusually long and was usually based upon childhood memories. There was a greater expanse than in any other truth commission between the personal experience of harm and the narration of it.

Finally, more than in any other truth commission, the TRC on Indian Residential Schools was concerned with mental illness, with trauma following from institutionalized violence. It was also concerned with healing from trauma and mitigating its widely ramifying effects in the lives of individuals, communities, and the nation; and for this reason it had much to say about how one can and should recover individually and collectively from the traumatic past. It was unusually active in its involvement with mental health intervention, and hence with promotion of the ideas and categories associated with mental illness and recovery, above all with post-traumatic stress disorder and historical trauma. This quality of the Commission also explains its inclusiveness and encouragement of witnesses who might otherwise have been reluctant to testify about experiences that were painful and felt to be shameful, experiences that in some cases had not even been shared with close family members before finding their way to the stage, before an audience, cameras, and microphones. In my review of many hours of testimony (the subject of chapter 4), I have found that first-time witnesses tended to conform to the Commission's guidelines or "templates" to the extent that their testimony reflects the Commission's encouragement of painful, deeply personal experience. At the same time, they sometimes used the permissiveness of the various statement-gathering venues to add complexity to the stereotypes of the victim/perpetrator dichotomy or to press beyond the Commission's mandate by giving expression to other grievances, often more current, sometimes even expressed with more urgency and passion than their traumatic memories of the abuse they experienced in school.

Although it is not always on the surface, there was arguably more disputed, mutually contradictory meaning-making in Canada's TRC than in any truth commission elsewhere. Under these circumstances, the Commission faced an unusually difficult task: it will have succeeded if it convinces a sufficiently large number of citizens of the harm done by the schools and the need to overcome it, and it will have failed if too many remain unpersuaded of the reality of these harms and if few possess the will to bring the history of the school experience to life with their own tangible participation in its remembrance.

THE ETHNOGRAPHY OF LEGAL PROCESS

It is now commonplace to observe that the trans-human networks of people, groups, communities, and organizations are everywhere reconfiguring the boundaries (and boundary-less forms) of human interaction and membership. As a consequence of this, every ethnographer now has an obligation to define what the anthropological project means to them, and how their particular approach to method relates to the people and problems on which they have focused their attention.[8] No one approach, no one solution, can be recommended to everyone. It has to be done anew each time.

In keeping with this requirement, the first thing I am called upon to do in this study of Canada's Truth and Reconciliation Commission on Indian Residential Schools is rethink the idea of "ethnos" at the heart of "*eth*nography." This absence of a clear ethnos is now a familiar issue to most ethnographers, but is all the more acute in the effort to render the Truth and Reconciliation Commission ethnographically intelligible. What does "ethnos" mean when the main subjects of the study are diverse in origin and identity, when they are Inuit, Métis, and aboriginal (itself a category inclusive of great diversity) and come from hundreds of reserve communities or live "off reserve" in towns and cities across Canada and even a few in the United States? Moreover, what happens when I include among my research participants the priests, brothers, nuns, and laypeople who once worked in the schools? Where is the ethnos when the subject matter goes far beyond any one group, community, profession, or other territorialized, stable marker of identity—so far beyond, in fact, that it ceases to have any clear limits? And what does this ambiguity mean for the subdiscipline, the anthropology of law, that tries to maintain at least some connection to the supposed certainties of legal writing and process? For all the factual orientation and sought-for procedural clarity of law, conducting an ethnographic inquiry with such scope is a bit like trying to conduct a mining operation on a gaseous planet.

Then again, there is in the middle of all this a kind of person, the residential school survivor (sometimes written as "Survivor" with an honorific upper-case "S"), who embodies the schools, the trauma, the abuse of the policies and their impacts, and of course a certain resilience in the face of these things, who is therefore defined in common with others not so much by any one tradition or territory but by new and emerging notions of suffering, existence, and persistence. The survivor is not a category that follows from attachments to tradition, but from recognition of a common experience by which tradition was interrupted. In its widest usage, it is a new identity concept that materialized out of processes of justice lobbying, litigation, and efforts toward collective healing and securing a new place in history. It has entered our language to designate (and self-designate) those who experienced the horrors that define our time, like the Holocaust, the Vietnam War, and more personalized, stigma- and isolation-inducing traumas like rape and incest. In the particular iteration that I will discuss here, it emerged out of a rejection of unwanted ideas that might attach to former students of Indian residential schools, such as victimization, dysfunction, and assimilation.

By extension, the category of survivor as it developed in Canada's TRC stands opposed to the most readily identified agents of the schools—the priests, brothers, and nuns—from among whom come some of the most visible perpetrators of violence and abuse. Many of these agents of residential school institutions and policies are still alive and able to speak (and will speak in the pages that follow) with their own distinct memories, justifications, and abiding values that, taken together, stand in sharp contrast to the remembered experience and identities of survivors.

We should not be too concerned about making a secure connection to a discipline-specific method. In fact, doing so too narrowly can stand in the way of seeing what is before us—and of recognizing the significance of what is not. The subject matter of this book is situated not only in the different and sometimes opposed memories and identities of the survivors and the clergy, but in the publicly mediated ideas that occupy the space between them, in the charged particles of collective remembrance that can only be described by inference and imagination.

The centre of it all is survivor statements. By the time the TRC released its final report in December 2015, it had gathered nearly 7,000 statements, nearly all of them video or audio recorded. I made it my goal to attend as much of the public statement gathering as I could. I attended, took notes on, and, with the aid of research assistants, recorded and transcribed narratives from hundreds of witnesses in three levels of TRC event: "community events" in Iqaluit and Ottawa; a "regional event" in Victoria; and the "National Events" in Winnipeg, Inuvik, Halifax, Saskatoon, Montreal, Vancouver, and Edmonton.[9] Each of these meetings had its own character, with greater intimacy in the Band hall or school gymnasium settings of the community events, where it was apparent that most people intimately knew one another and were tolerant of the temporary scattering of strangers in their midst, in contrast to the crowded, multiple-venue regional and national events that took place in major public spaces: a public park/fairground (The Forks in Winnipeg), a sprawling high school campus (the Sir Alexander Mackenzie School in Inuvik), and a variety of hotel/conference centres (the Prince George and Sheraton hotels in Halifax, the Empress Hotel in Victoria, the Prairieland Park Trade and Convention Centre in Saskatoon, the Queen Elizabeth Hotel in Montreal, the Pacific National Exhibition site in Vancouver, and the Shaw Conference Centre in Edmonton). In each of these events, the Commissioner's Sharing Panels, the Sharing Circles with the Survivor Committee, and the Private Statement Gathering all happened simultaneously, punctuated by honorary witness ceremonies, expressions of reconciliation, keynote speeches, and town halls on reconciliation; while elsewhere participants could find concerts, film screenings, a Churches Listening Area, displays of photographs and artifacts in the "Learning Place," information kiosks occupied by a variety of public and private organizations, souvenir boutiques, and arts and crafts displays. Then there were spiritual activities: lighting of the sacred fire (on opening day), daily opening and closing prayers by invited elders and church leaders, and sunrise and pipe ceremonies. At one time or another, I was present in each of these activities, though my focus was on the most publicly visible venues of the national and regional events: the Commissioner's Sharing Panels, where survivors had their largest audience—with 50 to 800 people in the room at any one time, not to mention those several thousand viewing online.[10]

"Bureaucratic administration," Max Weber famously observed, "always tends to be an administration of 'secret sessions': in so far as it can, it hides its knowledge and action from criticism";[11] and, as a peculiar kind of bureaucratic organization, Canada's Truth and Reconciliation Commission was no exception. There were entire realms of activity undertaken by the Commission that were closed off from sustained scrutiny, not just behind the closed doors of its headquarters in Winnipeg, but temptingly within plain sight at the Commission's events. These included the secret-by-definition Private Statement Gathering sessions of each Commission event, the statement-gathering sessions that took place in penitentiaries, and the activities of the Missing Children Project, which made its first public appearance in an out-of-the-way broadcast-quality recording booth at the Atlantic National Event, staffed by a forensic anthropologist, there to privately record oral accounts of "children who died or disappeared while attending an IRS."[12] (While the Commission's mandate prevented it from making recommendations concerning civil and criminal liability, it was entirely free to gather and eventually report on information that points in the direction of such liability, including the serious crimes associated with missing and murdered children.) And while it was interesting to learn that forensic anthropologists stood at the ready to investigate credible accounts of burial sites connected to Indian residential schools—and that, in the event such sites were found, the Commission planned to sponsor commemorative feasts and "traditional ceremonies in those locations to ask the spirits of the Missing Children to return home to their communities"—this was an entire realm of Commission activity with a starting point in secret knowledge.[13] There was no crime-scene tape across the entrance to the booth, but there might as well have been, and my attention soon returned to the public spectacle of the TRC-sponsored events.

Because of their complexity, I approached the National Events as sites of what might be called "institutional ethnography" or "event ethnography," based loosely on the model of Marcel Griaule's studies of Dogon ritual, in which the richness and variety of the occasion calls for a small team of researchers observing from different angles.[14] Even though complete coverage of any one event was impossible, my student trainees (usually numbering one or two, with five in Montreal) and I would attend different venues occurring simultaneously, coordinating our activities through text messages (an advantage unavailable to Griaule).

From this starting point, I pursued the ideas at the centre of this study much more broadly. I interviewed, singly and in groups, eighteen Oblate priests in their residences in Montreal, St. Albert (near Edmonton, Alberta), Iqaluit, Ottawa, and Winnipeg. I also met with eleven Grey Sisters in two group interviews in Winnipeg. My research assistant, Marie-Pierre Gadoua, collaborated in these efforts by occasionally attending the interviews and conducting three on her own with Oblate priests in Ottawa, Montreal, and Rome; an Anglican minister in Inuvik; and a United Church minister in Saskatoon. I cannot claim that our coverage of the views of priests extends beyond the Oblates into other orders of Catholicism or denominations of Christianity, though I did also have informative conversations with clergy and laypeople from the Anglican, United, and Presbyterian churches at each of the National Events. The fact that the Oblate order was responsible for operating some 60 per cent of Canada's Indian residential schools was reason enough for me to follow up on unprecedented opportunities to conduct interviews with them. In order to get a proper sense of the range of opinions and experience among the priests, brothers, and nuns, it was important to conduct an adequate number of interviews. Extending this effort into other denominations—in other words, spreading the research effort more thinly and broadly—would mean sacrificing some thoroughness in rendering the views and experiences particular to each church. So my focus has been on the Oblate order, leaving the perspectives of clergy in other denominations to be expressed publicly by them and through future inquiry.

My assistants and I also conducted twelve recorded interviews with survivors and seven with health support workers (several of whom were also former residential school students) during and after TRC meetings. My conversations with former residential school students extend all the way back in time to my research for the Cree Board of Health and Social Services of James Bay in Chisasibi, Quebec, in the mid-1990s, near the former sites of the St. Philip's Indian Residential School and the Ste-Thérèse-de-l'Enfant-Jesus, as well as a period of two years from 1998 to 2000 in the reserve community of Cross Lake, Manitoba, former site of the St. Joseph's Indian Residential School. From there, it has continued through to the events and post-event interviews of the TRC, as well as, along the way, a two-day meeting in March 2012 of the Outreach Residential School Atlantic Committee under the auspices of the Atlantic Policy Congress of First Nations Chiefs Secretariat in Millbrook, Nova Scotia.

All of this amounts to the pursuit of an idea, or a complex of ideas, focused on Indian residential schools and their legacy, including the institutional remedy intended to overcome it. The grounding here is not to be found in vaguely similar meeting rooms and stackable chairs. It is in a continuity of thought, the thread that follows from one place to the next, from one speaker to another, in the exchange of ideas about suffering and belonging—all with a starting point in a systemic, historically proportioned human rights violation and source of trauma, an institutional wrong of church and state.

THE ETHNOGRAPHY OF PUBLICS

There is another sense in which this book deals with a nebulous subject matter. When the moderator of the Commission proceedings in Halifax proudly announced that 4,700 people were watching the live streaming of the event from ten countries and three continents, he indirectly introduced another kind of participant, evident only in the raw data on live-feed users, the number of windows connected to the TRC web link, and the sources of their Internet Protocol (IP) addresses.

Such public exposure has not always been a defining quality of truth commissions. The earliest commissions (in Uganda, Bolivia, Argentina, Uruguay, the Philippines, Chile, and elsewhere) did not even hear testimony in public out of concern that it would be too inflammatory or that it might inspire the accused (in some cases ousted members of the military) to retaliatory action. The reports of these early commissions reflected this reticent approach to testimony by offering only distilled, carefully edited summaries and cautious interpretations of what occurred in the past.

The South African truth commission broke with this pattern by opening up testimony to public view, permitting press and television cameras into hearings, widely disseminating verbatim testimony, making testimony the subject of national drama, and encouraging its final report to be the subject matter of open debate.[15] Canada's TRC did not attain the kind of exposure achievable through live television coverage to an engaged national public. It did, however, make use of the tools of digital technologies that were not available to South Africa's commission. It had a comparatively small audience of those who live-streamed the proceedings on the Internet; and it sponsored (directly and in indirect offshoots) information and discussion forums on Facebook, YouTube, and Twitter. There was also a long-term orientation to the use of media in Canada's TRC that included the goal of a permanent research centre with a digital archive of survivor narratives.

Statements presented in Canada's Commission hearings were therefore offered with some degree of understanding on the part of participants that their audience went beyond those present in the room, beyond even those who may have been watching a live video broadcast, extending out to many spectators who could only be perceived in the abstract, including future public audiences. There is every indication from the testimony itself that witnesses were motivated by this aspect of the event, perhaps in a way that corresponds with the stock phrases "wanting their voices to be heard" and "being a part of history." Audience members in a side meeting in Halifax titled "How to Share Your Truth," for example, characterized the purpose of sharing as being "in order for ... Canadian mainstream society to really understand ... where we've been ... what has happened to us," and "so that future generations will know exactly how we were treated, and why. So it doesn't happen anymore."[16] We can gather from this that some survivors at the microphone, besides speaking most immediately to those in the room, were also often addressing a Canadian public audience in the present—"out there in cyberspace"—and perhaps an even less knowable futurity that could only be imagined: the readers, listeners, or viewers of an archive, meant to influence opinions or judgments yet to be made, perhaps by people yet to be born.

One exception to this deference to the media presence (and by extension the viewing public) occurred in the Urban Inuit Community Hearing in Ottawa in August 2012. There, for the first time in all the meetings I attended, one of the survivors—a thin, diminutive Inuit man in his fifties—requested that the cameras be turned off before he began his statement. The camera operators, with a nod from Commissioner Marie Wilson, duly pointed their cameras to the ground and walked to the back of the room. He then leaned toward the microphone and explained, "I have trouble with authority figures."[17]

We can only commend his choice. In acting on what he later referred to as "trust issues" by sending away—of all possible people in the room—the present and future viewing audience on the other end of the cameras, he exercised his rights with a startling implicit truth: taken together, these anonymous viewers were indeed the authority figure with the greatest potential to pass judgment on him and influence the way he felt in presenting his testimony.

So it is clear that the TRC was directed toward, and in some ways responsive to, the public (or, because publics can have distinct compositions and characters, I will often use the plural form "publics"). But what more precisely do we mean by "the public," or by the other terms that relate to its influential ideas, like "public opinion" and "popular will"? Despite the currency of these concepts, there is no ready-made answer. We seem here to be faced with a kind of entity that has been neglected by ethnographers, probably due to the fact that publics are almost entirely abstract and anonymous and hence not easily subject to the immediate, personal, face-to-face dynamics of ethnographic inquiry.

The public, as Gabriel Tarde presciently observed more than a century ago, is "in the midst of becoming, in the contemporary theatre, like the chorus in a Greek tragedy, the principal interlocutor that one addresses and who responds—or fails to respond."[18] This observation seems to reach across the century since it was written, speaking to us directly about the public ideas and activism, supported by new media with global reach, that have become central to the legitimacy, effectiveness, and conceptual reach of human rights. Several studies have noted the significant place of public persuasion in human rights reporting and activism, oriented toward an "amorphous public sphere often referred to simply as the international community."[19] One of the central claims I am making here is that engagement with public audiences, in a sense the "consumers" of justice claims, has important implications for the development of collective experiences of harm, injustice, and ultimately, the self. The processes by which distinct people define who they are—above all the ways they articulate and defend their collective rights and shape and represent their essential attributes—are now more than ever before negotiated and "mediated" (literally and figuratively) in collaboration with mostly unknowable, abstract masses of people whose preferences and inclinations are formed and manifested through media.

In this study of the TRC as a publicly oriented legal remedy, the assertion of ideas, the expression of emotion, and the formation of identity must include the influence of these abstract, impersonal, largely unknowable and unpredictable "publics." Partly because they are impersonal and nebulous, publics have in particular not really been given their due in studies of legal process. By their very nature, they offend positivist sensibilities; they thwart the will toward factuality, clarity, and certainty. Still, it is a bit disappointing that they should be featured with such one-sided prominence in commercial marketing strategies and media-driven, pre-reified political contests. Our language about them is impoverished. In English, for example, the word "poll" is the same for both the process by which opinion is statistically measured and the procedure by which opinion is acted on in an election, as in a "polling station." (French does a bit better in this regard: the word for measuring public opinion, *sondage*, is derived from the process of geological or deep-water sampling. Either way, the unintentional metaphor built into this one word is apt: it evokes either the hidden knowledge that lies beneath sedimentary layers of rock or, better yet, the information to be found in the murky abyss among unseen currents that move in one direction or another.)

In *Public Justice and the Anthropology of Law*, I describe some of the qualities I have found in those publics that are often the targets of justice lobbying, based in part upon observation of a variety of media-oriented campaigns in the international movement of indigenous peoples.[20] Here I find that if publics were to be given the attributes of human personality, they would be complex characters indeed, perhaps even suffering from something akin to bipolar disorder, compounded by narcissism, immaturity, and passive-aggression. They are also potentially compassionate, wanting and willing to help, to get involved, to pursue utopian ideals, to change the world for the better. Whatever attributes we apply to them, it is clear that the ideas they respond to—and express, when their opinions are manifested through such things as editorials, blogs, flash mobs, rallies, protests, and riots—are inconsistent, sometimes even starkly contradictory, to an extent that we would not find in a normal adult individual.

They are also, to a limited extent, changeable and influenceable, which makes them a suitable target for lobbying. Nothing helps a justice cause like having increasing numbers of people rallying to it, advocating for it, or at least expressing ideas consistent with it. But publics can be persuaded to latch onto an issue only with great difficulty. They do not often have "aha" moments, as individuals do, which mark a sudden change from one viewpoint to another. They look first to see if similar others are of like mind before committing themselves to a cause. This means that simply putting information "out there" only once, no matter how compelling it might be, will almost never succeed in igniting a public's imagination. The message has to be repeated, but without monotony; it has to recur creatively and compellingly from different angles— hence the need for campaigns of justice lobbying to effect any significant degree of popular persuasion.

As Richard Sherwin has convincingly demonstrated, there are distinct logics to the media that produce visual culture, one of which involves making claims through image-laden storytelling. Consistent with these logics, legal argument, presented on a screen, motivates belief and judgment swiftly and powerfully. "We respond to images quickly, holistically, and affectively—the same way we perceive the world at large."[21] And through our visual proclivities and new opportunities for exercising them, visual meaning-making is becoming an increasingly significant aspect of judicial process. "The poignant dignity of a victim wrongfully harmed, the implicit malice of one who has perpetrated (or is about to perpetrate) an act of violence"—there is an eloquence and excess of meaning in those images that "move us with an uncanny power, a sense of presence that cannot be easily explained."[22]

But even while publics often respond to visual storytelling of the kind presented in courtrooms, on the whole they are easily bored and distracted. And who can blame them? With every NGO that possesses any amount of media access trying to persuade them of the urgency of this or that cause, publics (poor things) are being bombarded from all sides with pleas and persuasion. This means that a successful justice cause will make use of ideas and images that are striking and simple, that appeal at an emotional level, that in some way stand out from the claims of competitive others and focus peoples' attention on the one that matters. Ideas that instill compassion (sometimes by way of revulsion) are often expressed through images that reach into a human essence, that strike a primal nerve, things like a suffering child, corpses, wreckage, fire, blood, and tears. Such things have the power to capture attention. But then begins the real work of persuasion, of assigning responsibility for the harm that compelled the public's attention, and inciting collective action in a cause for justice.

A Facebook posting by Isabelle Knockwood, a former student of the Shubenacadie Indian Residential School and activist/organizer in the Mi'kmaq community of survivors, makes clear the goal of persuasion as she tries to rally her cohort into greater unity in a struggle to make known the ongoing effects of the residential school experience:

Publicity is a very powerful tool. We should use it. Let the public know what has been going on in Shubie these last 20 or 30 years or more and is still going on. I'm radical to begin with that's why I think we need a consensus on what to do ... we have to take action. But everybody has to do the same thing. It can't be just one or two people. One or two people are not even going to be noticed. That's my take. Am I right or wrong? signed, Just another angry Indian! and I make people mad too. If they get mad enough they MIGHT do something or say something or write something to stick up for themselves.

Knockwood is acting on an insight that defines our era. Public sympathy has become *the* interim goal, the indispensable provisional prize on the way to the real prize of restitution, the central source of energy behind campaigns of justice. When all other recourse is exhausted, when an injustice remains unaddressed by all official avenues available, it might not be enough to rely on the judicial system at work behind closed doors. Under these circumstances it is common to see the sufferers of injustice engage with public audiences. Even a fraction of the indignation felt by the immediate victims and their families every moment of every day might be enough to move these strangers to action. If only they knew ...

This brings us to a fundamental question that will concern us throughout this book—a question that follows from the TRC's unusual emphasis on building awareness of the abuses of the state and churches as a source of national shame (as opposed to, say, South Africa's efforts to create viable nationhood in the aftermath of globally recognized crimes). How are publics persuaded? How does an appeal expressed through media garner attention? Out of all the possible claimants, and all the possible ideas they assert in making their claims, what makes one or the other stand out while the rest are, in varying degrees and with various speeds, forgotten? More to the point, what are the emotions at work in convincing people to involve themselves in a condition of unjust suffering or in the processes of bearing witness and historical remedy in a truth commission?

Few of us are used to thinking in any deep or systematic way about the emotions associated with justice. By this I mean not so much the histrionics of courtroom drama, but the emotions that give energy to claims and appeals to justice. The legal venues that offer the certainties of judicial process and opinion are by design hostile to the expression of emotion (anger especially) and try to keep it within limits. Less expectedly, anthropologists have not been much better in taking up emotions as a legitimate aspect of collective experience, perhaps because they are part of an essentially "soft" and subjective discipline that has long struggled to establish its empirical legitimacy.[23] But humans, being what they are, find ways to defy efforts to keep their very human emotions at bay. As every practising lawyer knows, even the formality of the staging and procedural rules of judicial process are not sufficient to produce a corresponding rationalism in participating human actors.

We can take this line of inquiry further, and in a specific direction. The focus on the emotions revealed in judicial process tells us little about the emotions provoked by injustice, about the *sense* of injustice that we see both in the foreground and in the excluded experience of witnessing in the Truth and Reconciliation Commission. And, because of this, there is much to be gained by considering the emotions associated with the sense of injustice as prime movers and motivators of legal process, including the remedies that take place in the aftermath of judicial procedure.

To illustrate the influence of emotion on public persuasion it may be useful to consider part of the testimony presented by Andrew Wesley (a school survivor and Anglican pastor) at the National Event in Saskatoon:

> Before [being sent to school] we were living in a trap line. We enjoyed life. Life was good. We enjoyed creation. Then a time came that I must go to school. I remember shortly after that when I was in school, I don't know what we were eating for supper, I threw up. I got sick. A worker came over. "What are you

doing?" Of course at that time I didn't speak English. She hit me over the head and said, "Eat your vomit." And just for a while try to think of yourself as a little boy being hit over the head and vacating your vomit on the floor. And you know how vomit splashes while you're crawling around. [Pauses, weeping] Crawling around on the floor, licking. Treated like that. I was so scared, so helpless. Nobody came. And I threw up for the second time after eating the vomit and being slapped on the face.

My nose was bleeding. I was told to "eat your vomit" again, with your blood. With your own blood. Crawling around, trying to save yourself. Nobody, nobody came. Nobody. Nobody came. Nobody.[24]

Judging solely by their tears and downcast faces, this testimony evoked particularly strong reactions from Wesley's listeners, but what more precisely might have been the emotion(s) behind their sorrowful reaction and the standing ovation that followed? Compassion, sadness, and disgust, certainly, perhaps in combination. But the answer is more complicated than that.

One of the terms used to describe the sense of injustice, with a deep history in Western thought, is *indignation*. This is not a term in very common use. Confronted with the kind of testimony offered by Wesley and asked to identify their emotional response, it is unlikely (but not out of the realm of possibility) that people would say "it made me *indignant*"—an awkward word, after all, with its three syllables and "g-n" elision. Yet indignation is in my view a close emotional correlate of injustice. And, in the context of the truth commission, it is all-pervasive.

This merits some elaboration. Martha Nussbaum defines indignation as "a moral response appropriate to good citizens and based upon reasons that can be publicly shared."[25] As with many concepts associated with justice, it has been infused with rationalism and order. It is, in fact, widely seen as the correlate of order and sound judgment. The emphasis here (which, Nussbaum informs us, might well be traceable to the legal rationalism of Aristotle) is on the constructive response to a wrong or harm, a response that pursues collective judgments based on the "public exchange of reasons." Indignation conceived this way serves as a contrast to disgust, an emotional response to pollution, based in a kind of magical thinking that seeks to preserve the self and society from contamination. Wesley's testimony certainly seemed to provoke such a response of sympathetic disgust. But Nussbaum argues for the removal from judicial process of any recourse to disgust as a source of decision making, any invocation of the viscerally rejected properties of "sliminess, bad smell, stickiness, decay, foulness—[that] have repeatedly and monotonously been associated with, indeed projected onto, groups by reference to whom privileged groups seek to define their superior human status."[26] That is to say, ideas of pollution are not just formulated in the abstract, but have been targeted toward particular groups. "Jews, women, homosexuals, untouchables, lower-class people—all these are imagined as tainted by the dirt of the body."[27] By extension all these categories of people, by virtue of such attribution of pollution and invocation of disgust, have been treated unjustly in political and judicial process. And that has to stop.

This argument, convincing as it is, leaves room for thinking further about Nussbaum's point of contrast with disgust. Indignation, I want to argue, is not as straightforward or constructively rational as it might at first seem. As an emotion, indignation does not stand by itself, but is influenced by other emotions that lie adjacent to it. Love as a sense of sympathetic connection, of brotherhood and sisterhood, is vital to motivating distant strangers to go beyond a mere perception of injustice, toward a feeling of indignation and a willingness to act on it through participatory citizenship. The sense of injustice or indignation is clearly set in motion by simultaneous feelings of love, loyalty, and compassion. Indignation builds energy through personal or personalized relationships that are close to the source of error or harm at its origin. A simple example might be the emotional response to a wrongful conviction. In such circumstances, the feeling of injustice will be felt more keenly by those with close relationships with the sufferer of injustice than by those with no other connection to the case than television news or a Netflix documentary. Indignation concentrates its energy through the human relationships that are closest to its source. By extension, it is more difficult to feel indignant toward a situation of injustice involving people we care little about, who may be superficially unattractive in ways that have nothing to do with their claims. The most responsive publics, activists sometimes note, have strong, sometimes inconvenient preferences for recognizable innocence, for objects that readily lend themselves to nurturing and compassion, toward situations involving, shall we say, young children, or animals that appeal broadly (baby seals come to mind)—the species known to experts on animal rights activism as "charismatic mega-fauna."[28]

Coming from another direction, disgust also lies adjacent to indignation and can also be used to provoke the sense of wrong, but through an association of contamination with the harm done. This connection between disgust and indignation was evident in the testimony by Wesley and the audience reaction to it. This is to say, Nussbaum's strict contrast between indignation as rational and disgust as irrational may in this sense be misleading. Indignation is only superficially rational, while it is constantly stimulated, provoked, and possibly even influenced to action by irrational passions.

At the same time, the sense of injustice is an emotion that corresponds with nothing we usually describe as expressive or affecting. It lacks the explosiveness and temporariness of anger, though it is often confused with anger or even the extremes of rage and fury, the kinds of things that lead to setting cars on fire rather than the strategic pursuit of a grievance. People simply can't survive rage or anger for very long. Over the long term, conditions of health and senses of judgment are impaired by the intensity of these kinds of emotion. But in the absence of a venue for expression and action, indignation lingers, constricts, and suffocates. Jakob Wassermann is one of very few writers to explicitly describe this aspect of the feeling of injustice [*Ungerechtigkeit*] in his 1928 novel, *The Maurizius Case*: "I cannot describe to you how I feel when I experience injustice—my own or someone else's, it's all the same. It goes right through me, hurting body and soul. It is as though someone had filled my mouth full of sand and I had to choke on the spot."[29] Only by considering a strong emotion of this kind—a deep, suffocating sense of injustice—can we understand both the testifiers' narratives of suffering and their trespass beyond the bounds of on-the-topic testimony to the expression of unrecognized experiences that exceed the mandate of the Commission.

The sense of injustice has some of the energy of violent emotions, except on a slower burn, allowing for more reasonable communication and strategic action. Other than in passing moments, it does not have the flash of feeling and instant energy of anger; nor does it readily succumb to the passivity of sorrow. It is an emotion that allows people to think—even adding energy to their thought and ability to strategize. It comes with a sense of something being out of place in the symmetry of justice. It emerges from a kind of collectivist sympathy that sees in the experience of others a threat to the security and prosperity of all. Injustice is a readily generalizable condition. And, as the emotional correlate of injustice, indignation enables activism with a simultaneous emphasis on compassion and the common good.

PERSONHOOD

One of the outcomes of the public representation of injustice is a new kind of person: the Indian residential school survivor. The emergence of the survivor concept as a new possibility for self-understanding and -definition illustrates a much wider phenomenon, in which legal claims and processes encourage the erection and patrol of boundaries that situate those who are (or who subjectively see themselves as being) subject to systemic injustice within closed ontological comfort zones, "communities of affirmation" or "solitudes" (discussed further in chapter 8).

Use of the term "survivor" as one who lives through a catastrophic event, with consequences of that event manifested in challenges to mental health and personal integrity, has influenced trauma studies and found its way into popular ideas over the past half century. The first iterations of this concept came from two psychiatrists who drew from both personal experience and work with patients who had survived the Holocaust to explore issues of resilience and trauma following incarceration in concentration and death camps. Henry Krystal's 1968 edited volume *Massive Psychic Trauma* introduced the concept of "survivor syndrome" to describe the mental health consequences of the death camps.[30] And a decade later Bruno Bettelheim's essays in *Surviving* offered an exploration of "concentration camp survivor syndrome" and introduced the idea of survivor guilt as a significant element of the syndrome that arises out of the survivor's strong will to stay alive while others perish, manifesting itself in self-blame that is morally ungrounded yet obsessive, destructive, and formative in the survivor's personality.[31] From this starting point in the study of post-Holocaust trauma, the concept of the survivor was soon taken up more broadly and popularly to refer to those who had undergone almost any kind of severe traumatic event, such as combat (with the Vietnam War as a focal point), a natural disaster, or childhood sexual abuse.

The concept of the Indian residential school survivor appears to be a later outcome of this popularization of the survivor concept, with an additional impetus from claims grounded in notions of genocide (hence drawing from the concept's original connection with the Holocaust) and sexual abuse. While a precise timeline of the emergence of this use of the concept is difficult to establish, several local organizations were founded in the 1990s that applied the word "survivor" to former students of Indian residential schools, perhaps the best known of these being the Shubenacadie Residential School Survivors. Three organizations were established in the early 2000s with the specific goal of centralizing and coordinating the work of survivor groups: the Indian Residential School Survivors Society, based in British Columbia (est. 2002); the National Residential School Survivors Society (est. 2003); and the Outreach Residential School Atlantic Committee (est. 2004).[32] With this move toward centralization, the concept of the school survivor soon became a reference point for the legal claims pursued or supported by aboriginal organizations, eventually achieving secure anchorage in the negotiations and media exposure leading up to the Indian Residential Schools Settlement Agreement of 2007. The Settlement Agreement, in turn, brought into being the Indian Residential School Survivors Committee to assist with the work of the Truth and Reconciliation Commission.[33] And, as we will see in the pages that follow, the TRC was itself active in naturalizing the concept of the Indian residential school survivor, with primary reference points in trauma and cultural genocide. With astonishing rapidity, the concept of the Indian residential school survivor had gone from obscurity, through organizational and legal anchorage, to a broad base of popular recognition.

To understand how new and emerging legal processes might influence categories of identity and belonging, we should consider more fully what happens on either side of the courtroom, during the before and after of judicial process. The pre-litigation process of identity formation and the way it played out in the lead-up to the Settlement

Agreement provides an illustration of the most basic correspondence between law and collective identity. Before a collective justice claim has the remotest chance of success through public lobbying and legal process, it first has to establish a recognizable community of claimants. Elaborating the rights of a people, community, or group calls for an unambiguous description of the beneficiaries of those rights. Who legitimately belongs to the category of rights-holders and who does not? Collective claims, like those pursued by the survivors of Indian residential schools, cannot succeed without a clear answer to this question.

The Settlement Agreement at the origin of the TRC took this logic of the law, which initially applied in specific instances, and extended it into historical identity on a national scale. The most obvious way the new community of survivors was defined was through the Commission's mandate, which included and excluded certain kinds of institutions, and hence narrowed the range of individuals who attended (or were incarcerated in) them. Beyond this, the Commission encouraged particular, preferred narratives through examples provided to potential statement givers and audience members that "set the tone" for the experience of bearing witness. It is therefore a fallacy to assume that a commission of this kind is simply and straightforwardly receiving, recording, and preserving narratives from witnesses. As I intend to show, it was actively cultivating them at the same time. Those who appeared before the microphone and cameras were not transferring remembered experience directly from their memories to recording devices in the manner of a USB cable or portable flash drive; they were selecting and reworking that experience. What is more, they were doing so in part through conditions of affirmation and encouragement established by the Commission. Survivors both conformed to and refused conformity with these preferences; but in their engagement with the process of bearing witness, in their choice of grievance and in their telling of it, they were also active agents of their identities, of who they chose to be in their moment at the microphone before an audience of friends, relatives, and anonymous others.

This brings me to my broadest conception of the subject matter of this book. It is about a transformation that is taking place, or has already occurred without much fanfare, in the process by which people acquire their identities, their knowledge about self and others, in the way that they come to know something about their innermost sense of being and belonging. I am referring to an aspect of the human rights revolution, situated in the legal and bureaucratic foundations of group membership. The part of it I am describing here begins with formal agreement and ends with a sense of common cause with like-minded others. It also ends with a view of the world, of moral obligations, and, perhaps most significantly, with a more acute sense of justice and of offence against it.

NOTES

1   Useful comparative discussions of truth and reconciliation commissions have been provided by Martha Minow, *Between Vengeance and Forgiveness: Facing History after Genocide and Mass Violence* (Boston: Beacon, 1999); Priscilla Hayner, *Unspeakable Truths: Transitional Justice and the Challenge of Truth Commissions* (New York: Routledge, 2011); and Robert Rotberg and Dennis Thompson, eds., *Truth v. Justice: The Morality of Truth Commissions* (Princeton, NJ: Princeton University Press, 2000).

2   Anthropological perspectives on South Africa's TRC are offered by Fiona Ross, *Bearing Witness: Women and the Truth and Reconciliation Commission in South Africa* (London: Pluto, 2003) and Richard A. Wilson, *The Politics of Truth and Reconciliation in South Africa* (Cambridge, UK: Cambridge University Press, 2001).

3   Hayner, *Unspeakable Truths*, ch. 10.

4   For a comparative discussion of criminal prosecution in the context of truth commissions, see Alison Bisset, *Truth Commissions and Criminal Courts* (Cambridge, UK: Cambridge University Press, 2012).

5   Nneoma Nwogu, "When and Why It Started: Deconstructing Victim-Centered Truth Commissions in the Context of Ethnicity-Based Conflict," *International Journal of Transitional Justice* 4 (2010): 275–89.

6   For further discussion of the TRC mandate in a comparative context, see Matt James, "Uncomfortable Comparisons: Canada's Truth and Reconciliation Commission in International Context," *Les ateliers de l'éthique/ The Ethics Forum* 5, no. 2 (2010): 24–35; and Matt James, "A Carnival of Truth? Knowledge, Ignorance, and the Canadian Truth and Reconciliation Commission," *International Journal of Transitional Justice* 6 (2012): 182–204.

7   See Joanna Quinn, "The Politics of Acknowledgment: An Analysis of Uganda's Truth Commission" (YCISS Working Paper no. 19, York University, March 2003); Truth and Reconciliation Commission, Sierra Leone, *Witness to Truth: Report of the Sierra Leone Truth and Reconciliation Commission*, 2004.

8   Some of the recent innovative approaches to ethnography include those referred to as "de-territorialized" ethnography, "institutional" ethnography, "multi-sited" ethnography, the ethnography of the contemporary, and of modernity or postmodernity. The anthropology of the modern is influentially discussed by Paul Rabinow in *Anthropos Today: Reflections on Modern Equipment* (Princeton, NJ: Princeton University Press, 2003); Michael Fischer's "Emergent Forms of Life: Anthropologies of Late or Postmodernities," *Annual Review of Anthropology* 28 (1999): 455–78, is an early source of guidance for a form of ethnography that

brings into view the influence of new technologies, including new visual and electronic media; and George Marcus is an early and path-breaking advocate of "multi-sited" ethnography in *Ethnography through Thick and Thin* (Princeton, NJ: Princeton University Press, 1998). Recent examples of institutional ethnography can be found in Annelise Riles, *Collateral Knowledge: Legal Reasoning in the Global Financial Markets* (Chicago, IL: University of Chicago Press, 2011); and Galit Sarfaty, *Values in Translation: Human Rights and the Culture of the World Bank* (Stanford, CA: Stanford University Press, 2012).

9 The number of community events included in this study was limited by the difficulty of obtaining the requisite research authorization within the limited time between announcement of the Commission's agenda and the date of the meeting.

10 For the Vancouver National Event, I participated online through the live feed, while three research assistants attended and reported to me on the setting and activities both during and after the event. I was, of course, not able to attend Private Statement Gathering sessions, though I did once offer testimony in one at the TRC Urban Inuit Community Hearing, Ottawa. My experience of it was probably so unlike those of the survivors who gave statements in this venue that I have elected to keep my perspective as that of the outsider looking in.

11 Max Weber, *From Max Weber, Essays in Sociology*, ed. Hans Gerth and C. Wright Mills (New York: Routledge, [1948] 2007), 233.

12 Truth and Reconciliation Commission of Canada, *Missing Children and Unmarked Burials: Research Recommendations*, report of the Working Group on Missing Children and Unmarked Burials, n.d., 4.

13 Ibid., 8.

14 Marcel Griaule's approach to method is outlined in his posthumous work, *Méthode de l'ethnographie*, ed. Geneviève Calame-Griaule (Paris: Presses universitaires de France, 1957); his team-based method is given particular attention by James Clifford in "Power and Dialogue in Ethnography: Marcel Griaule's Initiation," in *Observers Observed: Essays on Ethnographic Fieldwork*, ed. George Stocking (Madison, WI: University of Wisconsin Press, 1983), 121–56. See also Isabelle Fiemeyer, *Marcel Griaule: Citoyen Dogon* (Arles: Actes Sud, 2004). A contemporary ethnographic project that makes substantive use of research assistants is described by Daniel Goldstein in *Outlawed: Between Security and Rights in a Bolivian City* (Durham, NC: Duke University Press, 2012).

15 Robert Rotberg, "Truth Commissions and the Provision of Trust, Justice, and Reconciliation," in *Truth v. Justice: The Morality of Truth Commissions*, ed. Robert Rotberg and Dennis Thompson (Princeton, NJ: Princeton University Press, 2000), 5.

16 Speakers at the TRC Atlantic National Event, Halifax, 27 October 2011.

17 TRC Urban Inuit Community Hearing, Ottawa, 16 August 2012. Consistent with his request for anonymity by excluding the cameras, I am omitting the witness's name here.

18 *"En train de devenir, dans la comedie contemporaine, comme le chœur de la tragédie grecque, le principal interlocuteur auquel on s'adresse et qui vous répond,—ou ne vous répond pas."* My translation. Gabriel Tarde, *Les Transformations du Droit: Étude Sociologique* (Paris: Félix Alcan, 1893), 120.

19 Winnifred Tate, *Counting the Dead: The Culture and Politics of Human Rights Activism in Columbia* (Berkeley and Los Angeles: University of California Press, 2007), 175. See also Ronald Niezen and Maria Sapignoli, eds., *Palaces of Hope: The Anthropology of Global Organizations* (Cambridge, UK: Cambridge University Press, 2017), 34–36.

20 Ronald Niezen, *Public Justice and the Anthropology of Law* (Cambridge, UK: Cambridge University Press, 2010). See especially chapters 2 and 3.

21 Richard Sherwin, *Visualizing Law in the Age of the Digital Baroque: Arabesques and Entanglements* (New York: Routledge, 2011), 2.

22 Ibid., 3.

23 Charles Lindholm, "An Anthropology of Emotion," in *A Companion to Psychological Anthropology*, ed. Conerly Casey and Robert Edgerton (Malden, MA: Blackwell, 2007), 31.

24 Andrew Wesley, Commissioner's Sharing Panel, TRC Saskatoon National Event, 23 June 2012.

25 Martha Nussbaum, "'Secret Sewers of Vice': Disgust, Bodies and the Law," in *The Passions of Law*, ed. Susan Bandes (New York and London: New York University Press, 1999), 26–27.

26 Ibid., 29.

27 Ibid., 29.

28 Nigel Leader-Williams and Holly Dublin, "Charismatic Megafauna as 'Flagship Species,'" in *Priorities for the Conservation of Mammalian Biodiversity: Has the Panda Had Its Day?* ed. Abigail Entwistle and Nigel Dunstone (Cambridge, UK: Cambridge University Press, 2010), 53–81.

29 *"Du mußt wissen, daß mir Ungerechtigkeit das Allerentsetzlichste auf der Welt ist. Ich kann Dir gar nicht schildern, wie mir zumut ist, wenn ich Ungerechtigkeit erlebe, an mir oder an andern, ganz gleich. Es geht mir durch und durch. Leib und Seele tun mir weh, es ist, als hätte man mir den Mund voll Sand geschüttet und ich müßte auf der Stelle ersticken."* My translation. Jakob Wassermann, *Der Fall Maurizius* (Munich: Langen/Müller, [1928] 2008), 37–38.

30 Henry Krystal, ed., *Massive Psychic Trauma* (Madison, CT: International Universities Press, 1968).

31 Bruno Bettelheim, *Surviving and Other Essays* (London: Thames and Hudson, 1979). See also Didier Fassin and Richard Rechtman, *The Empire of Trauma: An Inquiry into the Condition of Victimhood* (Princeton, NJ: Princeton University Press, 2009), ch. 3, for an informative discussion of Bettelheim's contributions to trauma studies.

32 An unpublished document released in 2000 by Alvin Tolley, "Federal Rules of Engagement: The Government's War against Survivors and the Churches," concludes that "the most promising way to gain collective leverage and influence is for survivors to form their own organization." Accessed 21 May 2013, http://www.turtleisland.org/news/ours.pdf, 3. Tolley identifies himself on the title page as "A Residential School Survivor." This is a legally informed text that acted (with what success is difficult to determine) to further the organizational currency of the residential school survivor concept.

33 Government of Canada, *Indian Residential Schools Settlement Agreement, Schedule "N," Mandate for the Truth and Reconciliation Commission* (Ottawa: Government of Canada, 2007), article 7, accessed 20 May 2013, http://www.residentialschool-settlement.ca/SCHEDULE_N.pdf.

Chapter 2

THE UNFOLDING

THE RECOGNITION OF HARM

Indignation, as felt by the victim of injustice, does not arise inevitably and immediately from an illegitimate harm, but is often gradually realized. It grows through time out of negative, even self-destructive emotions in an unfolding of awareness and capacity to act. Like the cycles of grief, the sense of injustice goes through changes that correspond with an increasing detachment from the injury at its origin, or perhaps better, a detached awareness of it that still leaves room for rational thinking.

The immediate impact of the harm can be an impediment to representing it to oneself as injustice. This point, like so many other things that relate to collective injury, can be illustrated by the experience of the Holocaust. Primo Levi invokes the myopia induced by the urgency of the need for survival in his description of life in a Nazi concentration camp: "The prisoner felt overwhelmed by a massive edifice of violence and menace but could not form for himself a representation of it because his eyes were fixed to the ground by every single minute's needs."[1] Only by degrees, and only in conditions of at least partial liberation, does the full magnitude of heinous acts of the state become understood by its victims.

In cases of the abuse of children such as those that occurred in some residential schools, the distance between the offence and a collectively recognized and mobilized sense of injustice is particularly great. Young children in particular, by the very nature of early childhood, are often unable to see the injustices committed against them as injustices. They are subject to and depend for their survival on the authority of adults. And because of this, they have a tendency to internalize the harm done to them, to think of their suffering at the hands of others as somehow deserved.

Although residential schools varied considerably in the kind of environment they created for children, above all through their management of discipline, the very nature of the institution meant that disciplinary authority was often systematically enforced and pervasive. But listening to the many narratives given to the National Events of the Commission, it became clear that there were some schools being mentioned most often in association with experiences of abuse: Shubenacadie in Nova Scotia and the Alberni Indian Residential School in British Columbia come instantly to mind as prominent examples, among others. True, there were some children who responded to oppressive discipline through the techniques of "ordinary resistance," such as running away, stealing food, drinking sacramental wine, or even arson; but for many if not most of the students who experienced abuse in the schools, such behaviour was unthinkable. They experienced a kind of solitary shame in which they saw themselves as personally flawed and therefore responsible for the acts of which they were victims. There was a great deal of ground to cover between shame and repression of traumatic experience and the awareness of it as a collective harm, with a correlate in a judicially mobilized sense of indignation. The secrecy that followed from feelings of personal disgrace had to give way to a sense of solidarity among former students based on a shared awareness of their suffering as an outcome not only of wrongful acts but of institutionalized conditions that made those acts possible—an awareness, in other words, of a shared condition of injustice.

A similar gradual process of unfolding took place in the public recognition of the harms of state-sponsored institutions. It has only recently been formally acknowledged that significant, systemic harm was done to children who were housed in institutions intended in various ways to help and "improve" them. A Law Commission of Canada report in 2000 made specific connections between such institutions as orphanages, schools for the deaf, and, of course, Indian residential schools, pointing to the all-important fact that such institutions were in various ways removed from a wider society and were largely free from oversight; for this reason they often became havens for pederasts and sadists, who sometimes abused the children in their care for years, even decades, while being sheltered by the institution in which they acted. The prevailing situation within residential institutions of all kinds was one in which vulnerable children were placed under the control of caregivers whose authority was virtually unquestioned. This was, in the words of the Law Commission report, "a recipe for the abuse of power by predators."[2] To this we can add that aboriginal children more commonly suffered the experiences of radical dislocation from isolated, rural environments and of racism and cultural denigration in school, encouraged by the institutional goal of re-education away from the influence of their families and communities. That is to say, aboriginal children were especially vulnerable because the ultimate goal behind their incarceration in school was that of correcting the essence of their being.

We know this now—at least, those of us who are academics and policy-makers whose business it is to know such things. But this basic awareness was long in coming. Canada was not acting in defiance of widely held norms in the 1940s, 1950s, and 1960s when Indian residential schools were at the peak of their influence. The schools were a reflection of popular ideas, despite the existence of new human rights standards that, strictly speaking, made them illegal in international law. Public opinion, more than the flawed logic of individuals, is capable of holding adamantly onto contradictory convictions. And public opinion in Canada was either uninformed or steadfastly in support of residential school policy for the greater part of the century or so in which they were in full operation.

It is noteworthy that resistance to residential schools corresponds closely with basic conditions that enabled aboriginal people to pursue grievances. For many years their legal capacities were systemically thwarted. A 1927 amendment to the *Indian Act*, for example, prevented anyone (native or non-native) from soliciting funds for Indian legal claims without a licence from the Superintendent General of Indian Affairs. The effect of this law was that aboriginal people were unable to pursue their interests and act on their grievances and hence were effectively unable to defend the interests of the children in the schools.

A further amendment to the Act in 1951 removed this impediment to Indian legal representation and effectively opened the door for aboriginal participation in Canada's legal system. This condition of greater empowerment gradually made itself felt, and as the possibilities for acting on conditions of injustice were slowly realized, the emotions of injustice and the pursuit of grievances corresponding with these emotions also made their public appearance.

One of the first media representations of collective resistance to the residential school policy can be seen in *PowWow at Duck Lake*, a 1967 film produced by the National Film Board of Canada. This was part of a participatory film and video project entitled *Challenge for Change* (*Société Nouvelle* in French), aimed at highlighting the social concerns of disadvantaged communities in Canada from the perspective of community members themselves. The topic of residential schools comes up in this film when it documents an encounter between native participants in a powwow and a visiting priest:

MAN I IN THE CROWD, TO PRIEST: Would it not be a forward step to eradicate residential schools? And keep people on their home reserves, at home with their parents, where they have a home atmosphere?

MAN 2 IN THE CROWD: I just want to say ... we were literally beaten, not only in
the residential schools but in the day schools, when we were caught speaking
our language.

PRIEST: I find that the, eh, a lot, a good number, I would even say more than
half of the Indian parents that I have dealt with in twenty-five years, they
want their children to learn English very well.

MAN 1: Sure they want their children to learn English very well!

PRIEST: Let me finish. When I was in [indistinct] they would even tell me: "I
want you to oblige my little boy to talk English!" And I found this an injustice to the little child, but they told me: "I want you to teach them English!"

MAN 1: Father, we heard people stand up here and say they were beaten if they
spoke their native tongue.

PRIEST: But that's one fact against the other! [laughs]

MAN 1: ... in residential school ...

PRIEST: What does it prove? Nothing.[3]

The first noteworthy thing about this confrontation is the simple fact that it took
place. It would have been far less likely a few decades previously at a time when the
clergy still had considerable authority, not to mention the power that followed from
their ability to call on the government to bring about compliance from parents and
community leaders in their operation of schools. The exchange with the priest in
Duck Lake in 1967 does not reflect the kind of deference that would earlier have been
the norm. The aboriginal participants are outspoken. They are telling the priest how
it is (and was). And it is the priest who is on the defensive and who, further on in the
film, leaves the scene in frustration.

There are also significant things that are absent from this encounter. In their challenge of the residential schools, none of the people in the crowd mention sexual
abuse, which was later to become a dominant theme of claims, compensation processes, and testimony relating to residential schools. The topic simply did not come
up. This makes this film clip a kind of historical baseline for understanding the claims
against residential schools—claims that at first failed in the courts (recall the priest's
"that's one fact against the other!" which would have had to be overcome) but eventually culminated in Canada's largest class action lawsuit, the Indian Residential
Schools Settlement Agreement (IRSSA) (approved by the courts and entering into
effect on 19 September 2007), government apology, and the Truth and Reconciliation
Commission.

In a few short decades a complete transformation took place in moral outlook toward a national policy in Canada, from one in which the Indian residential schools were
a necessity for providing language skills (English), job training, personal discipline,

piety (note the many archived photographs, once used for publicity purposes, of children in rows, in their beds or at their desks, hands clasped in prayer), and security in a changing world, to one in which the schools were widely recognized as a vehicle of assimilation and a source of trauma for individuals, families, and communities.

DISCLOSURE

Policies of dispossession or assimilation did not significantly motivate the public indignation behind Canada's Truth and Reconciliation Commission. The principal source of outrage that gave energy to the public reaction against residential schools had little to do with violations of the distinct rights of aboriginal peoples. Above all, it had to do with the violations of their common humanity, the disclosure of the institutionalized victimization, particularly sexual victimization, of children. The traction behind official apologies, litigation, policy change, and, eventually, the TRC came more than anything else from the growing credence given to remembrances and claims of sexual abuse of children by former students, directed toward the people in whose charge they lived. It came from a change in perception that made it possible to see members of the clergy as perpetrators of sexual crimes. It came above all from the willingness of individuals to tell, and their audiences to compassionately hear, narratives of abuse with considerable emotional impact.

This did not happen all at once. The stigma associated with sexual abuse of children was attached not only to the perpetrators but also, unjustly, to their victims. Overcoming this stigma took place in degrees. It began with private, secretive association among those who later called themselves survivors, moving toward a few confessions from victims (such was the shame attached to sexual victimization that these took the form of confessions) and apologies from representatives of the institutions. The unfolding eventually gained momentum toward widely accepted conceptions of historical trauma, successful lawsuits, and regimes of remedy.

A major turning point in all of this took place on 31 October 1990 with a public disclosure by Phil Fontaine, then Grand Chief of the Assembly of First Nations (AFN), that he had been physically and sexually abused while attending an Indian residential school. The news coverage of this event reached a national audience, including many former students (not yet referring to themselves as "survivors") who had also been abused. They, in turn, recognized the experience in themselves and in many cases were then (and only then) able to communicate it to others, even to take on the process of disclosure as a personal cause.

Garnet Angeconeb, in a memoir prepared for the Aboriginal Healing Foundation (AHF), provides a glimpse into what appears to have been a widely shared process of self-awareness, personal struggle, and finding common cause with others. Angeconeb describes the effect of reading the front-page article on Fontaine's disclosure in *The. Globe and Mail* while having breakfast with a friend:

> I felt incredible pain build up inside me. Through this haze of pain, I struggled to admit to my colleague that I, too, like many former students, had experienced sexual and physical abuse while at residential school. I was also enraged by the psychological and spiritual scars inflicted on me and the other students from the colonialistic and genocidal approach inherent in the residential school system ...
>
> After a while my colleague quietly asked, "So you were abused in residential school?"
>
> Not knowing what exactly to say, I responded, "Yes, I was abused—sexually." I told him that a man at the school named Hands, who eventually became an Anglican priest, had abused me and many others at Pelican during the 1960s. I felt a wave of rage overtake me ... Then, as if a floodgate had been thrown open, I cried uncontrollably.[4]

As Angeconeb goes on to report, awareness and acceptance of this painful experience in his own community was an obstacle to be overcome: "In northwestern Ontario, there was a heavy layer of silence surrounding the issue. Some people even questioned my motives for pursuing my case suggesting that I was doing it for political gain. But as I learned about others who were taking action and began to connect with them, I began to feel supported. It gave me the strength to continue."[5] Gatherings of former students began to take place informally, providing a sense of solidarity behind their interruption of silence and stigma. They began to form a common identity based on shared experience. This occurred region by region, community by community, in groups that formed around particular schools. For example, the Shubenacadie Indian Residential School, jointly run by the Sisters of Charity of Saint Vincent de Paul and the Missionary Oblates of Mary Immaculate from 1923 to 1967, produced hundreds if not thousands of former students (who later identified as survivors) in the surrounding communities. It also produced expatriate communities in Maine and a concentration of former students in Boston, a kind of reverse-direction Underground Railroad where aboriginal people from Canada, seeking asylum from the schools and protecting their children from recruitment into them, formed the first communities of former students in secret meetings that took place in the 1960s, well before any formal support or litigation on their behalf.

The unfolding public awareness of Indian residential schools as possible havens for the sexual abuse of children did not happen in isolation, but can be seen as occurring together with worldwide allegations of clergy sexual abuse, with the issue coming to particular prominence in Canada, the United States, Australia, and throughout the

British Isles. *The Boston Globe* was awarded a Pulitzer Prize in 2003 for its coverage of a major Catholic clergy sex abuse scandal (the subject of the Oscar-winning film *Spotlight*), which arguably raised the profile of the issue more than any other media outlet. This coverage stood out for its victim-centred detail, acquired through a "tip box" that accompanied the first articles that appeared on 6 and 7 January 2002. This consisted of an email address and two phone numbers, one to reach a live reporter and another to leave a confidential message. *Globe* reporters later recalled in an email group interview that in the early months of the project, "that tip box triggered such a torrent of phone calls and e-mails from across the country and even overseas that we had to hire a student intern to help us answer our telephones, which rang around-the-clock for weeks."[6] With the publication of the *Globe*'s first stories, including those that pointed to the Catholic Church's protection of accused perpetrators by moving them to other dioceses, "many victims grew even angrier because they realized that the betrayal they had experienced was not an isolated event ... it made them more eager to share the indignities they had suffered." The Vatican, meanwhile, was slow to respond, aggravating negative opinion and provoking even wider awareness of the issue by tending toward public statements that a correspondent for the *National Catholic Reporter* characterized as "tentative and half-hearted." This kind of response reflected a prevalent view in the higher ranks of the Church that saw the reporting of sex scandals in the United States as a "manifestation of cultural depravity and a news media crazed by sex."[7] Such views could well have been reinforced by the Catholic Church's strength in Latin America, Asia, and Africa, where there are greater challenges to public discussion and prosecution of pedophile priests, and where, as a *Boston Globe* reporter expressed it, "neither the news media, the legal system, nor the public culture are accustomed to robust discussions of sexual abuse."[8]

Such robust discussion of sexual abuse as a central feature of Canada's Indian residential schools was of course not the only catalyst of legal action and remedy—there were at the same time other sympathies, other sources of movement among aboriginal, Inuit, and Métis peoples to defend themselves against "attacks on their distinct cultural identities as they work to reclaim their histories and revitalize their languages, governance, and legal systems"[9]—but the sexual abuse of children, as an ultimate source of collective shame, brought with it greater reputational (not to mention litigational) costs to the institutions of church and state than any counter-narrative of colonialism. We can speculate that neither the apologies offered by the government and the churches nor the Settlement Agreement and the Truth and Reconciliation Commission would have occurred in the absence of a common perception (in North America and Europe at least) of the churches, the Catholic Church in particular, as unresponsive and even unrepentant in their harbouring of pedophiles. And as the stigma of this worst-of-all-possible-scandals extended to the state and to its aboriginal policies, the government too was called upon to act and to atone.

APOLOGY

The public apology has become an instrument in the rehabilitation of states that are recognized as having committed gross human rights violations. There is a kind of institutional personification that happens when states or state agencies make apologies, through a shared expectation that they should express through their spokespeople deep human feelings of personal regret and desire for absolution. It is as though states have some of the characteristics of flawed, well-intentioned individuals, capable of personal growth and moral improvement. But the moral correction of states is a public process. Their correction happens through their willingness to take an active part in the persuasion of their domestic publics, in efforts to bring popular opinion, and above all public awareness of state history, more in line with the moral universals of human rights.

In the background to Canada's acknowledgement and contrition toward residential school policy, the churches provided a model for how to proceed. This somehow makes sense, given that the churches are readily able to draw upon ideals of individual contrition, moral improvement, and salvation for policy changes and correction at the institutional level. The churches performed the first official acts of recognition and contrition toward Indian residential schools in the late 1980s and early 1990s. The United Church of Canada issued an apology in 1986, followed by the Oblate Missionaries of Mary Immaculate in 1991, the Anglican Church in 1993, and the Presbyterian Church in 1994.[10] The Catholic Church, as a decentralized institution with considerable autonomy given to each diocese, responded to the call for acknowledgement and contrition in a somewhat more diffuse way, with individual bishops making their own decisions on how to respond to information on abuse in their schools. Some did not acknowledge the harm or the institutional responsibility for it, and did not see the need for public contrition, while others, like Bishop Rouleau of the Diocese of Churchill-Hudson Bay, made the decision to offer an apology, and included a written follow-up to a statement presented at a church gathering that included direct reference to physical and sexual abuse:

> By taking advantage of the trust that you and your families had given to the personnel of the school the abusers perpetrated a profound violation against you, physically, emotionally and spiritually but sexually as well. As Bishop of this diocese I am ashamed and outraged that this happened to you. I apologize with all my heart for the role that members of the church took in all that.[11]

Expressions of contrition such as this did not garner wide attention. They were directed primarily to parishioners, to local audiences of the faithful. Due to the organizational form of the Catholic Church, no one bishop could speak on behalf of others. But even within such limits, apologies of the kind delivered by Bishop Rouleau still had the effect of encouraging others, particularly former students, to talk about their experiences. A survivor who gave testimony at the National Event in Inuvik made this explicit:

> When I first start talking about it, when I wanted to talk about [the sexual abuse that I received], at first it just won't come out. Somehow something got stuck in my throat and I couldn't say anything until I start talking to one person or two that I really believe in who is not going to go around and talk about it and then later it was coming out freely. Back in 1993, when Bishop Rouleau in Igloolik made an apology to us, that really opened up the whole story about Turquetil Hall residential school. I start talking about it to the media and everybody.[12]

The official apology, it would seem, had the effect of negating the stigma associated with sexual victimization, of making it clear to those who were victims that they held no responsibility for what they experienced as children.

Like many ceremonialized ideas in public life, apologies were communicated with contagious effect within and between institutions. In the Catholic Church, the idea eventually found its way from those dioceses that offered the earliest apologies against a current of church opinion, all the way to the Vatican. On 29 April 2009, Pope Benedict XVI held a private audience with a delegation led by national chief Phil Fontaine that included some fifty elders and residential school survivors from across Canada.[13] At the same time, the Vatican released a statement affirming that the pope "offered his sympathy and prayerful solidarity" to those suffering anguish caused by some church members. Although the statement had shades of the tentative Vatican response to other scandals and did not include the word "apology," Fontaine was satisfied, saying "this experience gives me great comfort" and expressing the hope that the event would "close the book" on the issue of church apologies for residential school survivors.[14]

But while the churches were able to draw on an established idiom of contrition and moral correction, the state had more difficulty reaching the point of apology. State apologies are more consequential in terms of the connection between contrition and the need for indemnification. The government had to be prepared at the same time to implement remedial action. An overwhelming edifice of evidence of the state's responsibility in a matter of catastrophic harm was needed before the state would act in a way that might restore its honour.

Part of the evidence that moved the Government of Canada in this direction came from the Royal Commission on Aboriginal Peoples (RCAP). In 1991, four aboriginal and three non-aboriginal commissioners were appointed to investigate the issues surrounding Canada's Indian policy and advise the government on their findings. The commission's report, released in 1996, makes a sweeping condemnation of nearly every aspect of Canada's aboriginal policy. Residential schools, in particular, were often the subject of testimony in the commission's hearings and figure prominently in the final report. Under the subheading "Discipline and Abuse," the RCAP report goes beyond establishing the common reality of violence in the schools; it also, and more importantly, establishes the illegitimacy of the policy that gave violence room to occur:

> At the heart of the vision of residential education—a vision of the school as home and sanctuary of motherly care—there was a dark contradiction, an inherent element of savagery in the mechanics of civilizing the children. The very language in which the vision was couched revealed what would have to be the essentially violent nature of the school system in its assault on child and culture. The basic premise of resocialization, of the great transformation from "savage" to "civilized," was violent. "To kill the Indian in the child," the department aimed at severing the artery of culture that ran between generations and was the profound connection between parent and child sustaining family and community.[15]

The report of the Royal Commission, together with a mounting accumulation of other testimony, evidence, and activism, led in 1998 to Canada's reformulation of its aboriginal policy. Given the title "Gathering Strength" and accompanied by the establishment of the Aboriginal Healing Foundation, along with a dedication of $350 million to support community-based healing initiatives, the revision was intended as a policy-based response to the findings of the Royal Commission. All of this was accompanied by an official acknowledgement of the harm that occurred in residential schools, published and posted online under the title *Statement of Reconciliation*. It is worthy of note that in spite of the evident care that was taken in this statement to limit Canada's liability, it was delivered by then Minister of Indian Affairs, Jane Stewart, with tearful sincerity:

> The Government of Canada acknowledges the role it played in the development and administration of these schools. Particularly to those individuals who experienced the tragedy of sexual and physical abuse at residential schools, and who have carried this burden believing that in some way they must be responsible, we wish to emphasize that what you experienced was not your fault and should never have happened. To those of you who suffered this tragedy at residential schools, we are deeply sorry.[16]

This statement, as many critics were quick to point out, expressed regret for the most serious harm caused by the schools, but fell short of an apology for the policy at their origin. Despite its limitations, the *Statement of Reconciliation* encouraged public discourse about sexual abuse in the schools in much the same way that the church apologies did, prominently breaking the "barrier of silence" that inhibited discussion of sexual abuse. With this kind of public acknowledgement, there was no denying the fact that there was abuse in the schools. And because of this, public communication could now begin with a presumption of the reality of abuse and harm.

Not long after Jane Stewart's delivery of the *Statement of Reconciliation*, a change took place in the tone of the discourse surrounding Indian residential schools. I was witness to this transformation while living in Cross Lake, an aboriginal reserve community in northern Manitoba. At the Band office, there was sudden interest in archival work I was doing at the Diocese of Keewatin-Le Pas on the local history of St. Joseph's Indian Residential School. People gathered around a desk as I spread out copies of photographs I had received from the church archivist, and a discussion ensued about the identities of the children in the photographs and sometimes what later became of them. A few found themselves in the photos: "There I am!" One office worker pointed to a photograph of a nun standing primly beside a row of children, their hands clasped obediently on their desks, and exclaimed, "She's the one who always used to pull my ears!"

Remembrance received official sanction from chief and council. Elders were interviewed by a Band researcher and invited to speak publicly about their school experience at events broadcast on community television. There was also an inter-community exchange in which a speaker from the Gordon Reserve in Saskatchewan made a stop on a tour to a number of reserve communities across Canada. This was a two-day event abounding in stories of abuse at the hands of those who were supposed to be educators and caretakers, and of loneliness, addictions, and distorted capacities for love and sexuality in adult life, told with even more forthrightness than was later the norm in the Truth and Reconciliation Commission (or perhaps equal to it, with my own perception of the event influenced by the fact that I was hearing such testimony for the first time). Former students also talked about more positive things, about healing and repentance, struggling for and achieving sobriety, and re-establishing loving relationships with family members whom they had hurt and betrayed during the low point of their lives. The meeting had something of the nature of a Pentecostal revival meeting, with an atmosphere of extravagantly open confessions; tearful expressions of pain, regret, and repentance; and attestations of sobriety and healing.[17]

By this time, the accumulating mass of testimony also took the form of an edifice of litigation. Long before the TRC began its work, the courts became the most important venue by which an alternative narrative about Indian residential schools began to gain traction. Starting in 1989–90, prosecutions of former residential school staff took place in British Columbia and the Yukon, initiating an ever-widening circle of investigations, indictments, and prosecutions across the country. (In the TRC meetings in Victoria and Inuvik, those who had been involved as plaintiffs in these groundbreaking lawsuits were given special acknowledgement.) As the full extent of abuses that took place in some of the most notorious schools across Canada unfolded in the courts, the expectation of appropriate action from government gained support. Largely through the language of the courts, public positions of doubt or qualification concerning the harm resulting from residential schools had become untenable. No amount of media relations skill and resources could effectively counteract the accumulating impacts of court judgments. One of the more striking of these was handed down in 1995, when Arthur Plint, a dorm supervisor at the Alberni Indian Residential School, was convicted of sixteen counts of indecent assault. During his sentencing, BC Supreme Court Justice Douglas Hogarth characterized Plint as a "sexual terrorist," and elaborated by saying, "as far as the victims were concerned, the Indian residential school system was nothing more than institutionalized pedophilia."[18] Any defence of the schools from the churches or government in response to such plain-spoken language from the courts would almost inevitably come across as bad faith.

Local organizations of former students, using the word "survivor" to designate their common criterion of belonging, were also central to this awareness-raising momentum. In Nova Scotia, Nora Bernard began welcoming other former students of the Shubenacadie Indian Residential School to her kitchen in 1987, and eventually used the resulting network as a foundation for an independent association of survivors, today referring to itself as the Shubenacadie Residential School Survivors. By 1998 it had 900 members in Canada and the United States. This organization, in turn, was the source of a major class action lawsuit.[19]

Yet a government apology that met most of the expectations of a state apology did not occur for another ten years after the preliminary *Statement of Reconciliation*. Canadian Prime Minister Steven Harper delivered the *Statement of Apology* in Parliament on 11 July 2008, shortly after ratification of the Indian Residential School Settlement Agreement. (The apology was, in fact, a condition of the Agreement.) But this background to the apology seemed to matter less to most former students than the fact that it occurred and that the prime minister said what they expected him to say:

While some former students have spoken positively about their experiences at residential schools, these stories are far overshadowed by tragic accounts of the emotional, physical and sexual abuse and neglect of helpless children, and their separation from powerless families and communities. The legacy of Indian residential schools has contributed to social problems that continue to exist in many communities today. We now recognize that, in separating children from their families, we undermined the ability of many to adequately parent their own children and sowed the seeds for generations to follow, and we apologize for having done this.[20]

There are certain expectations attached to the state apology that were not met in the *Statement of Reconciliation* but that are met here. First, the state has to express a sincere regret by explicitly disavowing discredited policies and promising that the state will never return to them. The apology is also (but less explicitly) expected to construct a binary of perpetrator and victim in a reconfiguration of the past. The state alone is expected to take responsibility for harm and, in the short space allotted (apologies are also called upon to stick to the point), to radically simplify the history of the conditions behind institutional abuse. In doing so, the public apology usually contains a subtext concerning the essential nature of victimhood and suffering. It is to offer a clear portrayal of those who are the living victims of the state—in this case not just the former students but also their families, including the "generations to follow."

In its unusually encompassing admission of the scope of the harm done by the state's Indian residential school policy, Canada's apology offered yet another level of affirmation to those who could see themselves as survivors and, from this point on, with clarity and certainty, as "intergenerational survivors." With the Truth and Reconciliation Commission taking office in the same month it was issued, the apology contributed to conditions in which the shame attached to victimization in the schools was further diminished and in which public narrations of school experience could take place on a national scale.

HUMAN RIGHTS AND WRONGS

In terms of the schools' history, much has been written about the institutions themselves, the ideas behind them as national policy, the participation of churches, and the lived experience of the children. From the basic outlines of this history we can see that it was the failure of the goals of residential schools more than public reaction to the abuses that commonly took place in their implementation that led to policy reform and closure.

We know less about the ideas and motivations behind the schools' initial illegitimacy and abandonment than we do about their later recognition as institutional sources of abuse and trauma and, resulting from this, as subjects of remedy and sources of litigation, apology, compensation, testimony-gathering, and re-inscription in history. But one thing in this historical trajectory seems to stand out: the *moral* rejection of residential schools actually came later than one might suppose, and might even be considered a work in progress. The wide dissemination of the idea of residential schools as places of systemic abuse, horror, and trauma did not occur simultaneously with the change in policy that led to their closure. It is largely through the work of the TRC that an accumulating, self-reinforcing mass of testimonies, confessions, and apologies is becoming accepted as part of public discourse, even though it remains marginal (evidenced by the comparatively spare media coverage of hearings). The basic lack of awareness among the "general public" of residential schools and the abuses that happened in them may be diminishing, but somehow stubbornly persists.

At the same time, changes in shared values and perceptions oriented toward institutional responsibility and accountability have only recently made it possible to think about the predatory sexuality of some individuals who were authority figures in the churches. It is now widely recognized that institutions exercising total control over a powerless population readily become havens for a type of personality that finds satisfaction in domination, in pushing their little domain of power to its furthest extreme. Sexual predation is but one manifestation of this personal domination of the socially marginal. We could almost call it an aspect of human nature, except for the fact that it is not part of the makeup of every individual, and may even be a great rarity. But, judging by numerous reports of the experiences of incarcerated children that have only recently seen the light of day, it seems to occur with enough frequency to make circumstances of grossly unequal power tend toward institutionalized horror and atrocity.

In contrast to human rights violations that occur through visible violence, in which cameras are at the ready, the harms that took place in and through residential schools were mostly invisible. An apparatus of state- and church-sponsored publicity had to be overcome before the damage could be revealed and recognized. This was not something that could happen overnight. The impetus of opinion behind the Settlement Agreement began in isolation, where former students found each other and through their solidarity found the courage to defy the silence and shame imposed on them and their experience by making it known to others. From these first "confessions" of victims, there followed an ever-widening circle of revelation and reaction, with a corresponding extension of the reach of contrition, from local politicians to the prime minister, and from priests to the pope.

Within the limits of their good faith participation in human rights (by no means a given), states that are concerned about their reputations in the "international community" are now subject to moral self-examination and correction, almost in the manner of the personal growth of good, aspiring individuals. This means that another impetus behind the Settlement Agreement and the Truth and Reconciliation Commission was the fact that the wrongs of the state associated with the Indian residential schools began to be recognized as such, as constituting a major, systemic violation of human rights. From this point of view, it was not so much (or not only) the acts of violence and sexual victimization that made the residential schools the embodiments of institutionalized harm but the fact of their establishment as instruments of dispossession in the common parlance of a new era of human rights, and of the human rights of indigenous peoples in particular.

This rights-oriented awareness also has a recent history of unfolding. It was only starting in the 1970s that we began to see the appearance of a genuine social movement around human rights, understood by many "as a pure alternative in an age of ideological betrayal and political collapse."[21] The contrition and moral correction of states and state-sponsored institutions that seem to be broadly accepted (if not expected) today are, from any historical angle one might want to take, oddities that defy explanation. They certainly differ from nineteenth-century notions of progress, which tended to be linear, cumulative, and celebratory of state power. The idea of progress that we can now see in action is based on public scrutiny and moral accountability, in which the exposure of harms wrought by states are responded to by policy reform, apology, and public examination. The mostly implicit assumption behind this process is a deep suspicion of the goodwill of states if left to their own devices, accompanied by the requirement, which they often resist or comply with in limited, foot-dragging ways, that they at times interrupt the momentum of their designs and acknowledge and atone for their errors.

The phenomenon sometimes referred to as the rights revolution brought into being an idiom in which it was possible to see the systemic harm done by governments through "total institutions" and to put that harm into the languages of public indignation and legal remedy. Efforts to overcome the legacy of residential schools, in other words, reflect a shift in the consensual foundations of the state. The expectation that the state should act as a responsible moral actor is the most basic and compelling but also taken-for-granted idea behind the remedial response to the knowledge of harms perpetrated in and by means of state institutions. The public dynamics of human rights accountability are central to this personification of the state, with implications for the ideals of social justice and, beyond this, for the definitions of selves and social worlds.

NOTES

1 Primo Levi, *The Drowned and the Saved*, trans. Raymond Rosenthal (New York: Vintage, 1988), 17.

2 Law Commission of Canada, "Restoring Dignity: Responding to Child Abuse in Canadian Institutions" (Ottawa: Minister of Public Works and Government Services, 2000), 5.

3 National Film Board of Canada (NFB), *PowWow at Duck Lake*, Film (Montreal: National Film Board of Canada, 1967), 8:00. For more on the documentary

film project of which this was part, see Thomas Waugh, Michael Brendan Baker, and Ezra Winton, eds., *Challenge for Change: Activist Documentary at the National Film Board of Canada* (Montreal and Kingston: McGill-Queen's University Press, 2010).

4   Garnet Angeconeb, "Speaking My Truth: The Journey to Reconciliation," in *Speaking My Truth: Reflections on Reconciliation and Residential School*, ed. Shelagh Rogers, Mike Degagne, and Jonathan Dewar (Ottawa: Aboriginal Healing Foundation, 2012), 19–20.

5   Ibid., 22.

6   Christy Cox, "Abuse in the Catholic Church," *Dart Center for Journalism and Trauma*, 7 April 2003, accessed 2 March 2013, https://dartcenter.org/content/abuse-in-catholic-church.

7   John Allen, cited in Michael Paulson, "World Doesn't Share US View of Scandal: Clergy Sexual Abuse Reaches Far, Receives an Uneven Focus," *The Boston Globe*, 4 August 2002, A1, accessed 2 March 2013, http://www.boston.com/globe/spotlight/abuse/print/040802_world.htm.

8   Paulson, "World Doesn't Share US View of Scandal," A1.

9   Paulette Regan, *Unsettling the Settler Within: Indian Residential Schools, Truth Telling, and Reconciliation in Canada* (Vancouver: University of British Columbia Press, 2010), 3.

10 Aboriginal Healing Foundation, *1999 Annual Report* (Ottawa: Aboriginal Healing Foundation, 1999), 7, accessed 30 August 2009, http://www.ahf.ca/downloads/annual-report-99.pdf.

11 Reynald Rouleau, "To: The Former Students of Joseph Bernier Federal Day School and Turquetil Hall (1955–1969)—Chesterfield Inlet; From: Reynald Rouleau, O.M.I., Bishop of Churchill-Hudson Bay," unpublished open letter, Diocese of Churchill-Hudson Bay, 18 January 1996.

12 Speaker unknown, Commissioner's Sharing Panel, TRC Inuvik National Event, 30 June 2011.

13 This was an event prompted by a personal suggestion to the pope some six months earlier by Archbishop Weisgerber of Winnipeg. Interview with Archbishop James Weisgerber, Winnipeg, 19 June 2010.

14 "Pope Expresses 'Sorrow' for Abuse at Residential Schools," *CBC News*, 29 April 2009, accessed 2 March 2013, http://www.cbc.ca/news/world/pope-expresses-sorrow-for-abuse-at-residential-schools-1.778019.

15 Royal Commission on Aboriginal Peoples, *Final Report, Volume 1: Looking Forward, Looking Back* (Ottawa: Indian and Northern Affairs, 1996), part 2, ch. 10, section 3, accessed 18 October 2012, http://data2.archives.ca/e/e448/e011188230-01.pdf.

16 Indian and Northern Affairs Canada, "Notes for an Address by the Honourable Jane Stewart, Minister of Indian Affairs and Northern Development, on the occasion of the unveiling of *Gathering Strength—Canada's Aboriginal Action Plan*" (Ottawa: Indian and Northern Affairs Canada, 1998), accessed 30 August 2009, http://www.aadnc-aandc.gc.ca/eng/1100100015725/1100100015726.

17 I discuss this meeting in more detail in *Public Justice and the Anthropology of Law* (Cambridge, UK: Cambridge University Press, 2010), ch. 6.

18 *R. v. Plint* [1995] B.C.J. No 3060, at para. 14.

19 David Soosaar, "Bernard's Lawsuit Helped Natives Nationwide," *The Daily News (Halifax)*, 30 December 2007, accessed 17 June 2017, http://archives.algomau.ca/main/sites/default/files/2010-061_014_008.pdf.

20 "Text of Prime Minister Harper's apology," 11 June 2008, accessed 25 April 2009, http://www.fns.bc.ca/pdf/TextofApology.pdf.

21 Samuel Moyn, *The Last Utopia: Human Rights in History* (Cambridge, MA: Harvard University Press, 2010), 8.

Chapter 3

THE PROCESS

THE APPLICATION OF JUSTICE

How does one even begin to proceed toward a regime of compensation in the aftermath of the largest and arguably the most politically significant class action lawsuit in Canadian history? In the wake of a policy that had been revealed as a human rights disaster and a national shame, how does one make a transition from judgment to remedy, from rulings of the bench and legally mediated negation to the *application* of justice?

Everything that we associate with this Truth and Reconciliation Commission (and this I will describe in more detail in the chapters that follow)—including the ritual, the kinds of emotion publicly expressed, and the form and dominant narratives of testimony—is set within the wider context of this remedial challenge and the solutions found for it. Although regime change in fledgling democracies is a common background to most TRCs, it is not a necessary precondition. Canada's TRC—in common with, for example, the Greensboro Truth and Reconciliation Commission, which inquired into the deaths of anti-Klan demonstrators in North Carolina in 1979—is one of few that have taken place through a change in political outlook but in the absence of a regime change.[1] No war or revolution preceded it and gave it impetus.

The real force behind the Settlement Agreement and its terms of reference for the TRC was litigation. By October 2002, over 11,000 legal cases had been filed against the federal government and churches involved in Indian education.[2] In May 2005, the federal government, the churches, and the AFN signed an agreement in principle to negotiate a settlement to resolve the legal cases. Then, on 5 August 2005, the AFN launched a class action lawsuit against the federal government that sought $12 billion in general damages; $12 billion in special damages for negligence, breach of fiduciary duty, statutory duty, treaty obligations, and other common law duties; and $12 billion in punitive damages. Although a settlement was already underway with its terms largely decided at the time of its submission, this lawsuit made the AFN a plaintiff and a party to the negotiations, more than an interested advocacy group. With this strategic motive as an impetus behind it, the Indian Residential Schools Settlement Agreement (IRSSA) was reached on 10 May 2006 and entered into effect on 19 September 2007.[3]

One outcome of the Settlement Agreement's background of litigation and negotiation is that the federal government and the churches sought finality for judicial process and reparations, a circumstance, in turn, which favoured limiting the judicial powers of the TRC. A priority of the Settlement Agreement was to create a nationwide alternative to litigation. It accomplished this through two regimes of compensation. The Common Experience Payment (CEP) applied to everyone who as a child resided in an institution recognized as a federally operated Indian residential school, whether demonstrable harm resulted from this experience or not. The purpose of the CEP was to provide compensation to former students who were denied access to the language and culture of their families and communities. This corresponded with the argument made in class action lawsuits to the effect that the loss of language and culture was a significant harm that was not being addressed through litigation or the federal government's Alternative Dispute Resolution model of compensation, which was in place before the Settlement Agreement.

The Independent Assessment Process (IAP), underway at the time of writing, is a federally operated system for adjudicating specific claims of harm in the schools.[4] Former students seeking compensation for particular abuses that took place on the premises of a recognized Indian residential school through the IAP are eligible to be heard so long as the incident(s) took place on school property or in circumstances under which school authorities were responsible.

These two compensation regimes have cast long shadows. They became focal points of concern in aboriginal communities before the TRC began its work, and it is through them that processes of remembrance and re-experience were significantly set in motion. More than this, they established the conditions by which the priests, nuns, lay personnel, and sometimes even former students of the schools were identified as "Persons of Interest (POIs)," usually in the form of allegations of sexual abuse; and this in turn, as I will discuss further on in this chapter, had a determining effect on their participation in (or absence from) the Commission and hence the nature of testimony presented to it. In their widest significance, they illustrate the surprisingly direct way that legal structures can shape conceptions of history, identity, and boundaries of social membership. This, I hope, is sufficient justification for the attention I will now give to the Settlement Agreement's bureaucratically rendered conceptions and categories of compensable harm.

Survivors did not need to prove subjection to wrongdoing in order to qualify for the Common Experience Payment (CEP). Former students were awarded compensation simply by virtue of having attended a residential school for which the federal government was responsible; $10,000 for their first year spent at school and $3,000 for each year thereafter. By 30 September 2012, when the deadline for submission of CEP claims had passed, 106,023 applications had been received, with (thus far) 79,309 deemed eligible for payment and 23,927 ineligible. The average payment under this system has been estimated at $20,457. Nationwide, this amounted to a sudden influx of $1.6 billion into the aboriginal population.[5]

Predictably, money did what money does: it enabled the enabled, corrupted the corruptible, gave exploiters the opportunity to exploit, and allowed the addicted to nourish their addictions. Analysis of a complex event like this often resolves itself into a dualism of "positive" and "negative" effects. Just such a dualism was reported by an Aboriginal Healing Foundation (AHF) study that sought the opinion of 117 aboriginal people who had either themselves received the lump sum payments or observed the effects of them in their families and communities. On the positive side, there was much to be said for an influx of money into marginalized communities. Once the cheques arrived, many recipients turned their temporary financial gain into opportunities with lasting effects, helping out family members, clearing up debts, and investing for the future.[6]

More commonly, it would seem, the interviews pointed in the other direction, toward harms that followed the windfall. Recipients noted that the payments often led to increases in drug and alcohol abuse, pressure from family members for money, and encroachments by financial predators. Perhaps the most troubling result was the increase in drug and alcohol abuse. For one contributor to the study, the program of Common Experience Payments "took away from healing because money makes people 'go crazy.' Everybody in small communities will be affected by heavy drinking. Everyone is affected. When a group is drinking, this multiplies the burdens for individual families. Those who were living traditional lives—hunting and trapping—abandoned this way of life for the money. The government threw this money out and caused chaos."[7] This increase in addictive behaviour was also observed by social service providers, one of whom remarked that "payments not only amplified existing negative behaviours and problems in their communities, but they opened up doors to experiment with substances recipients could not afford before, like cocaine."[8]

In other ways the payments did not fit neatly into the positive effects/negative effects binary; they seem to have commonly produced a mixed feeling in the recipients, a condition of ambiguity that we can only imagine would follow from picking up one's mail and finding a government cheque, sent in compensation for time spent in a residential school as a child. One contributor to the AHF study described it as "humiliating," but at the same time encouraging: "It forced recipients to name their experience and to deal with it. People got past their denial. They revealed their secrets."[9] This symbolic aspect of the payments was connected to money, but at the same time was not "about" money. It was not the exchange value of the payment that mattered most but a kind of recognition value, a form of incentive to begin the process of "telling our story."[10] This quality of encouraging the narration of harm is a situation that makes compensation hearings markedly different from any other kind of civil litigation. And, as we will see, it was to have important, recognizable consequences for the later testimony presented to the Truth and Reconciliation Commission.

THE INDEPENDENT ASSESSMENT PROCESS

The essence of the Independent Assessment Process (IAP) is that it renders the victimization of children into a dollar amount and a cheque in the mail. According to an update released by Indigenous and Northern Affairs Canada on the implementation of the Indian Residential Schools Settlement Agreement, with figures valid as of 31 March 2017, a total of 38,096 IAP claims had been received under this agreement, 36,717 of which have been processed. Of these, 26,020 had been completed with decisions rendered, 4,343 resolved through negotiated settlements, and 6,354 not admitted, withdrawn, or dismissed. Total compensation to this date, including awards and legal fees and disbursements, had reached $3,117,000,000, with the average cost of each settlement standing at $111,737. With some 4 per cent of the IAP claims remaining to be processed, it can be estimated that the final cost of the IAP process will approach $3.3 billion.[11]

The IAP is an out-of-court process intended to be claimant-centred, non-adversarial, and efficient. In its handling of claims, there is no encounter between accuser and accused, no cross-examination, none of the drama commonly associated with judicial process. The possible vulnerability of claimants is built into the design of adjudication. Prior to any hearings in a case, the secretariat will have contacted those who are accused in the claimants' report—until they are convicted of a crime they are known as "Persons of Interest"—informing them of the allegations, and of the fact that they have a right to send a statement or to arrange a separate hearing with the adjudicator. The process is, as advertised, claimant-centred. On its "Frequently Asked Questions" page (now removed from the Internet), the Indian Residential Schools Adjudication Secretariat assured potential claimants, "You will not have to come face-to-face with your alleged abuser."[12]

Under this regime of compensation, credible survivor testimony is applied to a point system in which numerical scores are awarded under three basic headings, "Acts

Proven," "Consequential Harm," and "Consequential Loss of Opportunity," which are then further divided into different categories, ranked according to degree of severity. Of the seven categories for "Acts Proven," five concern sexual victimization. The first level of sexual misconduct awards the claimant five to ten points, and includes "one or more incidents of fondling or kissing," "nude photographs taken of the Claimant," employees of the school "exposing themselves," and "any touching of a student, including touching with an object ... that violates the sexual integrity of the student." From here the grid covers an entire spectrum of perversion and rape all the way to level 5, "repeated, persistent incidents of anal or vaginal intercourse" and/or "anal/vaginal penetration with an object," for which claimants are awarded 45 to 60 points. One category does all the work of defining and awarding points for physical harm in a catch-all that includes "one or more physical assaults causing a physical injury," "impairment or disfigurement," with, inexplicably, only one example of a specific resulting injury—"broken bones"—and a short list of possible causes of injury: "severe beating, whipping and second-degree burning."[13]

Once the claimant's experience of victimization is established and assigned a number between 11 and 25 points, a second set of criteria are applied, arranged under the heading "Consequential Harm," to arrive at points for the degree of suffering and disability experienced by claimants as a result of their victimization in school. These range from a first level of "modest detrimental impact," marked by occasional short-term "anxiety, nightmares, bed-wetting, aggression, panic states, hyper-vigilance, retaliatory rage, depression, humiliation, loss of self-esteem" (for which claimants are awarded 1 to 5 points), through to a fifth level, "continued harm resulting in serious dysfunction," evidenced by "psychotic disorganization, loss of ego boundaries, personality disorders, pregnancy resulting from a defined sexual assault or the forced termination of such pregnancy or being required to place for adoption a child resulting therefrom, self-injury, suicidal tendencies, inability to form or maintain personal relationships, chronic post-traumatic state, sexual dysfunction, or eating disorders," for any of which they receive 20 to 25 compensation points.[14] Claimants who demonstrate severe consequential harms can be awarded an additional compensation amount for "future care" of up to $15,000 for psychiatric treatment.

The third category, "Consequential Loss of Opportunity," is the most straightforward. It again has five ranked categories, ranging from "diminished work capacity" caused by reduced strength or attention span (1 to 5 points) to "chronic inability to obtain employment" (21 to 25 points). If detailed evidence of "proven actual income loss" can be shown, the point grid can be abandoned in favour of compensation based on amounts normally awarded in court decisions for similar income loss.

The scores for "Acts Proven," "Consequential Harm," and "Consequential Loss of Opportunity" are then combined to arrive at a total score, which corresponds to a range of dollar amounts for compensation. The lowest total of compensation points starts at 1–10, valued at $5,000 to $10,000, and from there it goes up by ten point increments to 110–120, worth $211,000 to $245,000, followed by a somewhat more open category, 121 or more, valued at up to $275,000. To this can be added 5 to 15 per cent (rounded up to the nearest whole number) for "aggravating factors," such as verbal abuse, racist acts, threats, intimidation, degradation, failure to provide care, sexual abuse accompanied by violence, abuse of a young or particularly vulnerable child, "use of religious doctrine, paraphernalia or authority during, or in order to facilitate, the abuse," and abuse "by an adult who had built a particular relationship of trust and caring with the victim," a category captured by one word at the end of the definition: "betrayal."[15]

The criteria that form the basis of the claims process that I have just described have the effect of clarifying, but at the same time heightening and making uncomfortable, the associations between financial compensation and traumatic experience. We can see this in the testimony of a school survivor who had been through the Independent Assessment Process and who made his feelings about it known to the Commission during hearings in Saskatoon: "I found it abusive. 'How many times did you get raped? That's another $5,000.' It's demeaning. It didn't work."[16] Others have seen the same effects of sudden windfalls as those that followed the Common Experience Payments, except that the amounts involved were greater. Chief Clarence Rodney Papequash, narrating his life story to the Survivor's Sharing Circle in Saskatoon, made a pointed observation about the destructive consequences of the sudden windfalls: "My sons got a-hundred-and-twenty grand out of Gordon's [Indian Residential School]. How many of you are drug addicts? When I was a drug addict, if I got a hundred grand, I would say 'Helllloo!' And that's what happened. They blew their money away."[17] And again, as with the CEP awards, there are those who see it as an opportunity to accomplish something otherwise impossible:

My brother Charlie [Wenjack] ... he died running away from school. He was only twelve. After being hit by a principal, after being sexually abused, sodomized by another older student. I wanted him to have been here, to say that all he wanted was to go home. That's all he wanted. He didn't want anything else. But it took us two days to get here ... And that's a long ways. He tried to walk that. In 1966, October 22, he froze to death trying to walk home.

... And whatever money I get from my IAP, I want to get a healing centre for my reserve, with Charlie's name.[18]

With the deadline for the submission of IAP claims looming at the time of the Saskatoon National Event in June 2012, the more sordid side of money-as-remedy made itself evident in a scramble for clients, ultimately for the fees that make up the lawyers' part of the damages-for-the-deserving. (The Indian Residential Schools Adjudication Secretariat recommends that lawyers charge not more than 30 per cent of the compensation award.) Two local law firms set up booths to solicit clients. As "hooks" to bring in potential clients, one offered free donuts and candy, the other sugar-free candy (an elderly woman, stopping to look, said, "Oooh, sugar-free? Then maybe I can have another!") and a raffle, giving away a blanket, a jogging suit with the firm's logo, and a small flat-screen television. A brochure at this booth provided information on the claims process, including the most crucial information: the amount of compensation possible through the process, which "range[d] from $5,000 to $275,000," with these amounts highlighted in red.

This brings us to another selection process at work before IAP hearings take place, in which lawyers gave priority to claims likely to be successful and lucrative. If a case was complex or likely to be only for a small amount, claimants were less apt to be taken on by a lawyer. Claimants were of course free to proceed through the IAP claims process without a lawyer, but this was discouraged.[19] The process also tended to exclude those who had clearly been abused in the schools but were unable to remember those basic details that were prerequisites of a successful claim, sometimes even what school it was and when they were there or, most commonly, the name of the person who victimized them.

These tendencies point in the direction of a structural contradiction in the claims process: it has disadvantaged some of those who were the most distressed, those who suffered lifelong mental illness, with all the attendant symptoms of trauma like trouble remembering and acute anxiety when faced with the challenge of recalling traumatic events. Jack Anawak, a former residential school student and Member of Parliament from Nunavut, remembered the trouble people had participating as witnesses in the litigation process: "Many people then had to face the difficulty of writing their statements and telling the world, and then speaking to them in a fairly sterile process ... Some could barely set it down on paper. Some could barely stand up while giving their testimony. Some fainted and fell to the floor."[20] A case worker who had once worked for the federal government in the Alternative Dispute Resolution program reported to me what it was like working with one such traumatized woman through the process of submitting a claim: "It took six or seven weeks. We would talk a little bit, get something down. Then it would be too much for her and we'd have to take a break. We would meet again later in the week and have a little more progress before she'd be unable to go on, until finally the claim was ready to be submitted."[21] The very same difficulties were faced by some former students in preparations leading up to IAP hearings.

This kind of struggle goes together with the possibility that the claimant will give up on the case, as one survivor at the TRC meeting in Victoria reported having done:

"I shared with my lawyer many deep, powerful, sorrowful things. I had to write it out on a computer. It got to the point I was ready to give up my sobriety, the pain was so great. I gave up my lawsuit because I didn't want to start drinking again."[22] Not every lawyer is willing to commit themselves to long-term efforts with emotionally fragile clients, particularly when there are others better able to recall their experience and tell their story, not to mention less likely to drop their claim because of the pain of traumatic remembrance. This experience of mental illness also sometimes finds its way into testimony at TRC meetings—"The biggest phase now that I have to fight is the mental illness that came as a result of, after the [IAP] hearings"—leaving one to wonder whether another personal struggle might follow from making a confession to an audience, live and online, of thousands.[23]

REVOLT OF THE ACCUSED

The Independent Assessment Process has greater significance than the occasional remarks about it in TRC hearings might lead one to expect. Not only did the IAP shape survivor statements through its conditions for the selection and preparation of testimony, it favoured the appearance or absence of certain kinds of participants—hence the inclusion or exclusion of distinct realms of narrative experience—in TRC hearings, above all, the experience of its aggrieved "Persons of Interest."

Listening to the life stories of some of the priests with whom I spent time outside the interview setting, a number of commonalities became apparent that might help explain their shared attitude to the judgments and processes of the Settlement Agreement. For many of the priests, their membership in an order and vow of celibacy was not just a calling of faith, but a commitment to human betterment. The order was an anchorage in an uncertain world, an institutional manifestation of the certainty they found in religion. During the time that residential schools were in full operation, a career in the service of a Christian institution was also highly respected, honourable, and a possible avenue to power and public influence.

Then in the space of a single lifetime came a change in public attitudes toward the Catholic clergy in Canada. Church membership dropped. Seminaries and convents attracted fewer and fewer new members. Positions in remote parishes had to be filled by candidates from Africa and Latin America (where the order still attracts new members) because none were available locally. Communities of priests and nuns shifted toward retirement residences. This was the professional and demographic impact of a broad shift in public moral outlook and opinion. Archbishop Weisgerber linked the decline of the Oblates' model of missionary activity to their disappointment—"shock" is actually the word he used—over the anger directed toward them from aboriginal people. "It hurt a lot of them," he said, and went on to relate a reference point for this sense of rejection by those steeped in Church history: "A small number of Jews killed Jesus but [every Jew] was targeted with them."[24] The Oblates' strong reaction against the Settlement Agreement, from their personal point of view, stemmed from a feeling of being unappreciated, subjected to ingratitude, "because you have given your life and it wasn't appreciated, it's been thrown back into your face and you are made to look abusive."[25]

Another level of disappointment and resentment followed from the experience of being subjected to false accusations, particularly accusations of sexual abuse, communicated via identification as a "Person of Interest" as an outcome of IAP hearings in a letter from the Adjudications Secretariat. In the normal course of things, any structure of mass testimony linked to a regime of material compensation will create incentives for factitious and false claims. Consistent with this incentive structure, almost everyone in the Catholic clergy I spoke to had a story connected to such claims. (The invitation to participate in an interview, in fact, would have selected in favour of those with such grievances.) This included Archbishop Weisgerber: "One old nun told me that she was accused of having taught a girl how to do oral sex. She said, 'I don't even know what that is!'"[26]

For others, the stories were first-hand and the counter-accusations more personal: "I got ... allegations against me, especially Fort Alexander. Only there. Not elsewhere ... You know, you put some money in front of you, you come and tell your story you know, a juicy one. And the lawyers and they say, well, we'll pay you. So they make lots of allegations. It was always of course the sexual allegations. But I know there was, wasn't anything from on my part."[27]

In a group interview with eight retired priests in their residence at Winnipeg, resentment toward the compensation process was a central theme, and money a central explanation for its failings:

> R.N.: Do you think the testimony that we're hearing today [at the TRC
>   hearings] is influenced by the compensation regime that it all started with?
> PRIEST 1: Well, of course, money talks.
> PRIEST 2: [two priests talking at once] ... money talks. A great deal.
> PRIEST 1: Money talks. There's no doubt about it.
> PRIEST 2: It's money, money, money, money.[28]

One of the priests then elaborated on the role of lawyers in the compensation process: "So they [the lawyers] started from the top ... and then, who, the, the people, the teachers who were there, the staff people, they all got letters." He then spoke in the voice of a recipient of compensation: "'Wow! Whooo! I could buy myself a truck. I could even buy half a dozen!'"[29]

Father Jacques L'Heureux, who participated as a representative of accused priests and nuns in over a thousand abuse allegations over the space of eighteen years, expressed bitterness toward the false accusations of priests and brothers (it happens much less frequently with nuns) in the IAP hearings. He contemptuously referred to the process as "parajudicial" proceedings in which "the students' affirmations were never put in doubt when it was proven that the school was not even built [at the time of the alleged offence]. The adjudicators' reasoning is clear: 'You have attended a Residential School, THEN you have been abused. From your story, the abuses you have endured entitle you to a monetary compensation at this level. Please sign the release form and we will send you the cheque.'"[30] An obvious reason for such expressions of righteous anger is the nature of Father L'Heureux's position in the Oblate organization, which puts him in regular contact with priests and brothers who relate to him their experience of false accusations, along with their feelings of rejection and betrayal. One Oblate priest who had been subject to an accusation that was later retracted, for example, wrote a letter to L'Heureux that characterized the IAP hearings as follows:

This business of "Residential Schools" where brothers, sisters, and friends are dragged in an unjust (and unjustified) way before a court of justice that does not deserve the name, to be judged on the grounds of everything that happened ... for no other reason ... than the most odious possible lies—but profitable (it's incredible!), as much for the accuser as for their lawyer.[31]

Father L'Heureux, in his role as representative of the accused priests, then weighed in with a letter to Dan Ish, Chief Adjudicator at the Indian Residential Schools Adjudication Secreteriat, describing the consequences of this eventually retracted accusation:

Since the reception of the letter, dated November 1st 2010, in which [claimant] H affirmed that he had been sodomized by Fr. C, Father C has gone through a whole series of feelings where rage and unbelief mix in. At the time [that the offence was alleged to have taken place] Father C was still studying in Ottawa and had no idea about his coming "obedience" for the Y Indian School. It has been 15 horrendous months for this classmate of mine who is a perfect gentleman ... Will Father C receive an official letter of excuse from the student and the Secretariat?... Since H can just turn around and accuse another Oblate, now dead ... and go away with $100,000 for his story and the pains he said he suffered, I was asked by my confrère to request from the Secretariat a similar amount of $100,000 for the real suffering endured by him over the last 15 months. For your information Father C is still working with First Nations people. He has always worked with them and it is not interesting to be looked upon as a child abuser by people who will not dare put in doubt the word of one of their nation.[32]

Archbishop Gerard Pettipas, representing the Corporation of Catholic Entities Party to the Indian Residential Schools Settlement, also wrote to Chief Adjudicator Dan Ish with concerns, in this case about what he considered biases in the 2009 Chief Adjudicator's Annual Report: "The adjudication process is contributing to the creation of an unreal image of the idyllic life of First Nation children prior to attendance at Residential Schools, and the equally untrue depiction of the Residential School as a grim environment directed only by sadists."[33] He then pointed to what he saw as the principal source of bias: "The undifferentiated reporting of the results of the applications and adjudications gives the impression to the reader that all applications are meritorious and deserving of compensation, thereby unfairly tarnishing, we believe, the reputations of former staff, their institutions and former students."[34] This disaffection with the compensation process, though mainly restricted to the close circle of retired priests, has important consequences for the nature of the Truth and Reconciliation Commission hearings. Their negative experience in compensation hearings means that most of those closely involved in the running of the schools were unwilling to testify to the Commission, and the Commission did not have subpoena powers to compel them to do so. It was common in my interviews for priests to make a connection between the accusations directed toward them, which they adamantly denied and which offended them to the core of their being, and the testimony being given at the TRC hearings. Let us consider some of these statements:

> Today I have been so abused with all the accusations, what do you call them? Allegations against me. Even being here [in the interview] is difficult for me. The meetings they have now, what do you call it? Truth and Reconciliation. If you ask my opinion, I don't believe that. I don't believe half of what they say ... In my school in five years I never heard of physical abuse and sexual abuse. Years later this comes and all of a sudden you find out you are a criminal. That makes me mad. I've lost hours and hours of sleep over that business.[35]

The key to this statement is the priest's use of the word "abused" in reference to himself, which, whether intentionally or not, defies the logic through which the term is being used in the IAP hearings. By including himself in the category of the abused, the priest is calling into question the entire regime of compensation, just as Father L'Heureux attempted to do by making a claim to the chief adjudicator for compensation on behalf of a priest who was the target of an accusation eventually proven to be false and retracted.

The connection between such accusations and the testimony given to the TRC was discussed by another priest: "These allegations there, the girls even have allegations of me that I would phone somebody, send me a girl, send me Stella or whatever to my office and I would beat her or abuse her sexually. This is false! It's against my basic principles. These are the same people that come and report at the Truth and Reconciliation people. That's enough." [At this point, he ended the interview.][36]

Finally, one of the priests with whom I spoke gave further insight into the reasons for the Oblates' absence from TRC hearings: "Me, I haven't gone to the Commission. I'm not afraid to say it. Because there are those who are waiting just to know that I'm still alive. They're waiting just to find out where I live ... Because then they can easily say, 'Up 'til now we haven't got him; and now we will.'"[37] The real source of concern here seems to be about the possible loss of anonymity following from participation in Commission hearings. And from this point of recognition, the priest is hinting at a fear of confrontation and accusation, perhaps even of a civil suit by one of those former students who opted out of the Settlement Agreement. The common denominator of these statements is a sense of *their* victimization, of the violation of *their* rights and dignity, not through the residential schools themselves (which, as we will see, they tend to remember with fondness), but through a sense that the restitution process was systematically encouraging falsehood and injustice toward *them*.

But accusations of sexual abuse and identification as a Person of Interest in IAP hearings are not restricted to priests or others who had positions of responsibility in the schools. Former students are also sometimes identified by the claimants as perpetrators and are identified in the adjudicator's report as "POI." As with the accused priests, the adjudicator then follows up by informing the accused individuals that they have been named in the hearing as a Person of Interest. This could take the form of a phone call, but more often is done by means of a letter that mentions the details of the hearing, including the name of their accuser. The most immediate consequence of the arrival of letters of this kind that reach former students is shame and fear of criminal prosecution, even though they were children at the time of the offences they were alleged to have committed. In some instances the effects of the accusation letters have reached further, mostly due to the near impossibility of keeping secrets of this magnitude intact in reserve communities. Stories about these letters ramified broadly in some communities, revealing along the way something of the mistrust with which the compensation process was held, even while the benefits of the process were widely sought after and often appreciated. In Nova Scotia, for example, a community health worker who had a prominent role in the health supports of the Atlantic National Event reported to me that where mailboxes are shared with community members with the same last name—and there are many who share the same name as descendants of common ancestors—letters from IAP adjudicators were sometimes opened accidentally by those who were not the intended recipient. And as the content of these letters became widely known, even the stationery of the envelope became enough to alert people to an accusation—and often the identity of the accused. In one instance a woman giving testimony in an IAP hearing mentioned her older sister as a Person of Interest, a woman who was later to file her own IAP claim identifying someone else from the community. On another occasion a man who did not know how to read—he had spent most of his time in school shovelling coal and doing other kinds of manual labour—asked a neighbour to read the letter with official-looking government stationery he had just received. It seems reasonable to assert, based on this outline of the IAP process and the stories surrounding it, that the manner in which former students are identified as Persons of Interest amounts to a process of re-victimization—a deep provocation of the sense of injustice.

Neither the accusations directed toward priests nor those that find their way to former students (and sometimes beyond, into the networks of gossip in their communities) were spoken about in the public forums of the Commission. The accusations and denials of sexual abuse were hedged about with shame and anger. Yet they form part of the essential nature of the TRC. They represent clear instances of the exclusion of themes and the individuals bearing them that are still not part of acceptable speech. This exclusion in turn, as the next chapter will discuss, impinges on the formation of distinct realms of common experience and the possibilities for communication and reconciliation between them.

NOTES

1 See the Greensboro Truth and Reconciliation Commission Report, Executive Summary, 2006, accessed 9 November 2012, http://www.greensborotrc.org/exec_summary.pdf.

2 Courtney Jung, "Canada and the Legacy of the Indian Residential Schools," in *Identities in Transition: Challenges for Transitional Justice in Divided Societies*, ed. Paige Arthur (Cambridge, UK: Cambridge University Press, 2011), 225.

3 Commissioner Marie Wilson, in her introductory statement to the TRC Urban Inuit Community Hearing (Ottawa, 16 August 2012) made a broader claim to the effect that this was the largest restitution agreement in world history. Even if so, however, it is probably soon to be outdone by the estimated $30 billion in fines, settlement payments, and cleanup costs related to BP's Deepwater Horizon explosion and oil spill on the Gulf Coast of the United States. The size and scope of Canada's Settlement Agreement is favoured by the number of claimants who have exercised their rights through it, including 102,282 Common Experience Payment claims and 37,648 Independent

Assessment Program claims. By the time of a 2007 deadline for opting out of the Settlement Agreement, only 340 former students (out of the estimated 86,000 of those alive today who had attended an Indian residential school) had done so, and thereby retained their right to take independent legal action over their residential school experiences.

4   According to statistics provided by Indigenous and Northern Affairs Canada, updated as of 31 March 2017, 96 per cent of the IAP claims submitted for adjudication had been resolved. See Indigenous and Northern Affairs Canada, "Statistics on the Implementation of the Indian Residential Schools Settlement Agreement," accessed 17 June 2017, https://www.aadnc-aandc.gc.ca/eng/1315320539682/1315320692192.

5   This information is for the period 19 September 2007 to 31 March 2016, provided by Indigenous and Northern Affairs Canada, accessed 17 June 2017, https://www.aadnc-aandc.gc.ca/eng/1315320539682/1315320692192.

6   See Linda Popic, "Compensating Canada's 'Stolen Generations,'" *Indigenous Law Bulletin* 14, no. 7, issue 2 (2008), accessed 31 July 2012, http://www.austlii.edu.au/au/journals/ILB/2008/4.html.

7   Madeleine Stout and Rick Harp, "Lump Sum Compensation Payments Research Project: The Circle Rechecks Itself" (Ottawa: Aboriginal Healing Foundation, 2007), 31.

8   Ibid., 32.

9   Ibid., 30

10   Ibid., 27

11   Indigenous and Northern Affairs Canada, "Statistics on the Implementation of the Indian Residential Schools Settlement Agreement," accessed 17 June 2017, https://www.aadnc-aandc.gc.ca/eng/1315320539682/1315320692192.

12   Indian Residential Schools Adjudication Secretariat, "Frequently Asked Questions about the Application Process," accessed 16 February 2013. The web page has since been removed.

13   Government of Canada, *Schedule "D," Independent Assessment Process (IAP) for Continuing Indian Residential School Abuse Claims* (Ottawa: Government of Canada, 2006), 3, accessed 29 July 2012, www.residentialschoolsettlement.ca/schedule_d-iap.pdf.

14   Ibid., 4.

15   Ibid., 5.

16   Aubrey Quenwezance, Commissioner's Sharing Panel, TRC Saskatoon National Event, 22 June 2012.

17   Clarence Rodney Papequash, Survivor Committee Sharing Circle, Saskatoon, 23 June 2013.

18 Speaker unknown, Women's Circle, TRC Winnipeg National Event, 17 June
    2010.

19 Marie Wilson, in her introductory statement to the TRC Urban Inuit Com-
    munity Hearing in Ottawa on 16 August 2012, was among those who encour-
    aged survivors who qualified and had not done so to sign up for the IAP claims
    process before the September 19 deadline, with the advice that claimants should
    seek "legal supports."

20 Jack Anawak, Truth and Reconciliation Commission Community Hearings, Iqa-
    luit, 26 March 2011.

21 This is closely paraphrased from a discussion, which was not recorded, with an
    official who spoke on condition of anonymity. Halifax, 9 March 2012.

22 Speaker unknown, Truth and Reconciliation Commission Regional Gathering,
    Victoria, 13 April 2012.

23 Beatrice Burnheart, Commissioner's Sharing Panel, TRC Inuvik National Event,
    30 June 2011.

24 Interview with Archbishop James Weisgerber, Winnipeg, 19 June 2010.

25 Ibid.

26 Ibid.

27 Interview at Résidence Despins, Winnipeg, 20 June 2010.

28 Ibid.

29 Ibid.

30 Jacques L'Heureux, "The only politically acceptable speech about the Indian Resi-
    dential Schools," unpublished open letter, 29 June 2011. Despite the fact that his
    name ironically translates into English as "the happy," this is not a pseudonym.

31 *"Cette affaire de "Pensionnats" où confères et amis(ies) sont traînées de façon aussi in-*
    juste (et injustifiée) devant un cour de justice qui n'en mérite pas le nom, a en juger par
    tout ce qui s'y passe ... sans aucune raison ... sinon par suite d'un mensonge des [sic]
    plus odieux qui soit ... mais bien "payant" (c'est incroyable!) tant pour lui que pour son
    avocat." Letter to Father Jacques L'Heureux, Maison Deschâtelets, Ottawa, 15
    December 2010.

32 Father Jacques L'Heureux, unpublished letter from Les Missionnaires Oblats
    de Marie Immaculée, Ottawa, Ontario, to Dan Ish, Chief Adjudicator, Regina,
    Saskatchewan, 1 February 2012. I have slightly altered the text of this letter to
    maintain the anonymity of the individuals mentioned in it.

33 Letter from Archbishop Gerard Pettipas, Chairman of the Board, Corporation
    of Catholic Entities Party to the Indian Residential Schools Settlement, to Dan
    Ish, Chief Adjudicator, Adjudication Secretariat, Re: 2009 Chief Adjudicator's
    Annual Report, 27 May 2010.

34 Ibid.

35 Interview at Résidence Despins, Winnipeg, 21 June 2010.

36 Ibid.

37 "*Pis mois je ne suis pas allés à la commission, pis j'ai pas peur de le dire, car il y en a qui attendent juste de savoir si je suis encore en vie, ils attendent juste de savoir où je demeure ... parce qu'ils peuvent facilement arriver de dire 'on l'a pas eu jusqu'à date, on va l'avoir.'*" Interview at Résidence Despins, Winnipeg, 21 June 2010.

Chapter 4

TEMPLATES AND EXCLUSIONS

SAYING THE UNSAYABLE

It is widely recognized by survivors of residential schools that only a few decades ago hardly anyone spoke about their school experience, even to those in their immediate families. The topic was forbidden and repressed. This was also noted by a British Columbia trial judge in a case involving sexual abuse in a residential school: "When the evidence is examined closely, one is drawn to the conclusion that the unspeakable acts which were perpetrated on these young children were just that: at that time they were for the most part not spoken of."[1] This observation is consistent with the challenge faced by commissioners of the South African TRC, who found that testimony formed patterns around what was "sayable," with the subject of the worst crimes avoided or narrated incompletely; and in consequence their concern was that "the Commission might not obtain the 'whole story' of gross violations of human rights committed in the period under review."[2]

These accounts of witness reticence as a norm are in contrast with the frequency of brutally frank narration of child sexual victimization in Canada's TRC. It has only been a short time since the silence was broken by the willingness of many survivors to provide public testimony in courtrooms, compensation hearings, and, most publicly, the recorded, Internet-streamed, archive-destined statements of the TRC's Commissioner's Sharing Panel. This makes it important to understand how the emotionally laden, powerful narratives presented to the Commission have, in a relatively short period of time, become not only "sayable" (and "hearable") but, as I intend to show here and in the next chapter, dominant to the point of excluding or overshadowing other forms of remembered experience. What is the process by which the unspeakable became sayable, and the sayable a kind of protected and protective orthodoxy? How does something remain invisible, unthinkable, unspeakable, and then over the space of several short decades become publicly visible and subject to active representation, to narration by traumatized school survivors, even to the point of being a prevalent theme in their statements?

This problem, I find, extends to what remains "unsayable," the topics and opinions that tend to be absent or approached with caution. When we look for these forbidden areas we have a tendency to concentrate our search on things that are too emotionally intense to be articulated, conforming to the idiomatic expression "too horrible for words." But what we find in the statements presented to the Commission is just the opposite: horrible, sorrowful, traumatizing experiences are the sorts of things that *were* remembered and narrated. As we considered in the conclusion to the previous chapter, there are topics associated with shame, above all the kind of corruption of childhood that blurred the boundary between victim and perpetrator. The things not said also tend to be the stories that do not evoke strong emotion. Former students tended not to come forward to publicly narrate ordinary experience in residential schools, the more commonplace, quotidian indignities of excessive discipline and the shared, yet deeply individual, loneliness of removal from families. Those who thought of themselves as having suffered only minimally or not at all also often thought of themselves as having nothing to say.

The category of the unsayable extended to the perspectives of those once involved in the day-to-day operation of the institutions: the nuns, priests, other clergy, and laypeople who once ran the schools. These perspectives were not meaningfully represented in the TRC's witnessing activities, nor were those church members who remain disaffected with the accusations against them engaged in any form of encounter or exchange with those former students who were, in a sense, claimants and accusers in the process. As we have seen, the Oblate priests, brothers, and nuns with whom I conducted interviews often told starkly different versions of suffering, particularly of the suffering *they* experienced personally through the structures and processes of accusation. This realm of experience rarely found its way to the proceedings of the Commission, and if it did, it was usually veiled, discreet, and indirect.

The issue of included and excluded narration is complicated by the permissiveness of the hearings, and by the fact that there were no explicit limits to what one may or may not say into the microphone and before the cameras. Survivors were not overtly guided or interrupted in their statement giving. They were not even reminded of the time if they went on too long, at least not until they had finished speaking, and the admonition then seemed intended more for the speakers to follow than for the one immediately responsible for the breach of etiquette. With this non-interference as a given, how might the TRC have still channelled narrated experience into basic, complementary essentialisms, while excluding the representation of unwelcome countervailing meaning? What were the processes that made it possible for some forms of experience—and not others—to become, in a relatively short period of time, an essential, normal, natural, meaningful aspect of the self in company with others and, in narrative performance, before others? My focus here is on the processes by which shared, stigmatized experience is brought out of isolation, affirmed, given conceptual form, perceived, felt, and acted on. While much of my attention later on will be on the selectiveness and omissions of discourse, here I intend to explore the ways that suffering is affirmed as legitimate and expressed in the form of ritual and visual representation; in material depiction of distinct, iconic forms of suffering; or in online communities of affirmation. I am attentive here to what Linda Garro and Cheryl Mattingly refer to as the "imprint of institutional practice and ideology" in the ways that narrative is constructed and the way, in turn, that narrative constructs.[3]

Taking this line of inquiry further, it is possible to see the Commission's forms and strategies of affirmation and encouragement as processes by which disparate experiences are shaped into a common historical narrative and idiom of personal experience. Out of the mass of possible statements, those that were presented somehow corresponded with an essence of the school experience, visually, materially, and testimonially manifested at the sites (including websites) of the events. These controlled, often symbolic expressions of school experience, whether intentionally or not, act as templates that establish narrative themes and encourage survivors to present their painful memories publicly; and in the process they give shape to emotional expression, opinion, and understandings of the history of institutional practice, ultimately to be made manifest in new categories and criteria of distress and belonging.

There is, in the very nature of truth commissions, a judgment that has already taken place and receptiveness to a form of knowledge that makes it possible for witnesses to come forward with their confessions and narrations. The confessional qualities of hearings are particularly salient in so-called victim-centred truth commissions; and it is no accident that Christian churches have been leading participants in some of these, most notably in South Africa.[4] It should be recalled, however, that Canada's Truth and Reconciliation Commission faced the distinct challenge of making its existence and the subject matter of its mandate known to a public audience. In pursuit of this goal, the Commission was oriented from the outset toward public exposure, staging noteworthy and newsworthy events, garnering press coverage, and reaching out to a global audience via the Internet—all with a focus on victim narratives.

The most explicit source of guidance and encouragement for those planning to give statements to the Commission took place in meetings held on the first day of National Events, entitled "How to Share Your Truth Information Session." These sessions were voluntary, attracting between approximately sixty (in Halifax and Montreal) and fifteen (in Saskatchewan) participants (I have no explanation for the difference), mostly those who might be planning to speak in the public hearings of the Commissioner's Sharing Panel, the smaller Survivor Committee Sharing Circles, or Private Statement Gathering sessions. The meetings included presentations by TRC representatives and health support workers who took turns providing an outline of the various venues, paying particular attention to the differences between the short, fifteen-minute public presentations to the Commissioner's Sharing Panel and the hour-and-a-half permitted (even encouraged) in Private Statement Gathering sessions; and to the availability and importance of health supports in each venue, followed by question-and-answer sessions with the audience. In Halifax this meeting also included a screening of a TRC-sponsored film that reiterated, in somewhat more detail, practical information on the various venues, repeating in generic language the importance of health supports ("Regardless of what option you chose to share your IRS experience, the TRC team will strive to make sure you are comfortable during the recording process"). The film then added more information on the utility of survivor statements for a planned national research centre, and concluded with "this is a great chance for Canada to come clean about its history ... The Truth and Reconciliation Commission of Canada offers this one chance to build a better Canada, and this is it."[5]

Before the hearings began at each event, there was also at least one statement (and usually several) by a commissioner or invited participant to the effect that the testimony soon to be heard would be affecting and possibly deeply disturbing, as indeed it usually turned out to be. Murray Sinclair, in his welcome address at the National Event in Saskatoon, did this almost in passing: "You will hear that pain, you will see these tears."[6] Eugene Arcand, a prominent member of the Indian Residential School Survivor Committee, added more detail: "We're going to be shedding tears, sharing a lot of guilt and shame ... We're going to have a chance to shed those secrets ... I invite church leaders to share their shame."[7] Even community hearings included such preparation of audiences for emotionally affecting testimony, as with a preparatory declaration by an organizer at the Urban Inuit Community Hearing in Ottawa: "The survivors will be sharing a very painful past. Let us be mindful of that."[8]

At the occasion of the third National Event in Halifax in October 2011, with numerous community events behind them, the dominance of statements based on the themes of sadism, sexual exploitation, victimhood, and lifelong suffering was becoming clear, and the commissioners seemed to feel the need to respond to it. Murray Sinclair, opening the meeting, made his expectations explicit: "It is not our intention to require you only to share your pain with us ... We need you to look not only at the sadness and pain, but to talk about the good things that happened in the schools ... It is important for your grandchildren to know why you survived."[9] And Commissioner Wilton Littlechild similarly prodded potential witnesses with the suggestion that their testimony "provides a great opportunity to hear good stories."[10] But in the course of seven National Events, there was very little response to this call for "positive" statements. Despite the commissioners' encouragement of "positive" stories along these lines, I witnessed a consistent pattern in the statements presented to them, in which emphasis was overwhelmingly placed on the traumas of the schools and their continued effects in adulthood, usually in the form of addictions and failure in parenthood.

It is useful to consider the preparatory statements as addressing not only the audiences about to listen to statements but also the survivors who are about to give them. The characterization of the testimony as powerful, emotional, painful, and disturbing in the opening remarks of Commission events contributed to the sense among survivors that their own remembrances that conformed to these "viewer discretion" warnings were normal, acceptable, and even encouraged. It is instructive to consider, as I will now, some of the ways that the meeting room of the Commission became a locus for what Pottage refers to as the legal techniques that "fabricate persons and things," mobilizing a repertoire of "legal techniques of personification and reification";[11] and for what Borneman describes as a "temporal sequence of experience" in which "loss and political crime become invested in objects—persons, places, and things—that make them meaningful in new ways."[12]

TEARS FOR THE CREATOR

One of the most important things to note about Canada's TRC meetings is that, whether participants and audience members were aware of it or not, the events in which they are taking part were sacred. The sacred qualities of the meetings were not accidental or tangential. The chair of the Commission, Justice Murray Sinclair, aside from his qualifications as a judge appointed to the Court of Queen's Bench of Manitoba in 2001, is a member of the Midewiwin (Grand Medicine) Society of the Ojibwa; and whether it is through his direct influence or not, the events of the Commission unmistakably included the ceremonies and values of the secret medicine society and, in a spirit of ecumenism, of other aboriginal traditions and of Christianity. Even before the opening prayers and speeches of the inaugural National Event in Winnipeg, for example, a sunrise ceremony and lighting of a sacred fire was performed by members of the Midewiwin Society and other spiritual leaders and healers. A few teams of journalists were there to shoot images of the symbolic first ceremony sponsored by the Commission, all other events being—literally and figuratively—secondary. They were surprised and visibly disappointed when they were told in no uncertain terms by an organizer of the ceremony that to photograph the sacred fire was forbidden. Some stayed for later ceremonies, which included prayers by Ojibwa and Christian leaders, lighting of a sacred pipe followed by its distribution to aboriginal leaders (including commissioners Sinclair and Littlechild), and a drumming ceremony symbolic of

FIGURE 4.1: Journalists filming a drummer at the Winnipeg National Event.

the four directions. The more persistent journalists duly shot footage that was later broadcast on the local evening news, spliced together with clips from the later official, more predictable opening speeches from a podium.

The influence of the Midewiwin Society and the model of pan-Indian spirituality in TRC events even found its way into hearings in the far north. A local organizer in Inuvik was dismayed to be told by someone from the TRC headquarters in Ottawa that she should be responsible for providing a supply of sage for the "smudging" to take place in the upcoming meeting. The challenge she faced was that sage is a plant that grows in arid regions, the closest being the dry interior of British Columbia, and none of the people of the western Arctic customarily make use of it. Whatever the solution eventually found, the National Event in Inuvik had a copious quantity of sage available for the spiritual purification of participants.

Some effort was made to make the ceremonies and the people leading them appropriate to the setting in which the meetings took place. In the Arctic events, for example, the lighting of the *qulliq*, the Inuit oil lamp, took a prominent place in the opening ceremonies, accompanied by drumming and prayer. Each of the female elders who lit the lamp and led the prayer also provided an explanation of the lamp's significance for the Inuit people. An elder named Singoori, conducting the ceremony at the opening of the TRC Urban Inuit Community Hearings in Ottawa, made the occasion less formal than it had been at other events. Speaking in Inuktitut through French, English, and

Ojibwa translators, she remembered the use she made of the lamp when she was young, joking about how important it was not to make it too hot and thus hasten the melting of the igloo. "In the past it was the only source of heat we had," she explained. "We didn't know any better life. But today we live in houses with government assistance, and we appreciate that. It is impossible to go back. I'm grateful that we can turn the thermostat on to heat the house." And with that she concluded: "Let us pray." In Singoori's introduction to the *qulliq*, the government emerges as the entity having the greatest impact on the lives of the Inuit; and the argument could well be made that this is without question an appropriate perspective to bring to a hearing on residential schools.[13]

The Commission did not just import ritual and spiritual meaning from existing traditions, as in the ceremonies of the Midewiwin Society or the opening prayers of the Christian tradition; it also creatively adapted and invented them.[14] Several of these had a focus on the sacred fire. Ashes from the fire at each National Event were collected in a basket, to be ceremonially deposited during the lighting of the fire at the next event, with the explanation by a master of ceremonies that this chain of continuity represents the common experience and unity of all survivors.

Another invention connected the sacred fire with tears shed during the hearings. Before any testimony was heard at national and regional events, the audience was given an explanation by the master of ceremonies about the positive nature of tears. He or she would point out that tissues were available, with a full box placed on every fifth or sixth seat. (In Montreal, tissues were distributed in smaller packages

FIGURE 4.2: Offering prayers to the Sacred Fire at the Inuvik National Event.

that displayed the logo of the Indian Residential Schools Resolution Health Support Program and the toll-free numbers of a helpline.) A team of "health support workers" (mental health volunteers, with a variety of backgrounds and professional qualifications) would then be introduced, identifiable by their brightly coloured vests or T-shirts and logos, unique to each event. During the testimony, they kept watch over the audience and approached anyone who seemed to be weeping, to comfort them and collect their used tissues in brown paper bags. Sometimes after testimony that had an emotional impact on almost everyone in the room, they simply moved through the audience, gathering the tissues in bags—less systematically than in a church collection, perhaps, but with much the same purposeful gravitas. As the master of ceremonies introduced the support workers, he or she also explained the purpose (aside from the obvious housekeeping goal of order and cleanliness) for which some of the tear-soaked tissues were gathered. In the Atlantic National Event, two baskets made by the Nicolas family of Tobique, the Maliseet reserve in New Brunswick, were placed at the commissioner's table and at the location for the Private Statement Gathering. As Andrea Colter, representing the health support workers at the National Event in Halifax, explained to potential witnesses, these baskets were given to the commissioners with the intended purpose of receiving gifts, and were since then "honoured by providing a place for when survivors shed their tears of healing." As she described it, "These Kleenex that they [witnesses] use are carefully put into this basket, and at the end of the day, the fire-keeper takes the tears and places [them] in the sacred fire so that they can be released to the Creator as part of their healing."[15] The ritual offering of tears to the Creator has been a feature of each of the major hearings. At some of these National Events, the emcee introducing the process to the audience will elaborate on the Creator's power to heal, to comfort, to release the weight of sorrow. At others, no further explanation is given. In most ritual acts involving prayer and sacrifice, the ultimate purpose is left unarticulated.

One of the works sponsored by the Commission stood out with words and attitudes of veneration toward its sacred power. The kerfed, or bentwood, box made for the Commission by Northwest Coast artist Luke Marston found a prominent place in representing and shaping the dominant themes of the Commission. At the inaugural Commissioner's Sharing Panel in Winnipeg, Marston explained that the inspiration he received for the front panel of the box had come from his grandmother, whose badly misshapen fingers had been a mystery to him until, toward the end of her life, she revealed that as a girl in residential school she had been thrown down a flight of stairs by a nun and had severely broken her fingers. They were not given proper treatment and healed badly, the disfigurement compounded later in life by the effects of arthritis. The common experience of suffering that unites survivors is manifest and made specific in the box's stylized image of the grandmother, whose contorted fingers

FIGURE 4.3: The bentwood box and a drum centre stage at the Quebec National Event, Montreal.

were prominently turned to the audience in every meeting, an eloquent, powerful reminder of the abuses that took place in the schools and their lasting effects. The inclusion of Métis and Inuit figures on the side panels served as an explicit reminder of the common experience of residential schooling among all aboriginal peoples, and as "a lasting tribute to all Residential School survivors."[16]

The box was used in the Commissioner's Sharing Panel as a repository of material testimony, books, documents, DVDs, and a miscellany of other reminders of the schools, such as a wool army blanket under which the children in a school once slept (one of the first items deposited in the opening event in Winnipeg). In the first hearings, these items were deposited with little ceremony, simply with an introduction of the meaning of the object and its direct placement into the box.

In later meetings, however (I first noticed this in Inuvik), there was a noticeable change in the ritual aspect of the box. The material representation of suffering, resilience, and cultural recovery were given the additional qualities of sacred power. The functional aspects of these vermin-proof, airtight kerfed boxes—once used for storage of such foodstuffs as oolichan oil and dried fish, as well as a protective container for ceremonial clothing—became, in the context of TRC meetings, a ritual vessel connecting commissioners with participants. In each meeting, following opening prayers by aboriginal, Inuit, and Métis elders and speeches by the commissioners and their guests, a master of ceremonies provided an explanation of the intended meaning of the symbols and the sacred power of the box, including a recounting of the story of the artist's grandmother. Witnesses were invited to provide any object they might choose to place in the box. And indeed, at various points in the event, usually with invited speakers who had the time to prepare their choice of donated object, items were selected for an "offering." Reverence toward the box was expressed through what might be called rituals of deposition. Participants and commissioners each held an object to be deposited and together placed it on a blanket at the foot of the box, where it was publicly visible. In later events they placed it directly into the box, usually with an impromptu display of respect. Items were never thrown or dropped casually into the box. Bodily movements, gestures, intentional slowness, respectful silence—and, on completion of the act of deposition, smiles, embraces, and applause from the audience all spoke to the perception of sacredness that the process had acquired.

There is, as anthropologists have long recognized, no better way to cut through distractions and focus attention than to convey messages through ritual performance, contextualized by prayer and sermons. Because of this explicitly contextualized ritual, each time an object was placed in the sacred box, the audience's attention was drawn to the messages of the box itself. Whatever else the ritual accomplished, it also bracketed the testimony within a kind of ontological invulnerability. There can be no contestation of opinion, no alternative historical narrative with any broad power of persuasion when it runs up against the perceived infallibility of sacralized truth.

TEMPLATES

Let us consider further the ways that the context of a witnessing event can influence what the witness will be encouraged to express, whether with awareness of these contextual influences or not. The phenomenon I am referring to as a *template* consists of anything presented in the forum setting that provides imitative meaning, with the effect of shaping the ideas and/or behaviour of participants. As we have seen, the TRC's templates are clearly recognizable in the opening meetings, speeches, and early stages of the Commissioner's Sharing Panel in which the organizers are "setting the tone," or more instrumentally trying to establish thematic and behavioural patterns.

A further illustration of the influence of templates took place during the appearance of the first witness in the TRC Urban Inuit Community Hearing in Ottawa, held in August 2012. The witness, a small Inuit man with a long grey beard and ponytail, was overwhelmed with grief as he sat before the microphone. He was comforted by a woman, his "support person," who put her hand on his back and shoulder as he spoke. Try as he might, he could not talk past the sobs and constriction of his throat that took away control of his voice whenever he approached the topic of his abuse as a child in school. He eventually stopped his testimony, pulled his chair back from the table and wept deeply, his body heaving, while he received a long, comforting embrace from his support person. When he had regained enough composure he got up to return to his seat. The audience was itself sympathetically grief-stricken and silent. Commissioner Wilson moved her hands as though to clap, as had been done after every presentation by every witness in every other meeting to that point, but then stopped her hands in mid-motion. After a brief look of confusion, she pulled back her chair and stood in a silent gesture of acknowledgement of the witness. This gesture soon established a pattern. After the next witness spoke, again no one applauded, but about half the audience stood. At the conclusion of the third witness's testimony, everyone in the room was silently standing to honour them in a way that was now established as customary and that continued throughout the meeting.

In several of the Commission's major venues the preparation of audiences and potential witnesses seemed more intentional. On each of the opening days of the National Events in Inuvik and Halifax, for example, the Commission screened a film in the main venue consisting of a sequence of fragments of testimony from the community meetings that had taken place during the preceding weeks. These films were similar in thematic content and structure to material later posted on the TRC website, the main difference being the wider scope of the online video, which was able to draw from several National Events.[17] In these films, the Commission was able to select from the many hours of video from community hearings those moments that resonated, the sound bites that deftly captured not only what the speaker was trying to say, but more significantly, what the Commission was trying to convey. These selected narratives of the "highlight reel" emphasized the themes of loss and suffering, both within the schools and in adult lives broken by the experience, the heightened emotion of grief (but within certain bounds of self-control and composure), and in a closing narrative, a positive story of healing and rediscovery of that cultural heritage once slated for destruction through the schools.

The statements selected for this film are worth citing at length, because they represent the preferred narratives of the TRC, the themes that the organizers found poignant and memorable, as presented to an audience that included those about to give their own testimony.

I wasn't meant to be abused. I wasn't meant to be hurt. I was only supposed to be a boy. I can't even remember being, I can't remember being happy.[18]

No one told me how special I was, what a good little girl I was ... No one said that. Instead, they told me what a dirty little Eskimo I was. And then they proceeded to beat me, or give another type of abuse.[19]

I seen a lot of abuse. And going to the bathrooms at night, you'd see kids sitting on the bowls with blankets over them, just scared they might pee their bed, they might be the [indistinct] in the morning. They'd rather sleep on the bowls all night.[20]

There was one thing I wondered about. I wondered which was the worst, the students who came from the communities and couldn't go home until the end of school in June, or like me, I could look out the window, see my mother walking around and I couldn't go across.[21]

It was hard for me when my mom died, oh my ... I didn't know what to feel, what to do, where to go. Because my mom died in Boston in 1962. We didn't have nothing, you know. We didn't [indistinct] say no prayers for us. It's just like a regular day. When I went to bed at night, I cried. I cried for my mom, and that person said, "Stop your crying! Stop crying, everybody wants to get to sleep," and most of them wasn't even asleep at all, you know. Yeah ... stop crying! Because it was hard for me, difficult the things what happened. It was hard for me to accept the things, and it was not easy.[22]

Commissioner Sinclair then appears on camera to provide context:

The general reaction from Canadians, once they hear about what went on in residential schools, is a lot of shock. That this is something that happened in their country is difficult for them to believe. And that this is something that went on in their country that was hidden from them by government and by political and church leaders is also something that shocks them.[23]

This is followed by a statement from Father Robert Michael:

We had no idea, no idea, not myself as a child, nor my parents, nor the community in which I lived, had any idea that these things were taking place in the 50s and in the 60s and in the 40s [sic]. It was only after I became an adult that I came to hear about the stories of the residential school in Shubenacadie. It was only after I became an adult that I heard about the tremendous abuse of the members of the church, priests and sisters, who abused young people. Having been so ignorant, once I found out and discovered it, the shame was overwhelming.[24]

After this, several more excerpts are shown from survivor statements in community hearings:

That's when I cry many times. When I think about them. If the government and priests [indistinct] to change the people that they should be so ... everybody should be so happy, the children and my people. Now, it's so many people very, very sad and sick.[25]

All of my friends that passed on was basically abused by this priest. They always talked about it. All of us who is still around, we still talk about it. Sometimes we laugh, sometimes we cry about it. I want this ... I want to see this priest tell me "I'm sorry." But I don't think I'm gonna hear that from him.[26]

Our experience is our evidence, our experiences are our truth. The church members haven't told us about their experiences. The pedophiles, the clergy pedophiles haven't told us their experiences. The abusers, the ones that didn't ... that punished us so severely, they didn't tell us how they feel when they were punishing us. The government is not telling us how they felt when they put us on Indian reservations and how happy they were to build Indian residential schools in order to kill the Indian in the child. When are they gonna tell us how that felt like?[27]

I didn't hear my dad speak Mi'kmaq until two weeks before he died. Although he was fluent, he could still speak his language, he never taught us. And though he spent eleven years in a residential school, forbidden to speak his language, he never forgot it. And two weeks before he died, his family came from Cape Breton to visit him, and they used to come in the room and start talking Mi'kmaq to my dad. And I'd say, "Oh, Dad, don't speak Mi'kmaq, because I don't speak it," and he started answering them back in his language, and I started to cry because I realized it was another loss. What he lost was the value of his culture and his language. They didn't beat his language out of him, but they, they beat the value ... and how he could have passed that on to us.[28]

Let the Commission put out the truth. That's what you are here for. Do not let your government stop you and put in some more little trinkles [sic] towards you, and say do not write that, or do not put this out. 'Cause I swear that's what they're gonna do to you. They're gonna stop you, in somehow, some way, of putting out the truth. And we want the truth put out there, so the government of Canada and the rest of the world could see what they have done to our people in the residential schools.[29]

About fifteen years ago, everything changed for my life. I became a dancer, I became a traditional dancer. Man, I love that powwow music today. I have more respect for my people compared to the Roman Catholic Church. I respect myself, I honour myself, and I love myself. Who I am today? So a residential school is not there no more. No more nuns, no more priests, no more punishment. And this is my life story, who I was, and who I am today. I am a survivor.[30]

The film closed with a montage of drummers, dancers, people singing, and a woman holding a baby, continuing the theme introduced by the last speaker of survival through rediscovered traditional identity.

As with any uncertain venture, like crossing a doubtful bridge, deciding what to do comes best from watching others go first. In most of the Commissioner's Sharing Panels (an exception was the fifth National Event in Montreal) this kind of security was also provided by preliminary, vetted, rehearsed statements in which individuals with experience in public speaking presented their testimony. This first set of presenters at several of the National Events had been invited, it would appear, not only because they tended to be confident in front of large audiences, but also because they had previously touched on themes emphasized by the Commission. Effective stories have the capacity to shape the narrations and audience responses that follow.[31] This was explicitly acknowledged by Robert Watt, co-director of the TRC Inuit Sub-Commission and master of ceremonies in the TRC National Event in Halifax, who introduced the first speakers as being there "to set the tone, to set the context." The first among these was Isabelle Knockwood, introduced as having six children, fourteen grandchildren, and a degree in anthropology and English from St. Mary's University in Halifax, which she undertook at the age of fifty-eight. She is also the author of *Out of the Depths*, a self-published book about her experience at Shubenacadie Residential School from 1935 to 1947. She accomplished the challenge of setting the tone, not so much by narrating stories based on personal experience but with emphasis on a more general history of dispossession and removal:

> When they put us on reserves and Indian residential schools the purpose was for land. And when they, and when they established the Indian residential schools they entered into a joint venture with the church. And in any joint venture, each of the parties expects to benefit. And the government expected to benefit from our land, and the church expected to benefit from our souls. Those were the two things they wanted from us. And Indian residential school schooling did that. Their purpose was to kill the, kill the Indian in the child.[32]

The most personal part of her testimony challenged the idea that education in Indian residential schools promoted her personal development: "I do not remember talking, feeling, crying, or even growing. My life at the Indian residential school, for the first 4 or 5 years, flatlined."[33] She then closed with a positive statement that struck a chord with the audience and resonated through the rest of the meeting, invoking a fragment of conversation she had had with another survivor: "I don't want to carry their garbage anymore. I'm happy, I'm happy with my life. I'm helping the survivors. That's what I want to do, and I'm happy. My happiness is my revenge."[34]

Even before any testimony is heard, starting with the first efforts to delimit the justice issues involved (the human capacity for the experience of injustice being boundless), the people who actually appear before the microphone are defined in various ways. From the outset, truth commissions usually have narrowly defined and enforced mandates that limit testimony to a specific kind of rights abuse, demarcated in terms of action, institution, time, and place. In Chile, for example, the first post-Pinochet commission investigated only those cases in which the victim died under torture, excluding all those who were tortured and survived and who were understandably angry and alienated from the commission's work.[35] The mandate of Canada's TRC excludes all institutions for which the federal government had no operational responsibility, even those private and provincial residential institutions that were explicitly established for Indian education. We have also (in chapter 1) already touched on the facts that the Commission had no subpoena powers, and was therefore unable to summon witnesses who did not wish to appear voluntarily; and that it was prevented from "naming names" unless the act in question was a crime for which the person was convicted. The mandate of the Commission emphasizes information gathering, raising awareness, and historical (re)appraisal. Being legally bound to its mandate and having no authority to redraft it, the Commission was limited in the kind of information it was able to gather.

But even as an instrument of knowledge, the Commission faced structural limitations. The most obvious way that the federal government was able to influence the scope of its responsibility was through the formal definition of a residential school, as recognized in the Settlement Agreement. In article 12 of the Agreement, an institution must satisfy a two-part test in order to be included: 1) it must have been a residence that took children away from their homes for the purposes of education; and 2) the operation of that institution must have been Canada's joint or sole responsibility.[36] The list of 1,531 institutions unsuccessfully claimed as residential schools is instructive.[37] Here the federal government is responding to petitions submitted through the provisions of the Settlement Agreement for the inclusion of an institution in "Schedule F" of the Agreement, which would have the effect of qualifying former students of these institutions for compensation. The federal government summarizes its response to these claims with a 125-page spreadsheet listing all those institutions excluded from the Agreement through decisions made by Aboriginal Affairs and Northern Development Canada. The list is bewildering in its variety. It includes convents, seminaries, schools for the deaf, orphanages, prisons, and colleges. Excluded are (to draw from the first few pages of the list) places like the Convent of the Atonement Home Orphanage in Edmonton, Alberta (rejected because of a lack of identified federal involvement);

the Edmonton General Hospital (with one word—"hospital"—without further explanation in the "reason for decision" column); the Goodfish Lake Protestant Day School (rejected as a "day school"); the Mannawanis Life Values School of St. Paul, Alberta ("Operated by Private/Nongovernmental Organization"); and so on.

Perhaps the kind of institution most commonly rejected for inclusion in the Settlement Agreement is known as the federal Indian day school. For many former students of these schools, the experience they had was indistinguishable from that of Indian residential school survivors:

> In those days when the schools came most of them were called federal day schools and the rule was that we could only learn in English. There was no place for our culture, for our language. There was routine physical abuse because of our Inuit-ness, because of our being Eskimo. We didn't even move anywhere. During negotiations of this agreement there was never any consideration of all of these [things] that I mentioned. I recognize that this issue does not fall in the TRC mandate but we are left out. It's like we are excluded.[38]

The rejections noted by survivors in statements to the Commission also include a scattering of bona fide Indian residential schools, even a few with some permutation of "Indian residential school" in the name, which are nevertheless excluded because they were operated by a provincial or territorial government, a church-based organization, or a private organization, and hence did not meet the basic criterion of *federal* involvement in the operation of the school for inclusion in the Agreement.

As a category of inclusion and exclusion, the federally operated Indian residential school is defined based on criteria that to most people are legal intangibles—such things as memoranda of understanding, transfers of funding, school inspections, even fire safety inspections by federal employees. In the course of their daily lives, in some cases the daily struggle for bodily integrity, students in the schools did not notice or care that the federal government was, through these intangibles, partially or wholly responsible for the operation of the institution in which they resided. What mattered, and continues to matter, for former students is the nature of their experience, the kind of institution they were sent to, the imposing size and structure of the buildings, the regimes of order and discipline, the supervision and surveillance, the new language and the way it was spoken, the prohibition of their language and the way it was enforced, the religious instruction and the way it was imparted, and for some, above all else, the absence and exclusion of family. All of this, of course, is aside from (or in addition to) the worst abuses of the very kind commonly reported in the Commission's hearings. The Settlement Agreement is structured in a way that is legally sensible, applying clear criteria for the inclusion of institutions as well as a process for petition and possible revision; but this is seemingly in defiance of a much wider, very tangible common experience that is fundamental to survivor identity.

The Commission dealt with this disjuncture between law and experience by taking a permissive approach to the inclusion of survivor statements. Those who were excluded from the Agreement still had a place in the speeches, ceremonies, and testimony gathering of the Commission. Clément (Clem) Chartier, president of the Métis National Council, appeared (wearing his finger-woven Métis sash) at a number of Commission events. He spoke as a self-avowed outsider who spent ten years at the Ile-à-la-Crosse Métis School. To him, the exclusion of this school from the Agreement is an obstacle to achieving the goals of the Commission: "To reach full reconciliation there has to be two parties. It can't just be the Métis nation speaking to itself."[39] As it now stands, only those few hundred Métis students who attended a federally recognized Indian residential school are covered in the Common Experience Payment and Independent Assessment Process, as outlined in the Settlement Agreement, leaving thousands of others without compensation (or apology) despite having attended specifically designated Métis residential schools. The Métis National Council is pursuing litigation to remedy this situation, but meanwhile their exclusion from official participation in the TRC is a *fait accompli*, informally addressed by the Commission by inviting their participation in the ceremonies and hearings of TRC events.

Other survivors relate a similar sense of exclusion and absence of remedy following from their experience as children in other kinds of institutions, sometimes institutions that seem only remotely related to Indian residential schools. Shirley Waskewitch, having suffered a mental breakdown and suicide attempt under a regime of discipline imposed by a nun whom she described as someone who "lived for punishing students in the school," was sent away to the infirmary of a convent for four months to recover. (Perhaps what she called "punishment" would more appropriately be termed "torture" since, according to her testimony, on one occasion it involved an earnest attempt by this nun at extracting one of her molars without anaesthetic.) This convent was among those institutions excluded from the Settlement Agreement, and because of this she did not receive compensation through her IAP claim for the time she spent there. This was a decision that she did not fully understand and that she experienced as an injustice worthy of simple and direct mention in her statement to the Commission: "They don't want to compensate you after going through stuff like that."[40]

An even further encroachment across the boundary of the Commission's mandate came from those who as children were subject to abuse in institutions that were not specifically designed for aboriginal children. The TRC Quebec National Event in Montreal, for example, included the participation of several "Duplessis orphans" (and their descendants), former child inmates of the notorious orphanages that were established by the Quebec government of Maurice Duplessis and operated by the Catholic

Church from the 1940s into the 1960s. A participant who might be described in the Commission's terms as an "intergenerational survivor" of the orphanages took the opportunity to speak in an open session for the public, referred to in the program as "It Matters to Me: A Call to Action on Reconciliation," where he expressed his need for justice as a force that defines his life: "I've lived with the anger for twenty years. I'm perpetually an angry man. I hate that. I hate the fact that I have hate in my heart. That I wake up every day—I hate the fact that I wake up every day and know that my mother never got justice. It pisses me off that I see people talking about forgiveness and asking for forgiveness for crimes that you don't deserve forgiveness for."[41] To this participant, the scope of justice should include prison for all those pedophile priests who acted with impunity in a variety of institutions and for those who protected them. "How can you excuse, how can we forgive ... any organization that does that?"[42]

Such trespasses across the boundary of the TRC's mandate are consistent with the narrated experience of many others who were subject to a wide range of institutional interventions established with similar intentions and with many of the same consequences as those of Indian residential schools. The Commission accommodated this wide range of abuse and grievance through a permissive approach toward the statements presented in its hearings. Those who sat before the microphone were given wide latitude in their identifications of institutional harm. At the same time, however, the Commission worked with a mandate that defines Indian residential schools with a specific focus on federal responsibility. In the course of carefully delimiting the institutions within its purview, the Settlement Agreement bracketed out myriad other institutions that incarcerated children within living memory and through this exclusion, the agreement could well be misrepresenting the era and the errors that the Commission was established to overcome.

There is a flip side to this long list of rejected claims by former students, to be found in an exception to it. Following a decision of the Ontario Superior Court of Justice, two schools from northwestern Ontario were added to the list of eligible institutions in "Schedule F" of the Settlement Agreement: the Stirland Lake High School (in operation from 1 September 1971 to 30 June 1991) and the Cristal Lake High School (from 1 September 1976 to 30 June 1986). Both schools were established by the Northern Youth Programs, Inc., an independent missionary organization dedicated to assisting aboriginal youth in accordance with the teachings of the Mennonite Church. The background to this amendment provided by the court points out that the Stirland Lake school was opened in response to "numerous requests from parents in Northwestern Ontario's First Nation communities [to the NYP missionary organization and Indian Affairs Canada] for the establishment of a rural residential high school at which Indian students could receive a high school education, without the stresses associated with adjustment to urban living," with similar circumstances later applied to the Cristal Lake school, a residential school for girls.[43] Starting in 1983, both schools were operated with the assistance of the Northern Nishnawbe Education Council, an aboriginal organization headquartered in Sioux Lookout, Ontario.[44] The participation of an aboriginal organization in the operation of these schools may have initially been the cause of their exclusion from the Settlement Agreement. But this was consistent with the way many of the schools were decommissioned through an initial transfer of responsibility to local aboriginal school boards, starting with the Blue Quills Residential School near St. Paul, Alberta, in 1971 and continuing through to the last seven schools still open in 1993, all administered by aboriginal organizations. There is no immediate explanation for the initial exclusion of these two schools from the Settlement Agreement, aside, perhaps, from their late arrival on the scene and the broadly participatory approach to their establishment. In any event, the immediate effect of this decision was that former students of these schools were entitled to the same regime of compensation under the Settlement Agreement as any other former student of the (now) 138 recognized Indian residential schools.

It could be that these schools were a solution to high dropout rates, delinquency, and by extension the loss of culture and connection of youth with their families and communities through urban education. And this exception should do nothing to change or challenge the former students' experiences of abuse in residential schools. Nor should it alter the conclusion that, taken as a whole, the schools were inherently misguided and part of a policy oriented toward assimilation of aboriginal societies into the Canadian mainstream, and hence had the effect of a systemic denial of their distinct rights. But the mere fact that two schools were established in response to wider social challenges, through a broadly consultative approach with aboriginal leadership, might add a single, small element of nuance and complexity to the history of residential Indian education as a force of assimilation, a point of irregularity on the surface of the Commission's narratives of cultural genocide and historical trauma.

A certain kind of personhood is developed through the work of the Commission. This can be seen not just in the formal inclusions and exclusions of the Commission's mandate and categories of witnesses, but more affirmatively in the setting of the lobby and hallways of the conference centre. It was here that those who referred to themselves as survivors were able to form close-knit support groups, particularly in those communities in which a significant number of former students were victimized in their school experience. Survivors were set apart in the Commission events as the beneficiaries of T-shirts and name cards worn around the neck that both privileged and identified them as distinct from other participants. The words most commonly used at the desks for registration and inquiries were "Are you a survivor?" and "These are for survivors only."

At the TRC National Event in Halifax, as at the TRC's other meetings, the organizers provided coffee, juice, bottled water, sandwiches, cookies, and a fruit plate for the survivors who were waiting to give testimony. Around this thoughtful provision, they constructed a boundary of belonging. The Resolution Health Support Workers—readily identifiable by their black shirts and brightly coloured, stylized RHSW eagle logo, who were there for the day to provide mental health services to survivors—were, according to the rules of the meeting organizers, not to have any of the refreshments, not even the coffee. This ignored the fact that some of these support workers were also former residential school students. A coordinator of the health support workers later told me that at one point a representative of the TRC secretariat confronted one of the health workers while he was serving himself coffee, pointedly reminding him that "the coffee is for survivors only." His reply was simply, "I *am* a survivor," as he continued to prepare his coffee.[45] The instruments for the construction and naturalization of social boundaries can take the form of everyday things that in other contexts hold very different meanings. By endowing them with rules, even fruit and coffee can objectify a line of segregation.

EVASION

The stories of abuse and trauma commonly narrated to the Commission are not just personally difficult; they are also institutionally dangerous. Childhood memories of residential school abuse and the stories of parents whose children were forcibly taken away are cumulatively persuasive. They influence audiences at an emotional level. There is no denying the harms inflicted by the worst of the schools, not when days on end can be spent listening to personal remembrances of heartless regimes of discipline and specific acts of sadism, sexual molestation, and the subsequent trauma, addictions, and failed careers and relationships, all without nearly exhausting the stories to be told or completing the lists of those waiting to tell them.

These public remembrances corrode the legitimacy of those institutions identified as being responsible. Ultimately, they can even challenge the basic legitimacy of church and state. So another set of features of the TRC to which I will be paying close attention (here and in the chapters to follow) involves institutional responses to this challenge, the way that the state and churches take responsibility—or avoid it—in efforts to minimize the reputational costs of the abuse for which they have been found responsible. The evocative powers of cumulative remembrances—the sights, sounds, smells, textures, and feelings—of childhood trauma presented by witnesses are deflected, avoided, and contested in a variety of ways by the institutions to which they are directed. The TRC, in other words, is a site of active contest over history and opinion.

One of the things that makes this particularly noteworthy is the fact that, as a fundamental starting point, the direct contestation of testimony and denial of institutional responsibility are inherently illegitimate and in themselves morally wrong. Refusal to conform to the templates of history and trauma of the TRC is an act of bad faith, done in defiance of the opinion of those who matter most in this process: the afflicted-as-children. Institutional resistance by those in the categories of the culpable therefore has a tendency to be oblique, manifested in absence and exclusion, rather than in ways that are readily identifiable and contestable. There was a cold contest over history and institutional reputation taking place behind the scenes of the TRC, evident mainly in selective avoidance of evidence and opinion.

In the Truth and Reconciliation Commission proceedings, the assignment of responsibility for the schools was directed almost exclusively toward the churches. Meanwhile, the federal government kept its presence at the TRC meetings to a minimum. There was no participation by the federal government in a large regional gathering in Victoria in April 2012. (This absence was publicly noted by several witnesses, but no statement about it was made by the commissioners.) In the largest gathering in Saskatoon, the Minister of Aboriginal Affairs and Northern Development, John Duncan, having missed the opening ceremonies without sending anyone else from his department, took his turn to speak in a panel of dignitaries invited there by the Commission to present their views on reconciliation. He began by saying that reconciliation cannot be expressed "unless we talk about [it] from a personal point of view." This was a lead-in to an autobiographical statement about how as a child his family was displaced from the town of Crowsnest Pass in Alberta, which was economically depressed and slated for demolition, and moved to Kamloops, British Columbia; how as a youth he worked as a busboy for the Pacific Railway; how, after getting a forestry degree, he worked in logging operations in which many of his fellow workers were aboriginal; and how he eventually "met a wonderful woman" with whom he had "three wonderful children, all with [aboriginal] status." His final point was expressed succinctly: "I know about your culture. I know about your pain." Then he left early to catch a plane.[46]

This spare federal participation in the National Events of the TRC does not mean that federal officials formerly responsible for administering the schools are not alive today. In the eastern Arctic in particular, the last region in which the residential school policy was abandoned, officials who had responsibility for the schools are alive and well, even young by some standards. Nor does it mean that by virtue of the distance of their offices (literally and figuratively) they had no real responsibility for what happened in the schools. With this in mind it is worth noting that there was a wide disparity in the attribution of wrongdoing between the courts and the Truth and Reconciliation Commission. In one of the lawsuits that immediately led up to the

Settlement Agreement, *Blackwater v. Plint*, the trial judge apportioned 75 per cent of the fault to the federal government and 25 per cent to the United Church of Canada (the Church defendant in that particular lawsuit). This apportionment of responsibility was later upheld by the Supreme Court of Canada.[47]

The TRC has symbolically reinforced the lack of federal participation in its events through its own formal categories of inclusion and exclusion. This can be seen, for example, in the registration form that had to be completed by witnesses before giving testimony, which provides a limited range of choices under the heading "Relationship to Indian Residential Schools." These consist of "Survivor," "Intergenerational Survivor," "Former Staff," and "Other (specify)." It is telling that the registration form does not include a category of "Government Official," which, besides administrators in the Department of Indian Affairs, could have applied to a wide range of federal employees with responsibilities related to Indian residential schools, including former food inspectors, building inspectors, police officers, and even, in some instances, guidance counsellors.[48]

The lack of federal government presence and participation at the TRC meetings was, for the most part, quietly accepted. The commissioners did not draw attention to it. And even when it was noted by survivors, as very occasionally happened, the focus of the hearings soon returned to the churches as the most immediate, remembered source of their suffering. Those with experience administering and operating the schools, whether under the auspices of the federal government or the churches, rarely had any interest in sharing their stories, and the Commission had nothing to compel or induce them to do so. The Commission was able to offer school survivors respect, reverence, affirmation, healing rituals, and gift bags, but it was not able to bring wrongdoing individuals into the picture, to hear their part of the story, possibly to hear their expressions of regret; it was unable to overcome obfuscation, non-cooperation, and denial from responsible institutions and individuals. And through this regime of "truth telling," the federal government remains largely an abstraction, a source of policy, funding, and administration, putting forth nothing that attracts censure or gains traction with audiences.

Not only were priests, brothers, nuns, and lay supervisors the visible agents on the ground of residential school policy; by the very circumstances of their positions, and perhaps even by their own proclivity toward symbolism, they readily lent themselves to becoming symbols of it.

NOTES

1   Cited in *Blackwater v. Plint* [2005] 3 S.C.R. 3, 2005 SCC at para. 15; the original statement can be found in *Blackwater v. Plint* [2001] BCSC 997, at para. 135.

2   Fiona Ross, *Bearing Witness: Women and the Truth and Reconciliation Commission in South Africa* (London: Pluto, 2003), 17.

3   Cheryl Mattingly and Linda Garro, "Narrative as Construct and Construction," in *Narrative and the Cultural Construction of Illness and Healing*, ed. Cheryl Mattingly and Linda Garro (Berkeley and Los Angeles: University of California Press, 2000), 15–16.

4   See Megan Shore, *Religion and Conflict Resolution: Christianity and South Africa's Truth and Reconciliation Commission* (Surrey, UK, and Burlington, VT: Ashgate, 2009).

5   Truth and Reconciliation Commission of Canada, "How to Share Your Truth Information Session," Halifax, 26 October 2011.

6   Murray Sinclair, "Welcome to the Territory and Opening Ceremonies," TRC Saskatoon National Event, 21 June 2012.

7   Eugene Arcand, "Welcome to the Territory and Opening Ceremonies," TRC Saskatoon National Event, 21 June 2012.

8   Speaker unknown, TRC Urban Inuit Community Hearing, Ottawa, 16 August 2012.

9   Murray Sinclair, "Commissioner's Welcome," TRC Atlantic National Event, Halifax, 27 October 2011.

10 Wilton Littlechild, TRC Atlantic National Event, Halifax, 27 October 2011.

11 Alain Pottage, "Introduction: The Fabrication of Persons and Things," in *Law, Anthropology, and the Constitution of the Social: Making Persons and Things*, ed. Alain Pottage and Martha Mundy (Cambridge, UK: Cambridge University Press, 2004), 1.

12 John Borneman, *Political Crime and the Memory of Loss* (Bloomington, IN: Indiana University Press, 2011), viii.

13 The distinct approach taken by Inuit participants in a TRC event, within an emerging intercultural solidarity of survivors, is discussed in Marie-Pierre Gadoua, "The Inuit Presence at the First Canadian Truth and Reconciliation National Event," *Études/Inuit/Studies* 34, no. 2 (2010): 167–84.

14 In the remaining pages of this section, I draw from my contribution to Ronald Niezen and Marie Pierre Gadoua, "Témoignage et histoire dans la Commission de vérité et de reconciliation du Canada," *Canadian Journal of Law and Society/ La Revue Canadienne Droit et Société* 29, no. 1 (2014): 21–42.

15 Andrea Colter, "How to Share Your Truth Information Session," Halifax, 26 October 2011.

16 Truth and Reconciliation Commission of Canada, "Sharing Truth: Creating a National Research Centre on Residential Schools," accessed 16 February 2013, http://www.myrobust.com/websites/NRC/index.php?p=121.

17 See, for example, "Moving Forward," from the TRC website video page, accessed 8 November 2012, http://vimeo.com/50701589.

18 Speaker unknown, in Truth and Reconciliation Commission, *Let Our Truth Be Heard*, film screened at the Commissioner's Welcome, TRC Atlantic National Event, Halifax, 27 October 2011.

19 Kay Adams, in Truth and Reconciliation Commission, *Let Our Truth Be Heard.*

20 Margarette Paulette, in Truth and Reconciliation Commission, *Let Our Truth Be Heard.*

21 Jean Crane, in Truth and Reconciliation Commission, *Let Our Truth Be Heard.*

22 Benjamin Lafond, in Truth and Reconciliation Commission, *Let Our Truth Be Heard.*

23 Murray Sinclair, in Truth and Reconciliation Commission, *Let Our Truth Be Heard.*

24 Robert Michael, in Truth and Reconciliation Commission, *Let Our Truth Be Heard.*

25 Elizabeth Penashue, in Truth and Reconciliation Commission, *Let Our Truth Be Heard.*

26 Patrick Rich, in Truth and Reconciliation Commission, *Let Our Truth Be Heard.*

27 Isabelle Knockwood, in Truth and Reconciliation Commission, *Let Our Truth Be Heard.*

28 Doreen Bernard, in Truth and Reconciliation Commission, *Let Our Truth Be Heard.*

29 Frank Thomas, in Truth and Reconciliation Commission, *Let Our Truth Be Heard.*

30 Speaker unknown, in Truth and Reconciliation Commission, *Let Our Truth Be Heard.*

31 Mattingly and Garro, "Narrative as Construct and Construction," 18.

32 Isabelle Knockwood, Commissioners Sharing Panel, TRC Atlantic National Event, Halifax, 27 October 2011.

33 Ibid.

34 Ibid.

35 Kevin Avruch, "Truth and Reconciliation Commissions: Problems in Transitional Justice and the Reconstruction of Identity," *Transcultural Psychiatry* 47, no. 10 (2010): 35.

36 This follows the criteria set out in article 12 of the Settlement Agreement: "(i) The child must have been placed in a residence away from the family home by or under the authority of Canada for the purpose of education; *and* (ii) Canada must have been jointly or solely responsible for the operation of the residence and care of the children resident there (e.g., the institution was federally owned;

Canada stood as a parent to the child; Canada was at least partially responsible for the administration of the institution; Canada inspected or had a right to inspect the institution; Canada stipulated the institution as an Indian Residential School)." This can be seen in the context of Canada's decisions concerning claims for inclusion of institutions as IRS at Government of Canada, *School Decisions* (Ottawa: Government of Canada, 2012), accessed 16 July 2012, http://www.residentialschoolsettlement.ca/SchoolDecisions.pdf.

37 Indigenous and Northern Affairs Canada, "Statistics on the Implementation of the Indian Residential Schools Settlement Agreement," accessed 17 June 2017, https://www.aadnc-aandc.gc.ca/eng/1315320539682/1315320692192.

38 Speaker unknown, statement to the Commissioner's Sharing Panel, TRC Inuvik National Event, 30 June 2011.

39 Clément Chartier, TRC Saskatoon National Event, 22 June 2012.

40 Shirley Waskewitch, Commissioner's Sharing Panel, TRC Saskatoon National Event, 23 June 2012.

41 Speaker unknown, "It Matters to Me: A Call to Action on Reconciliation," TRC Montreal National Event, 27 April 2013.

42 Ibid.

43 *Fontaine v. Canada (Attorney General)* [2011] O.J. 3756, ONSC 4938, C.N.L.R. 111, at para. 13. See also the Schedule "A" notice on the Indian Residential School Settlement website, approved by the Ontario Superior Court of Justice, accessed 15 May 2013, http://www.residentialschoolsettlement.ca/English_Main%20Page.pdf.

44 Government of Canada, *School Decisions*.

45 Interview with Andrea Colfer, Millbrook, Nova Scotia, 7 March 2012.

46 John Duncan, "Commissioner's Welcome," TRC Saskatoon National Event, 22 June 2012.

47 On appeal, the court tried to apply a doctrine of "charitable immunity" to the United Church, which can be used to exonerate charitable institutions from liability resulting from well-intended (but ultimately harmful and tortious) acts and policies, and applied all liability to the Government of Canada. This was overturned by the Supreme Court of Canada, which restored the 75 per cent/25 per cent apportionment in the decision of the trial judge. See *Blackwater v. Plint* [2005] 3 S.C.R. 3, 2005 SCC, at para. 71.

48 The variety of federal employees with responsibilities in Indian residential schools is made clear in the BC Supreme Court's handling of the issue of responsibility for the harms of residential schools on the part of Canada and the United Church in *Blackwater v. Plint* [2001] BCSC 997.

Chapter 5

TESTIMONY

VÉRITÉ ET TÉMOIGNAGE

Few are likely to have noticed that Canada's TRC went through a change of name that lasted a little more than a year—a bit like someone trying a nickname that didn't quite take. Sometime in 2010, the French version went from "Commission de vérité et réconciliation du Canada" to "Commission de témoignage et de réconciliation du Canada," with a switch in the keywords from *vérité* (truth) to *témoignage* (testimony), then back again in 2011 to the original version. The altered French adaptation appeared on the TRC's website and some of its printed publicity material, but it never fully replaced the original. Because of the impenetrability of bureaucracies of this kind, I was never able to pin down the reason for the change (it was surely discussed sometime, somewhere in a meeting of organizers), but if I had to speculate my guess would be that the word *témoignage* was preferred in part because it made for a more uniform acronym, with TRC providing the same URL (at least using the same letters of the alphabet) in both French and English. But then the question of meaning as a reflection of institutional values arises: does the TRC really want to privilege testimony over truth? From my perspective (the one I would have expressed if I were present in the meeting with the Commission's name on the agenda), it is a question of the institutionally preferred form of symmetry: the one that produces a uniform URL or the one that produces a correspondence of meaning and values.

The ambiguity that arises from considering testimony or, in the Commission's practical terms, "statement gathering," which is reliant on personal memory and motive as an anchorage or even equivalent of truth, is one of the most significant qualities of the TRC. It is evident most explicitly in the public statements that were intended to reveal the Commission's purpose and to prepare audiences for what they were about to see, hear, and feel. Commissioner Sinclair, in his opening speech at the National Event in

Saskatoon, made a distinction between "factual truths," by which he meant the quantifiable dimensions of rooms, the numbers of students, etc., and what he called "relative truths," which would include how people felt as a consequence of what happened in the schools as well as the addictions and violence that followed from their experience. The TRC, he explained, is creating conditions for a kind of personal truth that favours the ability "to come to terms with the past and accept the impact of the past." At the same time, he pointed out, the Commission is pursuing a wider historical and educational agenda, which comes with an obligation to "give a balanced story at the end of the day."[1]

The idea of "relative truth" seems to correspond with what Donald Spence, discussing the truth value of patient reports in psychoanalysis, chooses to call "narrative truth." By this he means the rhetorically organized narrative, in which memories are shaped by the words chosen to convey them, in which "what is sayable may pre-empt what is really remembered," and in which the demands of coherence offer a temptation toward narrative fluency "in place of being accurate."[2]

The common denominator that brings these multiple forms of truth together is their close connection to testimony; hence the perceived interchangeability of *vérité* and *témoignage*. The Commission was committed to the idea that personal insight and healing were potential outcomes of bearing witness. At the same time, it made the claim that a new history of the nation is to emerge from the narrated experiences of those whose voices have long been silent or ignored. Here, as I intend to show, we see a slippage between different kinds of truths—what witnesses convey in their narratives is commonly understood to be unadulterated, veridical reports of lived experience rather than instrumentally limited reports that are subject to selectivity and omissions of memory and that are "rhetorically organized."[3]

Besides the reporting of experience being shaped by the rhetorical capacities and inclinations of witnesses, the TRC had the power (though it may not be explicitly acknowledged) to encourage and elicit testimony, even to channel testimony in particular directions, to provide models for self-perception and representation. Contexts were created by which certain kinds of "relative truths" could be spoken in preference over others. This situation is not altered by the fairness of the judgment at the foundation of the Commission's work or the deep personal and historical significance of survivor statements. It does, however, mean that there are more layers of truth that remain to be considered before we can more completely understand what the Commission did in practice and what, given its restrictive mandate, it realistically had the potential to accomplish.

AUDIENCES

In taking up this challenge, let us first consider the influence of the largest categories of participants in the work of the Commission, the entities that in their very nature defy (and, like it or not, increasingly define) the work of ethnography: temporary audiences and abstract, remote publics. The presence of masses of listeners—anonymous and personally unknown to witnesses—is central to the experience of witnessing, and this includes the intensity and creativity with which presenters conform to and shape emerging idioms of distress. The audience stands in relationship to the witness as an "other" who can respond in different ways to testimony. As Paul Ricoeur writes: "This other can be someone who responds or who refuses to respond, someone who gratifies, or someone who threatens. He may be, above all, real or a fantasy, present or lost, a source of anguish, or the object of a successful mourning."[4] We can expect that whatever qualities an audience-other possesses, they will have enormous consequences for the experience of survivors as they give statements, and they will influence the parameters within which narrations will take form.

Audience members attending Commission events appeared to be, with rare exceptions, already familiar with at least some aspect of the history of residential schools, often intimately so in the case of former students or their friends and family members. This already makes up a significant proportion of attendees, sometimes a considerable majority, to which we can add members of the public who attended in response to advance publicity (and even here we can assume, at the very least, sympathetic curiosity), a scattering of informed professionals, health care workers, researchers, former priests and nuns, and members of church congregations who were encouraged to attend by their pastors.

Live audiences are temporary gatherings that are limited to an event that occurs in a particular time and place. They tend to have their own preferences and inclinations particularized to the events that attract them. Audience members also tend to come to these events with shared knowledge of rules of etiquette and repertoires or vocabularies of expression. We are familiar with most of these, which range from applause that can be warm or scattered, to boos of dissatisfaction or disapproval, or whistles and whoops of joy and approval—all of which permit audience members to express judgment one way or another. (In the Commission event in Saskatoon the so-called "war whoop" expressed the highest level of approval, while in Montreal the most vigorous applause was accompanied by drumming.) Then there is the ultimate vehicle for expression of censure: the indignant exit. The thing that audiences do best, though, is express emotion in ways that are impossible for individuals to accomplish. If just a minor proportion of people in a large audience make the same sound simultaneously, a small "aaah" or "mmm" or even the rustle of clothing as they shift uncomfortably in their chairs, then a kind of emotional democracy of expression comes into play that manifests their feelings and magnifies them for all to hear.

How might the immediate audiences at TRC events have influenced what was said by witnesses? Given that many or most of those present at some of the National

FIGURE 5.1: Audience members at the Iqaluit community hearings.

Events and most of the regional hearings were survivors or members of their families, friends, and supporters, the audience was prepared to listen approvingly or at least tolerantly to a very wide spectrum of narratives about suffering. For those who came to narrate the traumas and indignities of their personal experience of the schools and their effects that have extended into adulthood, the audience makes the microphone a safe place to be. But there is a limit, almost a demarcation, beyond which it is difficult to cross without invoking the rejection or even the wrath of the audience. The preferences and indulgences of the audience not only influence the emotions of speeches and the readiness of witnesses to relate emotionally powerful testimony but they also seem to inhibit those with more "ordinary" or "positive" stories from appearing. This predilection for horror and heightened emotion is part of the nature of mass audiences, including abstract publics. They want to hear from the tortured and the damned, not from those left miraculously unscathed.

The survivors who appeared before the microphone, cameras, and live audience did not put themselves there to shout into the air and have their words evaporate; their intention was clearly to be listened to and ideally to have what they said preserved, not just in the memories of their listeners but noted, recorded, and archived. They seemed to be attentive to the fact that there were cameras in the room. And they were occasionally reminded by the master of ceremonies that the same words and images that they could see on the giant screens in front of them as they gave their statements were going out to a live feed on the Internet and that there was ultimately to be a

FIGURE 5.2: Audience members at the Commissioner's Sharing Panel in Saskatoon.

permanent archive of all testimony given to the Commission. This was confirmed by a leaflet placed on every seat at each event, which announced in block letters, "THIS IS A TRC PUBLIC EVENT," followed by a set of bullet points:

- The media or someone with a cell camera or recording equipment may record what you say and they may use the recording as they choose.
- Your personal information, including your image, is not confidential if you choose to participate in this public forum.
- What you say publicly during these events, along with a photograph or video of you, may be used in books, films, videos and audio clips or in any other multi-media presentations.
- The TRC itself may record the event. The TRC may use parts of the recording for public education purposes, on the TRC website, in the TRC reports and research, in short videos, and may make it available to documentary film makers, and others.

In case this set of contractual points had a dissuasive effect, an alternative to public participation followed in italics:

Participation in this event is voluntary. If you do not consent to the above, you are welcome to give your statement in a private session with the TRC.[5]

As this announced range of intended media use indicates, the broad communication of the TRC's events and testimony also included considerable efforts—perhaps greater than in any other truth commission—dedicated to posting information and broadcasting events via digital media. This was manifested, for example, in live streaming via the TRC website of testimony given in the Commissioner's Sharing Panels; in DVD copies of statements provided to those who gave statements, to keep and take away with them if they chose; and in a general awareness, promoted by leaflets and introductory announcements, that a digital record of the Commission's work was eventually to be made publicly available in a TRC-sponsored national research centre.

It was emotionally difficult for many survivors to present their testimony, both because of the confessional nature of the event—revisiting the experiences of powerlessness and pain that was the focus of most of their narratives—and above all because exposure to a large number of strangers (albeit compassionate ones) produces a deep sense of vulnerability. In particular, the presence of cameras (in National Events these cameras project live images of witnesses on several large screens) appears to have been hugely intimidating, especially to those unused to presenting themselves before audiences of strangers. In Inuvik there was even a link to two screens outside the gymnasium where the meeting was taking place, in front of a playing field where picnickers and passersby could listen to testimony—or were *compelled* to listen

FIGURE 5.3: The third day of the Commissioner's Sharing Panel in Inuvik.

(so some complained)—through a concert-worthy sound system with no means of timely escape beyond earshot by which children could be protected from sometimes graphic descriptions of sexual crimes and suffering. Nor were the cameras neutral or innocent in their effect on witnesses, with cameramen sometimes making artistic efforts to highlight whatever was poignant in a witness's struggles before the microphone, with close-up shots of grief-stricken faces, tearful embraces, and once (in Halifax) a lingering, voyeuristic focus on a female witness's trembling hands that were half hidden under the table.

CONTRITION AND DEFIANCE

It is probably easiest to see the way that statements in Commission hearings are shaped by public preferences through examples of widely approved church presentations. The expectation here, complied with by almost all participants (I will later discuss a few exceptions), is that church representatives will express contrition and a willingness to support efforts to overcome institutional harm. A specific venue was set up for this in the National Events: a space referred to as the Churches Listening Area, where survivors could sit down individually with a church representative of their choice and hear a private, personal apology. In most of the National Events these Listening Areas were sparsely attended, for reasons that no one there seemed able to explain, leaving the church representatives to spend most of their time at the event sitting quietly or talking among themselves.[6] Private expressions of contrition were simply not what most survivors had come to hear.

The greater expectation by survivors at TRC National Events was that church participation would involve public statements of apology. For the churches, this presented little difficulty. They possess hierarchies from which people can be selected to represent the institution and to present official statements. There is also a ready-made pathway for contrition built into Christian churches, with an established idiom of confession, even of self-abasement, and a compensatory promise of eternal forgiveness. The Anglican apology delivered to the National Native Convocation in Minaki, Ontario, in 1993 by Archbishop Michael Peers provides an example:

> I am sorry, more than I can say, that we were part of a system which took you and your children from home and family. I am sorry, more than I can say, that we tried to remake you in our image, taking from you your language and the signs of your identity.
>
> I am sorry, more than I can say, that in our schools so many were abused physically, sexually, culturally and emotionally.
>
> On behalf of the Anglican Church of Canada, I present our apology.[7]

Almost in the same way that apologies encouraged survivors to articulate their experiences of abuse publicly, this speech provided the model for Archbishop Fred Hiltz to offer a thematically similar but emboldened apology at TRC National Events, including his presentation in Halifax in 2011:

> The theme of this Atlantic National event, "It's About Love," moves me to think of a mother's love, a father's love, the love of brothers and sisters, the love of grandparents, and the love of an extended family. I am sorry. I am sorry that our church was part of a system, a policy of assimilation, in which we took you from your homes. I am sorry for the loneliness you experienced in those schools, and for what we have already heard today, the nights when you cried for lack of love. I am sorry for the years of lost love, and the terrible impact on your lives.
>
> "It's About Love" moves me to think of a child's love, how precious, and genuine, and trusting, and beautiful that love is. And I am sorry for the sins of those who abused children in the residential schools. I am sorry for the bruising of your bodies, the crushing of your spirits, and the violation of your innocence. For all these sins of physical, emotional, and sexual abuse, some committed in the sight of others, and so many more in secret, I am deeply sorry.
>
> "It's About Love" moves me to think of a people's love of their language, culture, and traditions, their heritage, and their hope. And I am sorry for the ways in which we forbid you speak your languages, and to celebrate your cultures. I am sorry for our aggressive efforts in remaking you in our image.[8]

It was precisely this apology that received a strongly favourable response from audience members with whom I later spoke or whose conversations I overheard from surrounding seats. It offered a clear disavowal of past practices and an emotionally honest recognition of the harms the church caused. There was no self-exculpatory justification, no explanation of motives, and no introduction of uncertainty or conditionality.

Resistant views, refusals of unconditional contrition, however, did very occasionally find expression. Only once did I see a church representative disrupt the narrative of contrition to the point of causing a furor. When Brother Cavanaugh, representing the Oblate order, made a presentation to the Commission at an event called "Expressions of Reconciliation," he came, or so it later seemed, with the goal of setting the record straight. Before an audience of some 800 people, consisting mostly of survivors and their families and friends, in a large meeting room of the lavishly appointed Fairmont Empress Hotel in Victoria, British Columbia, he expressed views that differed sharply from the usual paradigm of church contrition. Brother Cavanaugh spoke of his experience (which he introduced as "my truth regarding my experience") as a young man, twenty-one years old, appointed as a supervisor of the senior boys in grades 5 to 8 in the Christie Residential School at Kakawis on Meares Island (off the west coast of Vancouver Island), which he remembered as a place of love and dedication to learning, with the Sisters of the Immaculate Heart bearing a great responsibility for the education and welfare of the students, together with five Oblate Fathers and Brothers as well as eight First Nations support staff. When he said in passing that the 120 children in the school were "sent by their parents," there was a murmur from the audience. He went on, "Was it a perfect situation? No," and followed up with a statement that seemed to set things off: "There didn't seem to be any other viable alternative in providing a good education for so many children who lived in relatively small, isolated communities."

At this point there was a shout from the audience: "Truth! Tell the truth! You're not telling the truth!" From somewhere else in the room there was a loud wail, followed by agonized weeping.

Cavanaugh persisted through the interruption: "The Native staff who were related to a number of the children along with the other staff, I felt, provided a good education, as well as excellent care and guidance."

"Tell the truth! Shame on you! We never sent our children to residential school!"

"Parents were encouraged to visit the school and rooms were available, if they wished to stay overnight to be with their children."

"Tell the truth!"[9]

At this point, Commissioner Sinclair approached the microphone and called for "health supports" for the person who was still wailing and weeping loudly enough to be heard across the room. He then made a brief statement in which he argued for Brother Cavanaugh's right to be heard, and he concluded by saying: "We must ask that you be respectful." The presentation then continued without further interruption as it fell into the expected pattern. Brother Cavanaugh presented a book about a Catholic-sponsored healing initiative and placed it with hands joined with the commissioner into the bentwood box, and this was followed by handshakes and scattered applause.

The Commission's final report recalls this event, and adds that later the same day Ina Seitcher, who attended the Christie Residential School that Brother Cavanaugh spoke about, gave a very different account of the experience: "That priest that talked about how loving that Christie residential school was—it was not. That priest was most likely in his office not knowing what was going on down in the dorms or in the lunchroom." The Commission's report then attributes the absence of such direct exchanges between survivors and former school staff to the fact that, for many, "the time for reconciliation had not yet arrived."[10]

Such interruptions of the pattern, manifested in stress points or ruptures of uncharacteristic emotion, tell us more about the boundaries of testimony than does conformity to them. In this significant moment we have an audience rejecting a narrative truth ("my experience") that makes a claim to correspondence with a historical truth that wilfully runs against the orthodoxy of survivor experience. It is instructive in the context of this thematic rupture to consider a document that parallels Brother Cavanaugh's argument—an introduction to a petition, probably written in 1950, addressed to D.M. McKay, then Director of Indian Affairs:

> After seeing what is being done in Indian Residential Schools throughout the country, we have come to the conclusion that only a Residential School could be of any utility to us. We therefore hope that you will take into serious consideration the present petition, which has been signed by all the Indians of this Reserve and that you will grant us, in the year 1950, a Residential School large enough to accommodate all our children ... Thanking you in anticipation, we remain, Dear Mr. McKay, Sincerely yours,
>
> The Indians of the Obedjiwan Reserve[11]

Documents, too, can be taken out of context. What we don't see here is the background involvement of the Oblate priests (other documents in the file point in particular to a certain Father Plourde as the principal activist behind the scenes), who very likely worked hard to convince the Indians of the Obedjiwan Reserve of the benefits that would follow from the establishment of an Indian residential school on their reserve. But the document still points to a process of consultation of sorts—at least in this one instance—behind federal funding of a residential school.

Given the possibility, supported by documentary evidence from elsewhere, that Brother Cavanaugh was making legitimate (though audience-rejected) observations about the establishment and operation of the school in which he worked, what was it about his statement that provoked such a strong reaction from the audience? Though only two people expressed themselves volubly, one with anger and another with grief, it was clear from the sounds, facial expressions, and body movement that the audience as a whole was hostile toward parts of Brother Cavanaugh's presentation. What did he say that offended his listeners so deeply?

In passing, the phrase "sent by their parents," seems to have been immediately picked up by the audience. With this, he interrupted the boundary that separated the oppressed as a collectivity from those who have moral responsibility for their suffering. In effect, he made aboriginal peoples co-conspirators in establishing residential schools. In doing so, he questioned the foundational historical premise of the Commission itself, captured succinctly in the title of an interim historical report, "They Came for the Children." Second, he indirectly challenged the integrity of some survivors when he pointed out that once in school the students were in daily contact with aboriginal people from their communities who had been hired as support staff and that facilities had been provided for parents to stay at the school and visit their children. With this point, he called into question accounts by survivors of their isolation and loneliness, the commonality of suffering and cultural erasure as essential qualities of the residential school experience, and hence the credibility of those who testified along these lines, even though he did introduce his statement as "my truth," without generalizing his experience to all other schools.

More generally, it interrupted—we might even say violated—the memories and identities of those in the audience whose experiences of abuse in school, its disastrous consequences on their lives as adults, and whose later sense of affirmation through the process of becoming survivors had all become indispensable aspects of a troubled, complex sense of self. And when he invoked the historical inevitability of the schools, he shifted the source of moral responsibility and injury from the level of the institutions to the few individuals in authority within them who violated their trust.

There is a Christian subtext here: agency and sin are concerns of individuals who are individually responsible for the care of their souls; and by extension, there is little place on the political stage for apologies and truth commissions for acts that should instead be understood—and managed—as part of a personal spiritual economy of sin and repentance. This narrative was fundamentally at odds with a paradigm of institutional domination and cultural genocide. And more to the point, it was at odds with the widely shared expectation of unequivocal contrition by the churches in all dimensions of their participation in Commission events.

A similar offence against the expectations of repentance occurred when Bishop Gary Gordon of Whitehorse was called to the floor by Commissioner Sinclair without being aware that he was once again on the speaker's list. He had not prepared his second presentation. The statement he gave under these circumstances broke with the expected pattern of acknowledgement and unqualified contrition. It began predictably enough by offering an account of the healing and reconciliation programs for Church members sponsored by the Diocese. More surprisingly, it then replicated a common pattern of survivor narratives, focusing on personal suffering, except that the source of the Bishop's suffering as he related it was his experience as someone unjustly associated with the abuses of the schools:

As a young priest I was working in Saskatoon and I was driving up to the hospital to visit a family. Somebody was sick. And I was wearing the Roman collar. And so as I was parked at the stoplight, the guy walked by and saw the collar and he just went to moon me. You know, just kind of, to show me what he felt. I'd never seen him before and didn't know him but it was just the anger coming out.

Another time, just walking along with the collar on, and the finger flipped at me, you get the bird. Never saw that person before, didn't know [him]. And it's just little things, like you know like it kind of wears on a person after a while and it becomes where I even felt it was hard for me to wear a collar because there was so [much] anger that would be directed at it. It's a little thing but it is part of how we've suffered. We're suffering too.[12]

Here the perpetrators of injustice were the people who in their anger rushed to judgment, who associated him with the pain that they were only then, in that offending way, able to express. And their expression of that suffering was the cause of his own—his sense of rejection despite service and sacrifice, the indignity of exposure to insults and obscenity, and following from this, his reluctance to wear the collar, the symbol of his faith and belonging.

The proceedings of the Commission left little place for such exceptions, for such constructions of memory from those who represented the oppressors to most of those present, who came before them without contrition (or contrition of the right kind) in defiance of the survivor/oppressor partitions of memory and experience. The Commission had a prevailing narrative that manifested itself through those who appeared before the microphone and cameras that was even more clearly defined by the selection of material posted online; and beyond this, the narrative was defined through the collective preferences and opinions of those on the other side who were most immediately the audience in the room—those who were there to respond or react, who would even send up one or two of their own to cut things short and reinforce the norm, to shout and cry when a speaker stood out too far from the surface of consensus.

EXPERIENCE AND NARRATION

The nature of the statements presented to the Commission can perhaps be better understood with reference to those former students of residential schools who, for one reason or another, decided not to speak. This could have been for obvious reasons, such as the fact that the schedule of the meeting in Saskatoon overlapped with a major powwow, leaving a larger proportion than usual of survivors absent and proportionally more non-aboriginal people in attendance. But survivors who decided not to give testimony sometimes expressed more revealing sentiments. One is the sense that the story one has to tell does not convey the depth of suffering that would move the audience and make an impression on the Commission: "I almost feel guilty because, I mean, I had it rough in residential school ... Sister N wasn't the nicest person in the world. I didn't starve though. I had clothes. I had warm bed. I wasn't abused physically, you know, or sexually abused. Um, she was pretty rough on us, though. But my story compared to our elders ... it almost seems insignificant, if I could say that."[13]

Reluctance to testify was also expressed by those who had concerns about the possibility (or even likelihood) of revealing intimate details of their lives to members of their home communities in the audience: "We live in small communities where everybody knows everybody and you know each other's stories and you know how gossip gets around, so I didn't think many people want to rehash the whole thing."[14] Of course, the purpose of the Commission's Private Statement Gathering in each meeting was precisely to allay such concerns while making the testimony available to the Commission, eventually to be assembled in a public archive with protections of anonymity in place. But there seemed to be an all-or-nothing approach taken by those who saw the largest public venues as the only ones worth speaking to—a possibility, revealing in its own right, that points to an attraction-repulsion effect of intimate self-revelation to a large audience.

Many of the speakers at the Commissioner's Sharing Panels were people who were not used to appearing before audiences, at least not of this size, and because of this they were particularly vulnerable. They had filled in a form and put their names on an open speaker's list; and they were usually unknown to the commissioners, unvetted, and hence unpredictable in terms of what they might say. Unlike politicians or other kinds of celebrity, they could not count on an intangible force of opinion from outside to give them a reservoir of emotional support in the face of any one audience, nor could many of them imagine coming to the microphone again. For them, giving testimony in this forum was a once-in-a-lifetime event.

The TRC was oriented first and foremost to the needs of these kinds of witnesses: their need to tell their own stories that for a long time were not listened to, their need for support and affirmation as they struggled with psychological pain, and their need to complete a transition in the emotional composition of their identities, from shame—above all the shame that attaches to victims of sexual abuse—to personal and collective esteem. As the commissioners often pointed out, this is part of a slow process of healing that was only marked at one point by their participation in the events of the Commission. But at the same time, as many witnesses pointed out even as they sat before the microphone, the act of giving testimony to the Commission was a deeply emotional, meaningful, and at the same time terrifying event.

Survivors would sometimes begin their testimony with a succinct statement of their identity: "I am an Indian Residential School Survivor of cultural, physical, spiritual and sexual abuse by the Government of Canada and church officials, which were entrusted with my care as a child."[15] Occasionally they began with an equally pointed characterization of the schools: "It was a concentration camp where our spirit was taken away."[16] More consistently, however, the testimony of survivors evoked the lived realities of violence directed toward children, with beatings, sexual abuse, and sadistic regimes of discipline, humiliation, racism, and cultural denigration among the most common themes. One example among many can be seen in the following testimony presented in June 2010 in one of the opening Commissioner's Sharing Panels of the first National Event of the TRC in Winnipeg:

> To this day I suffer anxiety problems. I am claustrophobic. I was not old enough when I first started school so when they sent the kids off to classes, the nuns would put me in a locker and take me out at lunch to go and eat and then when the kids would go back to school I would be locked back into that locker. And when I first got there they scrubbed me raw. They cut my hair. I slept on a bed, I couldn't move. I had to sleep like I was on the cross. My skin was so sore. I had blisters. I bled. To this day I still have nightmares—a certain nightmare. I am floating in the air, I see my dad taking this little girl in and I'm saying, "don't take her, it's a bad place." But he goes in with her. As he goes up the stairs he turns and looks at me, he knows I'm there and they take me, they are all nice at first. They say they are going to take care of me, and as soon as they close the door that's when it starts. I didn't know how to speak English, I got many straps. I got abused by two priests ...

The narrative continues from this point with a discussion of the sexual abuse and the witness's struggles with and recovery from the experience.

For another witness, the shock of an early experience with racism was a reference point of trauma:

> "Indians, dirty people, wash some more, here, your skin is too brown." I remember one of those small little nuns took me in the tub and started washing me; she couldn't get the tan off me. She was mad. She spanked me for that.[17]

Survivor statements also commonly invoke the insidious, negative influence of school experience on life as an adult, as in the following statement from an Inuit man in his late thirties or early forties at the TRC Community Hearings in Iqaluit:

> I didn't want to do it. I didn't want to abuse anyone whether they are a female or a male. I promised myself I wouldn't do that but apparently it becomes a cycle and just happens. When I had a wife, that's when I made that mistake. When we were here, going to school in Iqaluit I used to take advantage of my wife's daughter and even impregnated her and that child is my son. I couldn't love my own son because of that mistake I've made. You will confuse sex and love. There's a

healthy sexual experience if you're in love with that person but there is a deviant sexual experience. You confuse it with love and I did that with my stepdaughter, I hurt her mother very much, my daughter's mother.

In 1994, when we were in Iqaluit, we lived in White Row [a low-rent housing unit], I tried committing suicide when she left. All this time I have been looking for her. My ex came with RCMP, with my son and my stepdaughter. But because of my denial, I blamed her instead and I'm going to kill myself now in front of you because you keep telling me to kill myself. I was just lying because it's not true. I punctured myself with a knife trying to stab at my heart, but fortunately it just went to the right and I stabbed myself twice. The police shot with the pistol, and shot me in the thigh. I am so regretful and I feel so much remorse for my son, his sister, and their mother that I stabbed myself in front of them. I gave them my anger in a different form.

I got incarcerated for almost four years. It was a blessing in disguise because I had to learn the mistakes I made and it was fortunate that I learned when I was incarcerated that what I went through and what I did were two totally different things. I learnt that through healing programs and healing. I decided that [when] we were given a choice of healing workshops or just being angry and being incarcerated, I was just thinking "I'll just be incarcerated." That was my first thought because I was angry, but then I started thinking "maybe I need to heal." . . .

I died for a minute or a period and I know where suicide people go. I know where they go because I came back from that. I'm sorry, they're not resting in peace. I saw where they go ...

I have to apologize. I have apologized to the people that I hurt. I really wanted to express myself eloquently and unfortunately I didn't but thank you.[18]

It is worth noting that this testimony and others like it that intimately revealed deeply troubled adult lives did not find their way onto the "highlight reels" of the Commission, even though the experience of intergenerational harm is a prominent theme of the hearings and of the Commission's preparation and interpretation of testimony. The secondary harms committed by school survivors blur the boundary between victim and perpetrator. And while a cogent argument can be made that connects this secondary harm to the experiences of children in residential school, it does not readily lend itself to the narratives demanded of effective publicity, in which one is called upon to be direct, with a single, simple message and in which the objects of compassion are not to be confused in any way with the sources of harm.

Closely connected to this kind of statement, but representing a separate category in the witness sign-up sheet, were those whose narratives were based on the experience of being an "intergenerational Survivor" or "Survivor of intergenerational processes" (note that the form uses the honorific upper case "S" in Survivor), that is, those whose lives were in some way adversely affected by the actions of a close relative with a background of traumatic experience in residential school.

> When I became a young person he became my husband. He was a very bad alcoholic ... This sometimes surprises me that my husband is an alcoholic; me I never drink. I don't like it when you drink, so stop drinking because I never grew up that way. And he wasn't going to be drunk for one day, he would be drunk for a whole week ... And every time he gets angry and he said something about residential school and we would all be scared. When I tried to ask him questions he would get even angrier. I used to be full of bruises from the neck down to my feet because he used to physically abuse me and beat me up. When he started disclosing in the beginning at least I felt better because I started understanding him ... When you are with a survivor the impact is really bad and it takes a long time to fully understand why they are being that way and it takes a while for us to understand the way they act.[19]

There are two boundaries crossed in this narrative. The first involves the unclear category to which the speaker belongs, with her obvious suffering as a secondary result of the residential school experience, but with a trespass across the term "intergenerational"—the abuser in this case was a husband, not a parent or older blood relative. She also at one point makes a subtle switch from addressing the wider audience to speaking to him directly in her narration—"I don't like it when *you* drink ..."—an indication that her abusive husband is in fact being addressed throughout and, with his repeated bouts of binge drinking and violence, may even have provided a part of the motivation for her to make a public statement.

Finally, the most consistent and possibly most necessary theme in survivor testimony is a concluding account of healing and redemption. For the witness in Iqaluit whose narrative I cited earlier, it manifests itself in the "blessing in disguise" of incarceration and prison therapy. It can take a variety of other forms, including rediscovery of aboriginal spiritual traditions, finding truth in Christianity (a faith commonly seen by survivors as being distorted and sinned against by those operating the school), achieving sobriety in a twelve-step program, or, as in the following excerpt, simply finding comfort in family life:

> But now I'm not that broken and hurt as I really was ... I made myself what I am today. I look after my family really good. People know that everywhere around here. My children, my grandchildren, I lend them ten dollar bills every time they want something.[20]

The account of redemption is not the most prominent narrative feature of survivor testimony—it is often slipped in, presented in passing—but it is probably the only quality of TRC testimony that can at some level be considered fundamentally necessary. The lack of it stands out, particularly if the witness concentrates on traumatic events, producing a sense that he or she remains exposed before the audience in an acute condition of distress. The account of redemption is not only for the benefit of the witness but also a salve to the audience and publics listening to affect-laden stories of broken, violated childhood. It puts a cap on the witnesses' suffering and by extension the audiences' need for sympathy, as though, if they were to express it directly, they would be saying: "But I'm okay now. No need to feel sorry for me. Let's move on."

WHILE I HAVE THE MICROPHONE ...

Among the most important things revealed by the templates of the Commissioners' Sharing Panels are not just the dominant narratives that they conveyed and encouraged but the ways (and messages) in which some witnesses refused to conform to them. The tangents that witnesses sometimes pursued reveal the motivations behind their participation more clearly than the testimony that stayed closer to the topic and the security of the templates. When witnesses strayed from the subject of their residential school experience it was to reveal another significant priority, usually something that produced in them a sense of outrage comparable to, or even greater than, that of their school experience.

Emmet Peters, the first to put his name on the speakers list in Halifax, began by conforming to the pattern set by others, alluding to his sexual victimization in school ("sometimes at night all you smell is bad breath and all you see is these big hands"), his loss of memory ("there are parts I can't even remember ... years I don't even know about"), his life as a young adult ("years after I quit drinking, I still felt a lot of shame"), and his recovery through finding his way to the American Midwest to learn the traditions of the Lakota ("I eventually found my culture that was taken away") and raising a family, guided by the values he discovered among the Lakota, away from the influence of the church ("our proudest achievement is none of our kids is baptized"). All this was clearly important for him to put on the record. But what he really seemed to want to express was his sense of being personally wronged by the usurpation of the traditional chieftainship on Prince Edward Island in the late nineteenth century through federally mandated elections for chief and council. This fed into his rejection of the current leadership of the reserve: "I'm old enough to remember Indian Agents," he told his audience, "and the saddest thing I see is our chiefs acting like Indian Agents." In closing, he had his nephew read an obituary of his ancestor, Chief Joseph, dated 8 July 1880, which evoked the virtues of a man who was both a skilled hunter and an effective leader, but who was unable to pass on the inheritance of his office of traditional chief, for which, under different circumstances, Peters would have qualified.[21]

The places where witnesses broke away from the templates extended as far as other injustices that fit within the same logic of the TRC's preferred testimony but that did not fundamentally contradict the basic notions of trauma, grief, and injustice as an outcome of state policy, directed toward marginalization or elimination of the distinct, collective, self-determining status of aboriginal peoples. A Commissioner's Sharing Panel in the regional event in Victoria, for example, began, before any other testimony was heard, with a plea from the mother of a child taken into custody by British Columbia's Ministry of Children and Family Development for the return of her son. When Commissioner Littlechild gave her the microphone, ostensibly for a brief announcement, she spoke at length, sometimes shouting, in a desperate attempt to generalize her sense of injustice and gain support from the audience. "Whenever I go to court, 98 per cent of the people are Aboriginal," she said, adding, "We haven't gotten very far from the days of residential schools." As the meeting continued, she handed out business cards to everyone in attendance (some 300 people), which displayed a school photograph of her son and the caption, "Native lawyer Needed for class action law suit Let's Help Each Other."

A similar theme of ongoing forms of institutional abuse was touched on by Linda Bernard Maloney in her testimony to the Atlantic National Event in Halifax: "You know it's still going on because of the news that you see on TV every day about what happens to the women, the women that are not being looked after, the women that died in the jails, left there to die in their own vomit."[22] The television news, it would seem, was not bringing enough attention to this cause. Aboriginal women were still being neglected, arrested without reason, and dying in jail. And perhaps the more sympathetic, attentive audience of the Commission hearings might be more apt to make the connection between these circumstances and the abuses that took place in the schools.

For Jerry Dan Raddi, the microphone at the Commissioner's Sharing Panel in Inuvik gave him a chance to talk not only about his traumatic experience in school, his own subsequent difficulties as a parent, and his eventual reconciliation with his six children, but it also presented an opportunity to set the record straight about his recent run in with the law:

[A] few years ago my name was smeared right across the territories and was on ... CBC territory news and I was slandered. They said I broke someone's jaw with a two by four. I was incarcerated ... I ended up in jail for three months for something I didn't do ... There was gossip there, there was jealousy, there was hatred in there ... Things didn't look good. I had seven charges pinned on me and they're indictable; they were all carrying 2 years. [If I was] found guilty on all seven it would have been 14 years ...

We had nine guys standing outside our house, hiding ... They were on our property. They were going to hurt us. I was scared. I didn't know what to do. I tried to call the cops. I was pretty shaky. I didn't know what to do. I couldn't dial the numbers. I wasn't functioning right and I went outside. I remember he was standing outside. We could hear the swearing out there so I had no choice but to take a gun and I walked back out and I said, "Let's do this now." They all vanished. I put my gun away ... They arrested me and they threw me in. That night was scary. I was locked up. Those guys were creepy. There was guns out that night. They would carry shotguns and rifles. When I complained to the complaints commissioner they investigated ... What they did was not normal.[23]

One last example of the many there are to choose from comes from the testimony of Beatrice Burnheart, also from Inuvik, for whom one of the current, most burning issues was racism in the workplace:

I quit my job. In the first time in my life I worked for three little months, I say, "what the hell is happening to me, why am I falling apart?" but you know I'm glad today I'm not working with them because I saw their attitude towards Native people, when I was working for [that] big company. They don't have to say it, the way they look at you, exclude you. How could they exclude me on my own land, my own home, in my own territory? I came from dog team people. I was born in an igloo ... We're strong people. We're Copper Inuit.[24]

If for no other reason than through their sheer frequency, we should consider such apparent digressions as central to the significance of giving statements in Commission hearings. It then becomes possible to see the theme of injustice as covering a wider spectrum of testimony than anyone might have expected. The subjects preferred by survivors and their audiences extended beyond the mandate of the Commission to include a variety of ongoing forms of state-sponsored exclusion, dispossession, racism, and assaults to the pride of (and sometimes originating from) the community to which one belongs. The "while I have the microphone" phenomenon reveals that, for many of its participants, the Commission was a venue for the expression of current experience. They rejected the boundary that separated their remembrances of the schools from other more current, personally felt wrongs. Publicly remembering the abuses of childhood led almost seamlessly into accounts of political usurpation, unresolved treaty claims, the indignities of criminal prosecution, the apprehension and fostering of their children by provincial child protection agencies, the experience of ostracism in reserve communities, even (and not entirely unjustifiably) the high prices in the fast food outlets of the Commission's events—any active, irritating, burning cause of indignation could find its way into witness's narrations. It is almost as though the Commission's hearings were an open court of justice in which any cause could be heard and in which, somehow, miraculously, a judgment could be passed and a condition of fairness restored.

Participants in the hearings spoke in order to win some kind of approval from their listeners. Under these circumstances, the rhetorical value of what they said took precedence over truth value. Following Spence, they were presenting their testimony in conditions that were favourable to "narrative truth." Feeling the press of potential judgment from their listeners, speakers would translate what they said into what they were seeking to achieve in the situation. If they wanted to tell a good story, they would round the edges of their narrative, clarify the roles and personalities of the actors they described, and sharpen the contrast between conditions of grace and those of defilement. If they were seeking sympathy, they would emphasize the brutality of their childhood experience and their present suffering resulting from it. There was also a performative need to impress or be accepted by their listeners—particularly the commissioners—by bringing in good information, offering something of use.

The conditions in which speakers offered their narrations, above all the presence and pressures of an audience, were readily overlooked, while historical truth was often imputed to their narrations. For the churches, the truth they were called upon to tell was centred on unconditional contrition, an unequivocal recognition of institutional wrong, the conditions of suffering it caused, and a pledge to contribute in some way to healing and reconciliation. In the Commission's encouragement of survivor narratives we find conditions of affirmation, in which narrations and expressions of emotion were permitted in nearly any form. The limit imposed by the mandate of the Commission—the inquiry into residential school experience—was crossed with impunity as survivors narrated conditions of collective harm and injustice in an almost bewildering variety of forms.

But the Commission did not just cultivate emotional conditions of affirmation; it situated the condition of being a survivor in a context of ideas about what this condition entailed. The events of the TRC, as I will discuss in the chapters that follow, were not just sites for gathering knowledge; they were also active in producing it. This was accomplished through concepts drawn from psychiatry, history, and human rights that were combined in ways that clarified the essence of the survivor experience and made it possible for the category to be inhabited with certainty of conviction.

NOTES

1   Murray Sinclair, "Commissioner's Welcome," TRC Saskatoon National Event, 22 June 2012.

2   Donald Spence, *Narrative Truth and Historical Truth: Meaning and Interpretation in Psychoanalysis* (New York: Norton, 1982), 280.

3   For further discussion of the instrumental limitations of truth commissions, see Erin Daly, "Truth Skepticism: An Inquiry into the Value of Truth in Times of Transition," *The International Journal of Transitional Justice* 2 (2008): 23–41.

4   Paul Ricoeur, "The Question of Proof in Freud's Psychoanalytic Writings," *Journal of the American Psychoanalytic Association* 25 (1977): 839.

5   Truth and Reconciliation Commission of Canada, Unpublished document, first distributed at the TRC Winnipeg National Event, 16–19 June 2010.

6   For reasons that I am not able to explain, the National Event in Edmonton included greater participation in the Churches Listening Area.

7   Anglican Church of Canada's Apology to Native People, a message from the Primate, Archbishop Michael Peers, to the National Native Convocation, Minaki, Ontario, 6 August 1993, accessed 13 September 2013, http://www.anglican.ca/wp-content/uploads/2011/03/15-The-Apology.pdf.

8   Archbishop Fred Hiltz, Statement of Reconciliation, TRC Atlantic National Event, Halifax, 27 October 2011.

9   Brother Tom Cavanaugh, Oblats de Marie Immaculée, statement to the Truth and Reconciliation Commission Regional Hearings, Victoria, British Columbia, 14 April 2012.

10 Truth and Reconciliation Commission of Canada, *Honouring the Truth, Reconciling for the Future: Summary of the Final Report of the Truth and Reconciliation Commission of Canada*, 2015, accessed 11 August 2016, http://www.trc.ca/websites/trcinstitution/File/2015/Findings/Exec_Summary_2015_05_31_web_o.pdf. For further discussion of this event, see Ronald Niezen, Templates and Exclusions: Victim Centrism in Canada's Truth and Reconciliation Commission on Indian Residential Schools, *Journal of the Royal Anthropological Institute* 22 (2016): 920–938.

11 Letter from the Indians of the Obedjiwan Reserve to Mr. D.M. McKay, Director of the Indian Affairs Branch, Maison Deschâtelets, Ottawa, File. No. 3D5/04 Manouane (correspondence 1950–1952).

12 Bishop Gary Gordon, Commissioner's Sharing Panel, TRC Inuvik National Event, 30 June 2012.

13 Lucy Kuptana, Interview with Marie-Pierre Gadoua, Inuvik, 11 October 2011.

14 Philip Morin, Commissioner's Sharing Panel, TRC Saskatoon National Event, 23 June 2012.

15 Speaker unknown, Commissioner's Sharing Panel, TRC regional event, Victoria, 13 April 2012.

16 James Cardinal, Commissioner's Sharing Panel, TRC Inuvik National Event, 30 June 2011.

17 Jimmy Ittulik, TRC Community Hearings, Iqaluit, 26 March 2011.

18 Speaker unknown, TRC Community Hearings, Iqaluit, 26 March 2011.

19 Speaker unknown, Commissioner's Sharing Panel, TRC Inuvik National Event, 30 June 2011.

20 Such "transgressive political statements" as a key feature of survivor truth sharing in TRC hearings is also noted by Rosemary Nagy in an article based largely on observation of Commission events. Rosemary Nagy, "The Scope and Bounds of Transitional Justice and the Canadian Truth and Reconciliation Commission," *International Journal of Transitional Justice* 7 (2013): 65.

21 Emmet Peters, Commissioner's Sharing Panel, Atlantic National Event, Halifax, 27 October 2011.

22 Linda Bernard Maloney, Commissioner's Sharing Panel, TRC Atlantic National Event, Halifax, 28 October 2011.

23 Jerri Dan Raddi, Commissioner's Sharing Panel, TRC Inuvik National Event, 30 June 2011.

24 Beatrice Burnheart, Commissioner's Sharing Panel, TRC Inuvik National Event, 30 June 2011.

Chapter 6

TRAUMATIC MEMORY

FLASHBACKS AND TRIGGERING

The federal government's information-oriented website for the Independent Assessment Process included an unusual and ominous warning: "Important: This web site deals with subject matter that may cause some readers to trigger (suffer trauma caused by remembering or reliving past abuse). The Government of Canada recognizes the need for safety measures to minimize the risk associated with triggering."[1] Similarly, the website of the Indian Residential Schools Adjudication Secretariat opened with a pop-up that reads, "Thinking about past abuse can trigger suffering and problems in the present. Make sure that you have safety measures in place to help you if that happens," followed by the toll-free number of a twenty-four-hour crisis line.[2] "Triggering" is one of the words commonly used among survivors and their health support workers in reference to a danger inherent in attending the Commission's events or viewing them online. It is the emotional consequence of a "flashback": the onset of a sudden, overwhelming traumatic memory. Left unaddressed, the experience is recognized as leading to other manifestations of mental illness including severe depression, addiction, and/or suicidal thoughts and behaviour. According to a newsletter article put out by the Mi'kmaq/Maliseet Healing Network Centre intended to provide advice to survivors who planned to attend Commission events, flashbacks can be described as a sudden, unexpected, incapacitating feeling of physical, mental, emotional, and spiritual pain that involves "seeing, hearing or feeling as if the trauma is happening right now."[3] To help avoid such a crisis event, the newsletter advises survivors to prepare a "safety plan" before attending TRC events, which might include discussing breathing strategies with a counsellor or clinician, preparing to act on the need to get outside for fresh air or splashing cold water on one's face, making use of a "comfort item" like a teddy bear or blanket, or, in the long term, involving oneself in "back to culture activities," turning to family for support, consulting a therapist ("if available"), and relying on other survivors "who may share similar feelings [and] memories."[4]

A survivor visiting the exhibits, films, and photo archives of the Learning Place in the Saskatoon National Event had such an experience when he saw a woman walk by with a clipboard, and in that instant it reminded him of a nun who habitually carried a clipboard just like it. The traumatic memories of his school experience suddenly rushed back in the form of heightened, uncontrollable emotion, a "panic attack," that required intervention from health support workers: removal to a quiet, private room to take a moment to calm down, possibly to make arrangements for follow-up intervention, or even given an immediate referral to a psychiatrist. These health support workers, one of their supervisors informed me, were stationed in the Learning Place precisely in expectation of events such as this.

Those few members of the clergy who consented to give public testimony in TRC events were subject to the same stresses as those reported by survivors. In an interview about his experience of giving testimony at the Saskatoon National Event, where he talked about his ministry in Bella Bella among survivors of the Alberni Indian Residential School, United Church minister David Moors found that when he was sitting at the microphone he was "wrapped in silence," that it was like "trying to take shards of my life, pieces of my life that've not come together yet." After returning to his chair he had the overwhelming feeling of having to "get out of there," and experienced the sense of "drifting through rooms." It took him two or three hours to regain his composure. His recovery required the help of a friend in the ministry and a health support worker, a visit to the Cultural Support room where he washed his face in river water, smudged with burning sage, and was brushed with cedar and eagle feathers, then finding a quiet corner in the (retitled for this event) Churches Listening to Survivors Area to lie on the floor where he finally got his breathing under control. "[I] just breathed, breathed, did some stretching, and then talked to my wife on the phone and cried a bit. [I was] fragile for the rest of the day. I was very, in a daze, I guess."[5] His experience differed little from that of survivors who reported the debilitating effects of triggering in the context of TRC events.

Private Statement Gathering was identified by the Commission as a locus of particularly intense emotion with an accompanying high risk of sudden-onset mental health crises. Here, survivors narrated their experience over a longer period of time than in the public hearings, and were therefore more likely to navigate their way into sensitive topics and discuss them in more detail. Health support workers were on hand to sit with statement providers throughout their interviews, and "personal supports" were also invited to attend. A registration form asked those intending to give statements to choose, yes or no, if they want the TRC or Health Canada to contact them later to ask whether they would like "follow up health supports"; the interview guide used by statement gatherers included spaces for notes on the "expressions of emotion from survivor," the "tone" (parenthetically defined as "accent or inflection of voice to express emotion or passion"), and the statement gatherers' own "emotional reflection," all of which indicate careful attention to the potential for crisis in the interview and afterwards that could possibly be brought on by the emotions involved in narrating such experiences as physical and sexual abuse in school or domestic violence, homelessness, and suicidal inclinations in life after school.[6]

There were other less expected stressors at Commission events that acted as triggers. A post-event interview with a health worker in Inuvik revealed, almost in passing, that "perpetrators" had attended the event and caused anxiety attacks among some former students. Given the range of institutional abuses that took place in those schools that protected sadism and sexual predation and allowed widely ramifying effects of their acts among the students, the category of "perpetrator" could well be more inclusive than one might initially imagine. And the stress of encounter and triggered memory could have been equally common at the event.

If "triggering" is the specific form by which psychological pain is expressed among survivors, the general background in which it takes place is often referred to as "trauma." In Richard McNally's overview of recent trauma studies we find a fairly precise description of the kind of experience associated with triggering: "For people with posttraumatic stress disorder, remembering trauma feels like reliving it. Traumatic events from the past are recalled with such vividness and emotional intensity that it seems as if the trauma were happening all over again."[7]

Applying this observation to the TRC events, activities, newsletters, and Internet postings, it is easy to see why the warnings of possible triggering were so prominent and why they included the number of a help line—an admission in itself that the adverse response to sudden traumatic memory may be intense and uncontrollable.

The space between traumatic experience and narration is mediated by memory. Primo Levi, one of the twentieth century's greatest explorers of this space, thought about the place of memory in the history of the Holocaust (and by extension other major events of collective trauma) with arguably more self-critical acumen than any other Holocaust survivor, in part because he returned to it as the subject matter of his writing throughout his career and made new observations as the distance in time from the experience of the camps extended. In his last book, *The Drowned and the Saved*, written some forty years after the liberation of Europe, he finds that the essential nature of Holocaust remembrance by survivors had changed: "The greater part of the witnesses, for the defense and the prosecution, have by now disappeared, and those who remain, and who (overcoming their remorse or, alternately, their wounds) still agree to testify, have even more blurred and stylized memories, often, unbeknownst to them, influenced by information gained from later readings or the stories of others."[8] There are convincing indications in the memory studies literature that Levi's intuitions apply broadly. In F.C. Bartlett's famous experiments in the social psychology of memory, processes of construction and conventionalization emerged as dominant qualities or (in Bartlett's nuanced understanding) capacities of recall. Several experiments involving the reproduction of folk tales and proverbs, involving subjects from educated backgrounds in England and India, found an effect of continuous change from version to version, "following constant drifts of change from beginning to end," which ultimately achieve "a kind of group stamp or character."[9] From such evidence Bartlett concludes that "if we consider evidence rather than presupposition, remembering appears to be far more decisively an affair of construction rather than one of mere reproduction."[10] The same tendency toward conventionalization is prominent in the studies of traumatic memory. As McNally reports, "information provided to witnesses after an event affects how they later remember it, or at least how they report it. Even subtle differences in the wording of post-event questions exert an effect."[11]

The instability of traumatic memory goes even further when we consider several influential studies that emphasize the processes by which diagnostic mental illness categories come into being. Allan Young's study of post-traumatic stress disorder, *The Harmony of Illusions*, argues that the classification of post-traumatic stress disorder (PTSD) "is the product or achievement of psychiatric discourse, rather than its discovery."[12] "Traumatic memory is a man-made object," Young writes, "It originates in the scientific and clinical discourses of the nineteenth century; before that time, there is unhappiness, despair, and disturbing recollections, but no traumatic memory, in the sense that we know it today."[13]

Ian Hacking argues persuasively in a similar vein that the supposed connection between early and repeated child abuse and multiple personality disorder was the product of a new configuration of knowledge; it is, in other words, "not an empirical fact, but a conceptual one."[14] "Events, no matter how painful or terrifying," Hacking writes, "have been experienced or recalled *as child abuse* only after consciousness-raising. That requires inventing new descriptions, providing new ways to see old acts—and a great deal of social agitation."[15]

Didier Fassin and Richard Rechtman in their masterful *The Empire of Trauma* convincingly illustrate some of the ways that, as a man-made object, trauma has undergone a dramatic transformation in the past century. To establish this point, they provide a sense of the extent to which the link between horrific experiences and painful memory has changed by discussing in considerable detail the dominant approach to trauma intervention in World War I. This was the context in which interventions in the problem of "shell shock" achieved professional credibility as the means to returning emotionally incapacitated soldiers to the front lines. Here, on both sides of the hostilities, the soldier suffering (or, as it was often understood, *feigning* to suffer) from battle neurosis was a challenge not only to the effort to maintain the number of combatants in the field, but also to maintain the patriotic fervour that sent them there. Soldiers who were mentally and emotionally incapacitated by their experiences in the trenches were seen as malingerers engaged in a subtle form of desertion in which they strategically avoided the summary execution that would likely occur if their cowardice had taken place on the battlefield.[16] It is from this insecure starting point that trauma eventually achieved mainstream status in psychiatric discourse and therapeutic practice as an accepted, if not dominant, idiom of distress.

Even within this context of professional acceptance and generalized use of the concepts of trauma and traumatic memory, it is striking to see the permissive, witness-centred approach to narration of traumatic events in the public hearings of the TRC. When, for example, a survivor in Victoria, British Columbia, reported his experience of blisters that appeared now and then on his back and legs as a kind of body memory, which he reported as a manifestation of a beating received as a child within his first few weeks at school, the sympathy of the audience in the room was (as we are inclined to say with respect to audiences) "palpable," audible in a collective sound of movement: shifting of clothing, low murmuring of voices. And when he then reported his occasional experience as an adult of crying tears of blood in response to his traumatic memories, the reaction was more pronounced—something like an intake of breath, a gasp, and a moan all at the same time. My sense in listening to this was that the tears of blood were neither conveyed by the narrator nor understood by the audience as an allusion, but as a lived experience. And as a report of experience, his story was not greeted with any indication of skepticism from the presiding commissioner or the audience, but with deep, quiet sympathy, as though his listeners could imagine such a thing happening to them. In this story there is no separation of the literal from the figurative. The tears that normally fall are sometimes incommensurate with a person's feelings of grief and have to come from a place deeper in the body.

Even a witness whose testimony did not include an account of abuse, but whose introduction to school seemed positive, with a sister who was kind and gentle and whose manner prompted him to ask his parents to send him back to school during the summer break, still found that he had strong reactions to the memory of residential school, above all to the experience of being "told what to do all the time." These reactions intensified over the years. As he put it, "I didn't know I was going through a slow trauma. It just creeps up on you over the years."[17]

The emphasis on trauma by survivors was facilitated by one of the important qualities of the public hearings discussed in the previous chapter: the almost total absence of any explicit limits to the subject matter that survivors as witnesses discussed or the amount of time they spent doing it. The commissioners did occasionally reiterate a recommendation in the central events, the panels attended by large audiences with translation services and a live Internet feed, to the effect that speakers should try to keep their testimony to within fifteen minutes; but this limit was more often exceeded—sometimes excessively—than observed. There was a shared value of participatory tolerance at work in which everyone expected those in front of the microphone to be allowed their say, as they wished to say it. This once (in Winnipeg) included a witness suffering the consequences of a stroke who passionately delivered unintelligible sounds into the microphone for twenty minutes until he finished what he had to say. He then nodded thanks and returned to his seat. And in Inuvik, a witness who introduced himself as suffering from schizophrenia went on to present a disjointed narrative for more than twenty-five minutes before Peter Irniq, a prominent Inuit survivor who was presiding temporarily, cut him short—the only occasion on which I have seen a witness asked to finish their testimony before they were quite ready to.

This permissive element of testimonial confessional has certain affinities with the "secret memory" of Christianity that long predates its adoption in psychotherapy. In Catholicism and Orthodox Christianity this takes the form of sins and transgressions, which reach the point of becoming a spiritual burden, to be released by rituals and confession.[18] And in some forms of Protestantism (especially Pentecostalism or Charismatic Christianity) the individual believer is similarly relieved of the weight of sin through rituals built on the conversion experience. The central difference between this confessional tradition and the TRC is that the latter was oriented toward a public unburdening, in which elements of personal moral weakness were understood with reference to the transgressions of others. Ian Hacking characterizes this emerging, therapeutic approach to confession in just these terms: "Ever since Augustine, conversion experiences have been associated with confessions—the retelling of one's own past, the true past that one had been denying. All that is familiar: therapy as conversion, confession and the restructuring of the remembrances of one's past. Then comes an almighty twist. Your confession is not *your* sins but your father's sins."[19]

The goal of healing through self-revelation was expressed by the Commission in nearly every opportunity it had to communicate with survivors. A preparatory film, *Sharing Your Truth*, first screened at the Atlantic National Event, stated this goal plainly and directly: "We ... aim to make the process of giving a statement to the TRC as much of a healing experience as possible. We are here to listen and we care deeply about your experiences."[20]

Commissioner Sinclair made a promise of healing even more explicit in his opening speech to the Saskatoon National Event: "It has contributed significantly to the healing of these individuals who have come forward. And it has contributed significantly to the healing of relationships between these individuals and their families and communities."[21] And Darlene Auger, TRC Regional Liaison for Alberta, gave the idea some causal specificity in a preparatory workshop for survivors:

> It is healing when you begin to talk about it because it becomes real, and you put it out in front of you and you can look at it. You separate yourself, you begin to separate yourself from it. You are not your pain. You are a beautiful, wonderful spirit, beautiful, wonderful human being that has had a really bad experience perhaps, a really painful experience. But it is not what you are all about. And so, to talk about it, to share it, and even more, to record it, to create a permanent record of it, so that the future generations can hear it, can see you, that's even more profound.[22]

There is, in fact, some support for these healing claims to be found in the work of psychologists who report on the experience of participants in group therapy. Several studies point to the therapeutic effect of the realization by patients that they are not alone with their struggle, but are part of a group for the very reason that others are just like them.[23] Irvin Yalom and Molyn Leszcz refer to this as "universality," meaning that patients often come to a profound realization early in their therapy that their social isolation and sense of uniqueness are unfounded, that others—potentially many others besides those in the group—share their feelings.[24] In the early stages of group therapy, the disconfirmation of a sense of loneliness through validation from others can be a life-changing event: "After hearing other members disclose concerns similar to their own, clients report feeling more in touch with the world and describe the process as a 'welcome to the human race' experience."[25]

Despite this plausible analogy with group therapy, it remains unclear just how truth commissions impact their participants. The "therapeutic ethics" of truth commissions tend to be driven by the priorities of remote institutions made manifest through the goals of local elites; and the experiences of victims have rarely been given systematic attention, certainly not enough to arrive at comparative conclusions.[26] It is even less clear that giving testimony can maintain the effects of a sense of common belonging in the absence of consistent, effective therapeutic support. In circumstances in which the mental health resources of the community were routinely understaffed and stretched beyond the limit, the TRC itself was seen by a local health worker in Inuvik as responsible for a crisis left in its wake:

> [The TRC] re-traumatized us. We went through the traumatization. We went through the residential school. Some of our people went through that again and there was nobody there to say, well what can I do to help you now? Do you want to go for counseling? They tell us there are facilities across Canada where our

survivors can go and get after-care. I know of people who have applied for after-care who are still waiting. Long lines. People who have waited so long they've gone right back into drinking.[27]

Despite the upbeat advance publicity put out by the Commission, there do appear to be risks inherent in remembrance and testimony, including the possibility of "triggering" in the context of minimal and reduced mental health resources. Besides this obvious point, an intrusive question, to which I have no ready answer, kept nagging at me as I attended commission events: given the persuasive, imitative force of trauma as an idiom of distress, how can it be overcome by fixing in place the witnesses' memories of abuse and powerlessness and making them an essential aspect of the self, one that is projected on jumbo screens and gift packaged in a carry-home DVD?

HISTORICAL TRAUMA

In most cases, the school survivors who appeared before the Commission were advanced in age and were there to talk about experiences they had when they were children. This means that there was ample place for the work of memory, for forgetting and remembering, or, in the neo-Freudian phraseology sometimes used in the context of the Commission, for "repression" and "triggering," for the salience of things to be considered, reconsidered, and re-manifested. The tension that follows from this shaping of the past goes much further than a mere controversy over the truth value of traumatic childhood memory and the testimony on which it is based. There is also a much wider division evident here between the values of affirmation toward the witnesses, which includes pre-recognition of the historical injustices about which they speak, and the revelation of flux, adaptation, and construction inherent in the illness categories to which their narrations tend to conform.

What gives coherence to the "history in our midst" when it comes from so many individuals with such varied backgrounds and experience, and with so many indignities and injustices to draw from? It should be clear at this point that the Commission was not just an inert vessel for receiving from witnesses their narrations and ideas; it was at the same time actively expressing concepts that, taken together, made up the context, frame, or schema in which narration took place. It becomes a challenge of the first order, therefore, to make the sources of this schema explicit: to show the Commission's guiding ideas, where they came from, and how they might act to influence others, including witnesses.

The main difficulty here is that the Commission's guiding principles and assumptions are already so familiar that it is nearly impossible to disentangle them from widely current ideas (or unknowable hegemonies, if one wanted to push the difficulty to its limit)—from the ideological air we breathe. This is where the pioneering ethnographers of, say, British social anthropology had it much easier. When Malinowski wanted to understand the kula exchange of the Trobiand Islanders, or Evans-Pritchard the logic of witchcraft among the Azande, their task, as they saw it, was to translate deeply unfamiliar ideas into the vernacular of their readership, to make the seemingly mysterious fathomable. The effort to explore the social workings of ideas that are already at some level deeply familiar, like those at the foundation of the TRC, is an altogether different challenge. It is, at the outset, grounded in ideas that many of us already inhabit. It calls for a kind of critical introspection that highlights the strangeness of these ideas, separating or disambiguating them from notions of history and humanity with origins in academic literature guided by the norms and procedures of critical scholarship.[28] The challenge here is to identify and separate the polysemy of terms being used by the Commission, which draws freely from social science and human rights concepts of oppression, liberation, and belonging that are essential aspects of the intellectual ether of our time.

The Commission's connection to the human rights movement and the ideas with which it is associated should be clear from the simple fact that truth and reconciliation commissions are in their nature *the* quintessential human rights remedy—the most broadly legitimate solution for overcoming the most serious systematic harms committed by states toward their own citizens—sometimes expressed in the language of national healing. Victim-centric truth commissions aspire to bring remedy from the realm of rights into the realm of therapy—on individual and national scales. Martha Minow makes such a connection between truth and reconciliation commissions and therapeutic process: "The rhetoric of healing reveals the conception of trauma and health undergirding the process. Like therapy for individual survivors of trauma, the TRC is supposed to overcome repression and a sense of powerlessness for the entire society as well as for individuals."[29]

But within the nexus of ideas that we call human rights, there are differences in emphasis and orientation. The TRC on Indian residential schools is no exception. It expresses its own distinct notions of human rights that are oriented toward understanding the harm done to individuals and communities. And the most significant harm done to the children in residential schools brought out by the TRC was to their mental health, both as children in the schools and in the aftermath of their traumatic experiences as adults. In keeping with this, one of the particularities of the TRC can be seen by going beyond human rights discourse to include, if not emphasize, social psychiatry's still-emerging paradigm of historical trauma.

The notion of "historical trauma" is a recent idiom of distress. It has yet to complete the transition (or transmission) from specialist knowledge to a "grassroots" form of contextualization and expression of personal suffering. As a tool or diagnostic category for the treatment of mental illness, it is unusual both in its focus on collective experience and in the distance in the past that one might look to find sources of trauma having an inimical effect on the well-being of individuals and communities. "Historical trauma" is based on the simple observation that standard diagnostic categories such as post-traumatic stress disorder (PTSD) capture only some of the symptoms experienced by victims of colonial domination and mass violence and their descendants (such as nightmares, flashbacks, debilitating stress responses, etc.). It adds a collective, historical dimension to mental illness symptoms, with an emphasis on the effects of multiple traumatic events occurring over generations and the transmission of trauma from person to person within families and communities.[30]

In this collective form, trauma has made a transition beyond the clinical setting to serve as a social concept: an understanding of the self as having been subject to collective violence and a corresponding shared, intergenerational trauma. It transitioned beyond the individual as a solitary sufferer to include family, community, and people, encompassing all those who can be conceived of as sharing the historical subjection to abuse and who collectively experience acute distress. In doing so, the diagnosis of mental illness established a connection with historical reference points for mass, intergenerational trauma, such as the Holocaust, the history of slavery in the Americas, the Vietnam War, and apartheid in South Africa.

Maria Yellow Horse Brave Heart can be credited with developing the concept's application to American Indian/Alaska Native communities by considering their "cumulative emotional and psychological wounding, over the lifespan and across generations, emanating from massive group trauma experiences."[31] She finds the constellation of historical traumas manifested in many of the things associated with PTSD, such as substance abuse, suicidal thoughts and behaviour, depression, anxiety, low self-esteem, anger, and difficulty recognizing and expressing emotions.

The grief following from historical trauma is intergenerational and socially systemic rather than understandable through exclusive emphasis on individual behaviour and life history. As Cynthia Wesley-Esquimaux and Magdalena Smolewski explain, "Aboriginal people were incarcerated on reservations and in missions, held against their will in residential schools and in prisons and forcefully assimilated and acculturated. Their own ways of life were impoverished, their culture rendered bereft and their needs as human beings utterly forsaken ... [T]here was no opportunity to grieve their tremendous losses or effectively heal their shock and trauma; there was no recovery time."[32] In particular, "the residential school experience, following right on the heels of four hundred years of epidemics, further served to ensure a sense of hopelessness and defeat."[33] The result has been a distinct form of collective malaise and manifestation of distress, referred to by Wesley-Esquimaux and Smolewski as a "dis-ease or cultural uneasiness," an outcome of "unresolved pain from repeated and multiple assaults turning themselves inward. Endemic stress disorder in the Aboriginal population has been repeatedly illustrated through rampant sexual abuse and incest, apathy, physical and emotional infirmities, spousal assault, alcoholism and drug addiction. Each of these maladies is indicative of a shattered and fragmented Aboriginal socio-cultural experience."[34]

In its interim report, Canada's Truth and Reconciliation Commission applies such observations of the long-term, intergenerational effects of colonial experience specifically to residential schools: "The impacts began to cascade through generations as former students—damaged by emotional neglect and often by abuse in the schools—themselves became parents. Family and individual dysfunction grew, until eventually, the legacy of the schools became joblessness, poverty, family violence, drug and alcohol abuse, family breakdown, prostitution, homelessness, high rates of imprisonment, and early death."[35]

We can continue this narrowing down of the concept of historical trauma to the witnessing events of the TRC. The survivor at the microphone may have privileged access to his or her experience in the past, but the idea of intergenerational suffering resulting from a colonially inspired policy provides a context in which that experience can be placed. Whether or not they are familiar with the concept of historical trauma, its basic outline is an essential aspect of the intellectual context of TRC events. It represents a publicly accessible paradigm in which survivors are able to represent their experience, in which relevant words can be chosen to convey a sense of it and its lasting effects on their lives, in communication with listeners who may or may not share comparable memories. It is a way of making experiences coherent as they are translated into words, and as words are shaped into a fully formed narrative.

The TRC on Indian residential schools can be seen as a vehicle for the transition (and translation) of the concept of historical trauma into the mainstream. We have seen that the Commissioner's Sharing Panels were not passive sources for receiving testimony but active venues through which witnesses and their audiences were educated in the proper narrative forms in which experience could be recounted, the historical context of their suffering could be situated, and possibilities and pathways could remain open for healing and redemption. And in the repertoire of the TRC's construction and communication of ideas, historical trauma, even in the absence of the term, can be seen as a key concept. Georgina Lighting, director of a film on the healing activities of the TRC posted on YouTube, for example, addresses the concept when she appears in the film to outline the purpose of the Commission: "We need to learn why we are the way we are. We need to understand and learn what transgenerational trauma is, why our parents were the way that they were, the effects it has on us, so that we can acknowledge its power, knowing about it, understanding about it, so we can recover from it."[36]

Not only do public statements expressed by representatives of the TRC frame the hearings around the concepts of trauma, cultural erasure, and loss in ways that are consistent with the concept of cultural genocide and historical trauma, but they also express the goals of spiritual rediscovery and collective healing in a way that emphasizes the therapeutic possibilities built into the activities of the Commission.[37] The wrongs of the past and the solution to be found through the work of spiritual/artistic self-expression are both evident in the Commission's long-term agenda and activities.

ONLINE AFFIRMATION

Internet venues are a means by which those who feel themselves to be rejected by their families and by wider society sometimes find acceptance, approval, and the comfort of belonging; so it should come as no surprise that the TRC has sponsored online forums in which those who identify as survivors or intergenerational survivors can establish communities that cultivate a sense of privileged belonging. Here, too, we can see the concepts associated with intergenerational trauma that are given expression to a public audience, except that here the nature of the venue favours those who represent the youngest generation to which harm has been transmitted: those with the ability and inclination to communicate online.

It may be useful to put this development in context. The ideological permissiveness of the Internet is clearest in the message boards, forums, and chat rooms constructed around ideas and practices that are not accepted in any wider society. Here we can readily see the coalescence of group identities supported by the unique capacity of the Web to create multi-user space that invites and facilitates the formation of close-knit communities.[38] For some Internet users, their online community can readily become a vehicle by which they reject unwanted judgment and intervention in their lives, all the while making use of the Web's powerful capacity for posting enabling information. A sense of belonging in an online community, however shallow and contingent it might be, finds expression in shared ideals and an ease with which self-revelation can take place and feelings can be expressed. The Internet is able to bring individuals together who would otherwise be ostracized and lonely. Through new forms of communication, such individuals are finding common-cause with others and forming cohesive and apparently durable online communities. I have chosen to refer to such forums as *communities of affirmation* to emphasize the potentially life-changing realization by marginalized individuals that the root cause of their social isolation is in fact shared with others, that through access to the Internet they have a way to belong, to be human in a distinct way in society with others.[39] Applying this insight to the concept of the Indian residential school survivor, we can see that the Internet has become a vehicle for those who see themselves as survivors and intergenerational survivors to express ideas about the traumatic sources of their suffering, and possibly (we can at this point only speculate) to recover from the worst effects of that trauma through relationships formed online.

In efforts to prevent, to the extent possible, shame, fear, judgment, insults, and misperceptions and to foster a climate of support, hope, compassion, and empathy, communities of affirmation usually establish their own rules of interaction. These rules were prominent, for example, in the "About" section of the Truth and Reconciliation Commission's Facebook page (taken down when the Commission completed its mandate): "We welcome all opinions on this page. This is a space where all people, elders and children alike, can voice their thoughts about the many issues stemming from the Indian Residential School system. Defamatory, racist, and abusive comments and comments containing profanity will be removed by the administrator."[40] The volume of participation on this page (with some 5,000 "likes") actually seemed to inhibit a sense of community, almost making its encouragement of all opinions superfluous by inhibiting the kind of intimate posting we see elsewhere. Posts on the TRC's Facebook page were mostly made by administrators, with a focus on information about the activities of survivors or initiatives being taken by indigenous peoples' organizations.

A more encouraging, expressive space can be seen on the page sponsored by the Indian Residential School CART (Critical Analysis & Radical Thoughts). On this Facebook page the "About" section is more detailed in its rules of participation:

> NOTE: we thank you for your input but please ... do not TALK OVER or PREACH TO Indian Residential School Survivors whose first hand experience is shared here ... The principles of democratic and respectful discourse will prevail in these discussions. Racism, sexism, homophobia, narcissism and narcissistic attacks, hate, & personalizing will not be tolerated.
>
> Please understand the fact that Indian Residential School Survivors who have been confined have unique issues and require that their unique discourse be RESPECTED.[41]

And respected they are, with members posting intimate, loosely composed, almost free-associating narrations of feelings, which usually receive supportive replies consistent with the capacity of the Internet to create affirmative space:

> N.D.: People tell me that I should forgive and let go because it is the way to healing, some people think I am wrong to not trust all for the sake of a few, but, those few are actually more, it is really the few who suffer because of the larger whole, they say not to hate, that I should love those who have wronged me, and all those I witnessed, and feel guilt for what I witnessed, everyday,

I struggle in my heart to be a good man, and I question that word, man, I question being a man, because they made sure we knew we are not human, so I have trouble thinking I am huMAN.

[REPLIES:]

BETSY TURTLE BRUYERE: am right with you brother ... and so are a lot of others.

RAY TONY CHARIE: Its really unfortunate ... I lived the life of a victim, ashamed and scared to face my abuse. I felt guilty and dirty, but today I feel i done no wrong, but was sexually abused. It is indeed a horrid thing to experience that whole situation, but today I feel too as you do. I will never let anyone be harmed or made to feel bad for anything. I feel will never know what was experienced by anyone until we talk to them. For years and years I could not be in dark rooms as I was sexually abused in a dark room by another male ... one of those catholic brothers ... today I feel abit [sic] better, but have the memories as you do ... take care and hope things are ok for you ... hugs as well.[42]

These two latter postings are the opening replies in a much longer thread that continues with support of the feelings expressed in the initial post by N.D. This exchange illustrates, as well as any other I have seen, the capacity of the Internet to create conditions of security through abstract distance, even in an "open" page in which participants expose their interventions to an online public. By the very nature of distant, anonymous-if-one-chooses, instant communication, it overcomes insecurity, making it easier to reveal one's innermost senses of shame and weakness and to express equally intimate compassion, not only in company with others, but before anyone with an Internet connection who cares to see.

The school survivors' communities online create connections between people who share common experiences. Whether members of the group attended the schools together or not, they exchange memories that give them a sense of wider belonging. Survivors post childhood photos taken in the schools of themselves and other survivors. Members of the group work together to identify faces in old photographs to help remember teachers' and pupils' names, to attach dates to particular events, collaboratively untangling their past and situating themselves more clearly in relationships with friends, relatives, and even teachers in the schools.

If anything, online communities are more effective in implementing their stated receptiveness to every kind of testimony than is the Truth and Reconciliation Commission, as in this posting about common experience between an Inuit student (the narrator) and non-Inuit in Grollier Hall, in the Northwest Territories: "Hahaha, we sure learnt to talk with our eyes, noses, chin, face! We weren't allowed to talk out loud so many times! I had lots of fun moments and times with my pals at school and in Grollier. I sure enjoyed going out in the bush near the cabin when the weather was warmer ... never thought this Inuk would ever go out in the bush! Lol."[43]

It seems easier here than in formal statements presented to the Commission to find examples of narration that are not imbued with guilt, grievance, and sorrow.

Of course, not every posting is supportive of residential school survivors. Web browsers might encounter a range of reactions from an anonymous public if they care to reveal their self-defining confessions in an open forum: from recognition, understanding, and support to rejection, ridicule, and "cyber-bullying." "Trolling," a form of Internet behaviour that involves posting inflammatory or off-topic messages in online communities with a view to provoking emotional responses, has had a formative influence on the dynamics of online discourse and on the forms (particularly in terms of the degrees of enclosure) that online communities take, including communities of residential school survivors and intergenerational survivors. A YouTube posting provides some insight into the sorts of things trolls are saying to survivors and intergenerational survivors online:

> Just a note for anyone wanting to post bullshit. I am not obligated to post racist (on either side of the spectrum), nonsensical ("at least they got an education," "the holocaust was worse so what are they complaining about," or "they should just pull themselves up by the bootstraps" just a few examples) comments or anything which just shows 1) you didn't watch the video 2) you have no knowledge of history or 3) you are an ass. Don't like it? Tough shit. My video, my rules.[44]

The widely known injunction "do not feed the trolls" is often taken further than the mere avoidance of any kind of response to provocation, through the cultivation of core communities of regular participants who shelter themselves from mockery and who protect themselves from its emotional effects with heightened collective expressions of support. Belonging and opinion online are made simultaneously more adamant. The following response to a YouTube troll (which willingly "feeds" the trolls in a back-and-forth thread marked by increasing vulgarity) provides an example:

> Oh and you racist prick, this happened not only in Canada, but in America too. It was cultural genocide all across North America. Pick up any history book on Native peoples, take a Native American studies class, you'll see its all true. People go to college and get degrees in that study, you think they're lying about that? You are a shame and a disgrace to humanity with your disgusting racist words. Watch what you say next time, MANY native peoples including myself take it as a personal insult.[45]

It can be argued that online communities are actually strengthened by the kind of un-charitable feedback to which this post is responding. It encourages a sense of common belonging and purpose among those who truly belong, who define their belonging in dialogue, discussion, and "chat" in global forums in immediate ways that have never before occurred. This results in a degree of personal identity affirmation that is equally unprecedented, resulting in new possibilities for focused immersion of the kind we see with particular clarity in online survivor groups.

Internet forums might even offer part of the explanation for how those who came to one of the Commission's events found the courage to narrate painful childhood experiences publicly and to expose their failures in adult life willingly. Some of those survivors who reveal their names online appeared (before or after their post-ing) as witnesses at a TRC event. The Internet has become one of the tools by which former students come to understand themselves as survivors in community with others. Having given a statement at a TRC event, it does not seem such an outlandish idea to expose one's innermost thoughts and experiences to the online public. Alternatively, having situated themselves in an online community and en-gaged in intimate (yet open to the world) exchanges with other members, it may not seem like such an overwhelming step for survivors and intergenerational sur-vivors to reveal themselves intimately onstage and to narrate their experience for the record.

NOTES

1 Indian Residential Schools Secretariat, accessed 31 August 2009, http://www.irsad-sapi.gc.ca/index-eng.asp. The website has been taken down since this pas-sage was written.

2 Indian Residential Schools Adjudication Secretariat, accessed 12 May 2013. The pop-up has been taken down since this passage was written.

3 Mi'kmaq/Maliseet Healing Network Centre, *Mi'kmaq/Maliseet Healing Net-work Centre Newsletter* 2 (Winter 2012): 7.

4 Ibid., 7.

5 Reverend David Moors, Interview with Marie-Pierre Gadoua, TRC Saskatoon National Event, 23 June 2012.

6 The TRC's interview guide consists of an unpublished form without a heading or any other reference information.

7 Richard McNally, *Remembering Trauma* (Cambridge, MA: Harvard University Press, 2003), 105.

8 Primo Levi, *The Drowned and the Saved*, trans. Raymond Rosenthal (New York: Vintage, 1988), 19.

9   Frederic Charles Bartlett, *Remembering* (Cambridge, UK: Cambridge University Press, [1932] 1995), 173.

10 Ibid., 205.

11 McNally, *Remembering Trauma*, 67.

12 Allan Young, *The Harmony of Illusions: Inventing Post-Traumatic Stress Disorder* (Princeton, NJ: Princeton University Press, 1995), 121.

13 Ibid., 141.

14 Ian Hacking, *Rewriting the Soul: Multiple Personality and the Sciences of Memory* (Princeton, NJ: Princeton University Press, 1995), 170.

15 Ibid., 55.

16 Didier Fassin and Richard Rechtman, *The Empire of Trauma: An Inquiry into the Condition of Victimhood*, trans. Rachel Gomme (Princeton, NJ: Princeton University Press, 2008), 48–9.

17 Stuart [surname unknown], TRC Urban Inuit Community Hearing, 16 August 2012.

18 Young, *The Harmony of Illusions*, 28.

19 Ian Hacking, *The Social Construction of What?* (Cambridge, MA: Harvard University Press, 1999), 142.

20 Truth and Reconciliation Commission, Canada, *Sharing Your Truth*, film screened at the TRC Atlantic National Event, 27 October 2011.

21 Murray Sinclair, "Commissioner's Welcome," TRC Saskatoon National Event, 21 June 2012.

22 Darlene Auger, "How to Share Your Truth Information Session," TRC Atlantic National Event, Halifax, 27 October 2011.

23 Peter Bieling, Randi McCabe, and Martin Antony, *Cognitive Behavioral Therapy in Groups* (New York: Guilford, 2006), 27.

24 Irvin Yalom and Molyn Leszcz, *The Theory and Practice of Group Psychotherapy*, 5th ed. (New York: Basic Books, 2005).

25 Ibid., 6.

26 Simon Robins, for example, finds a disjuncture between the Timor-Leste truth commission's emphasis on historiography and the private truths sought by victims, which were oriented toward dead and missing loved ones and meeting demands for bodies and burials. Simon Robins, "Challenging the Therapeutic Ethic: A Victim-Centered Evaluation of Transitional Justice Process in Timor-Leste," *International Journal of Transitional Justice* 6 (2012): 83–105.

27 Sarah Jerome, Interview with Marie-Pierre Gadoua, Inuvik, 14 October 2011.

28 Here I am using the term "disambiguation" from its meaning in computational linguistics, where it describes the effort to create processing languages that can deal consistently with words that have multiple meanings. I elaborate on this

effort in Ronald Niezen, "The Law's Legal Anthropology," in *Human Rights at the Crossroads*, ed. Mark Goodale (Oxford, UK: Oxford University Press, 2012).

29 Martha Minow, "Institutions and Emotions: Redressing Mass Violence," in *The Passions of Law*, ed. Susan Bandes (New York and London: New York University Press, 1999), 270.

30 Teresa Evans-Campbell, "Historical Trauma in American Indian/Alaska Native Communities: A Multilevel Framework for Exploring Impacts on Individuals, Families and Communities," *Journal of Interpersonal Violence* 23, no. 3 (2008): 317.

31 Maria Yellow Horse Brave Heart, "The Historical Trauma Response among Natives and Its Relationship with Substance Abuse: A Lakota Illustration," *Journal of Psychoactive Drugs* 35, no. 1 (2003): 7. See also M.Y.H. Brave Heart, "The Return to the Sacred Path: Healing the Historical Trauma Response among the Lakota," *Smith College Studies in Social Work* 68, no. 3 (1998): 287–305; M.Y.H. Brave Heart and L.M. DeBruyn, "The American Indian Holocaust: Healing Historical Unresolved Grief," *American Indian and Alaska Native Mental Health Research* 8, no. 2 (1998): 56–78.

32 Cynthia Wesley-Esquimaux and Magdalena Smolewski, *Historic Trauma and Aboriginal Healing* (Ottawa: Aboriginal Healing Foundation, 2004), 27.

33 Ibid., 24.

34 Ibid., 24.

35 The Truth and Reconciliation Commission of Canada, *They Came for the Children: Canada, Aboriginal Peoples, and Residential Schools* (Winnipeg, MB: Truth and Reconciliation Commission, 2012), 77–8.

36 Georgina Lightning, statement in "Winnipeg National Event," YouTube video sponsored by the Truth and Reconciliation Commission of Canada, accessed 28 October 2012. Since the publication of the first edition of this book the video has become unavailable on YouTube.

37 This can be seen, for example, in the "Open Call for Artistic Submissions" section of the TRC website. There, the following guidelines are posted: "The TRC invites artists to submit works relating to apology, truth, cultural oppression, cultural genocide, resistance, resilience, spirituality, remembrance, reconciliation, rejuvenation and restoration of Aboriginal culture and pride." Truth and Reconciliation Commission of Canada, "Open Call for Artistic Submissions," accessed 3 November 2012, http://www.trc.ca/websites/trcinstitution/index.php?p=194.

38 Lev Manovich, *The Language of New Media* (Cambridge, MA: The MIT Press, 2001), 258.

39 This section includes excerpts from my article "Internet Suicide: Communities of Affirmation and the Lethality of Communication," *Transcultural Psychiatry* 50, no. 2 (2013): 303–322.

40 Truth and Reconciliation Commission Facebook Page, accessed 3 November 2012. This page was taken down after the TRC completed its mandate. In its stead is a page organized by the permanent institutional successor of the TRC, the National Centre for Truth and Reconciliation, hosted by the University of Manitoba in Winnipeg. Accessed 20 June 2017, https://www.facebook.com/National-Centre-for-Truth-and-Reconciliation-933534973335967.

41 Indian Residential School CART (Critical Analysis & Radical Thoughts) Facebook page, accessed 3 November 2012, http://www.facebook.com/groups/107575132623439.

42 Ibid.

43 Beatrice Bernhardt, "Grollier and Stringer Residential School Survivors," Facebook page, 12 September 2012, accessed 3 November 2012. This page is no longer available.

44 Author unknown, "Indian Residential Schools in Canada: The Painful Legacy," YouTube, 17 February 2008, accessed 2 November 2012, https://www.youtube.com/watch?v=_4-TYwFS-Po. I am making an effort through this selection of online material to avoid citing trolls directly and in so doing providing them with incentive to further provoke.

45 Author unknown, "Canadian Holocaust—Try Not to Cry," YouTube, 30 September 2009, accessed 3 November 2012, https://www.youtube.com/watch?v=hqPIh-267fg.

Chapter 7

WITNESSING HISTORY

THE MISSION

I wondered before the plane landed in Edmonton's international airport whether I would have any difficulty finding the priest from Rome who had arranged to meet me. Through email correspondence that had grown increasingly detailed, he arrived at the idea that he might fly to Canada on an unused ticket, Rome-Frankfurt-Calgary. He could then take a bus the rest of the way to St. Albert and the Catholic residence on Mission Hill. It might be a good idea, he thought, to take a break from his work at the Oblate headquarters—and if I happened to be interested in learning more about Oblate missionary work and Indian residential schools and had been thinking of travelling to St. Albert anyway, this would be a good opportunity for us to meet. His arrangements for finding each other in the airport worked perfectly—"I am 5′7″ [and] will be wearing a blue cap"—but even if by some random chance everyone in the airport were wearing blue caps I probably would have been able to pick him out of the crowd: sixty-something, an average build, practical glasses, a light jacket over a plaid work shirt, attentively scanning the lobby—all casual and ordinary, yet somehow priest-like.

Father Piché shook my hand politely, asked the usual courteous questions about my trip, and guided me to a well-used, red Ford Ranger. It belonged to the Catholic residence. He had borrowed it for the occasion. He hadn't driven much lately, he explained as he unlocked the passenger side, and it had been years since he had navigated in and around Edmonton, but we'd just try to do our best. He drove cautiously, with a discomforting preference for the inside "fast" lane. Impatient drivers rushed up to the bumper, sometimes flashing their lights, but he was steady and imperturbable.

He concentrated as much on the conversation as on the road. I learned that he had lived among the Dene in the Northwest Territories and had been involved in various struggles for their rights over a period of about twenty years, from the mid-1960s to the mid-1980s. He then did an eight-year stint in Chateh, Alberta, with another Dene community. At various points in his career he had been involved with the Berger Inquiry, Project North, the Oka Crisis, the Royal Commission on Aboriginal Peoples, resistance to the impacts of pulp and paper mills, and the spraying of spruce budworm in northern Alberta. (He later spoke passionately about the impacts of resource extraction in a way that was consistent with this first conversation: "These [industries] are going to come and rape and exploit the land, they are going to come and then they are going to leave, but these people [the Dene] will stay.")[1] In 1995 he was named Provincial of Grandin Province and was soon caught up in research and litigation on Indian residential schools as well as church-sponsored healing and reconciliation efforts. More recently his career had become international, with involvement in efforts to build an intercultural K'iche' and Spanish teacher's college in Guatemala, six months spent in Bolivia and Peru, and Spanish studies at the Institute of Bartolomé de Las Casas; his appointment in 2007 to a church-based NGO based in Rome, called Justice, Peace and Integrity of Creation (not long after he had recovered from a mild stroke), had taken him to Sri Lanka and, just before we met, he had spent three weeks in the war-torn Democratic Republic of Congo. All the while he had worked with the Oblate provinces of Canada on the issue of Indian residential schools. He was an expert on this issue, having been a director of one of these schools during the time he had spent among the Dene.

I'm not sure how much of his biography I learned during our drive from the airport and how much I picked up in bits and pieces during the four days I spent in the residence in St. Albert. I do remember that we had plenty of time to talk during the drive because he managed to get so badly lost that we ended up on a dirt road in farm country. He had remained calmly focused the whole time on our conversation and didn't seem to be at all bothered by problems of navigation—a matter of priorities.

We eventually found our way back to the main highway by following the volume of traffic, just as one might survive being lost in the wild by going downstream from a tributary to a river and from there to inhabited space. When we arrived at the mission he showed me the residence—recently renovated, he pointed out—with new railings on the stairs to accommodate the aging population of priests using the building. Photographs of prominent Oblates decorated the walls, interspersed with native prints and works of amateur art, apparently done by parishioners who had illustrated spiritual themes that gave them special worth. The room where I was to stay was almost as expected: spare furnishings, plain white walls, a crucifix, and an Internet connection.

Later that afternoon Father Piché invited me to take a tour of the grounds of the mission: the chapel of Father Lacombe, the founder of the mission and of the Catholic Church in Alberta; the statue of the same Father Lacombe, with its multilingual inscription (including the Blackfoot language); and the Foyer Lacombe, a modern retirement facility for Oblates with its own chapel and dining room. Eventually we came to the cemetery and the burial place of the Oblate priests and brothers, with identical modest headstones arranged in order of date of death, and an open patch of grass at the end of the row. Father Piché seemed to know the life stories of most of those buried here, but lingered in telling about those few whose graves were marked with fresh flowers, those remembered, as he expressed it, for their sacrifice, service, dedication, and for those qualities not recognized or rewarded in other professions: a cultivated inner life, gentleness of spirit, and piety.

In an interview a few days later he elaborated on these thoughts:

> They had learned the language, they had grown to respect the people, to live among the people, and to share their lives with the people ... We just buried one two years ago here ... who was fifty-six years in one small native community in the North ... And so that's our story, for many, many years. Then of course TB struck, the hospitals and the sisters came, the Grey Nuns, especially in the North. And they built hospitals and they cared for the sick and they cared for the handicapped and for the orphans if they had nobody to look after them and crippled people sometimes that had no family. That was the role we played.[2]

As with many things that were not said to me in the course of my research, the absent part of this statement is perhaps more meaningful than what was spoken. The Truth and Reconciliation Commission on Indian Residential Schools was clearly the pivotal subject matter here, particularly the impact it has had on the personal legacies of the priests and the historical reputation of their order, but he approached it discreetly and indirectly.

Only later in the conversation did Father Piché arrive at the subject of his experience as director of a school. As he described it, it was a place where the children developed and grew. Despite a chronic shortage of funding from the federal government, they somehow managed to get by. A craft fair, for example, gave the girls a chance to show off their skills in beadwork and embroidery, gave them all a chance to dress up and present themselves to the public, and brought them enough money for a bus to get them home for Christmas. On the whole, the school was a good place to be. "They enjoyed it. In fact they were sad when we [the Oblates] closed it down when I left."[3]

Then we arrived at the most thorny issue: the experiences of abuse and trauma being reported by so many former students of Indian residential schools. Here again he approached the topic gingerly, with an answer based on his own experience:

> There was this sister that really didn't fit in. She was heavy-handed. And when I tried to talk to her, she couldn't change. So at Christmas ... I brought in a

layperson and I made arrangements to have somebody else come in that was more of an educator ... I would tell the sisters, "Look, those girls are not happy. Why should they be here, and why are we here, if they're not happy? The least we can do is make them happy while they're learning." But somehow her makeup didn't allow her to work well with the kids. If I hadn't changed her, I could've had a whole bunch of lawsuits on my hands later on.[4]

The same kind of presence of the absent and cautious emphasis on the positive came out in interviews I conducted with other Oblates. The four days I spent meeting with the priests and brothers in St. Albert (in common with my interactions with Oblates in their residences in Montreal, Winnipeg, Ottawa, and Iqaluit) emerged as a kind of indirect corrective to the Commission's historical narrative, a reply to the themes of genocide and historical trauma that publicly challenged the priests' sense of their biographies, that threw into question the formative values of their youth, the personal commitments and sacrifices they made in acting on them, and the moral integrity of the church and order to which they belonged. The interviews in St. Albert seemed to take on more purpose for them than mere cooperation with a research project. I, the interviewer, became a potential source of persuasion, possibly even a way to restore their deserved place in history. The public was a third party in our interactions. It became clear to me that they were looking for a way to get past the visible apologies of the upper echelons of the Church hierarchy, for an opportunity to express *their* understanding of their place in history, *their* view of justice and injustice, *their* feelings in response to (in their view) the many false accusations of aboriginal claimants and the betrayals of the state in giving these claimants, through the terms of the Settlement Agreement, a monopoly of institutional space and sanction.

LESSONS FROM GENOCIDE

Robbie Waisman (born Romek Wajsman in Skarszysko, Poland, in 1931) was an Honourary Witness in Inuvik and a keynote speaker in Saskatoon, where he presented a talk titled "The Resiliency of the Human Spirit." Waisman was among those liberated from Buchenwald by American forces on 11 April 1945, belonging to a group of 430 children rescued from the camp, some of whom came to be famous as "the Buchenwald boys." In each of these two meetings of the Commission his presentation emphasized the importance of history ("Forgetting the Holocaust is every survivor's greatest fear, and simply not an option") and the value of testimony of oppression and suffering to a receptive audience ("the ultimate *mitzvah* for me, an amazing good deed").[5] In both events, his presentation included the screening of a film about his experience, *To Tell the Story*, done in the 1980s by the Canadian Broadcasting

Corporation (CBC). In this film, the story of his liberation, focusing on his subsequent friendship with one of the African-American soldiers who helped accomplish it, is interspersed with scenes from the Holocaust. Anyone who has ever seen these images will remember them: starving, dying people, naked, helped to walk by their liberators; crowds of soon-to-be-liberated inmates shouting and pressing themselves against a fence; close-ups of emaciated faces with eyes deep in their heads; stacks of corpses, pelvises and ribs jutting beneath the skin, and corpses thrown unceremoniously into mass graves.

In Inuvik, some members of the audience reacted audibly to this footage: "Ooooh!" In Saskatoon they were more quietly attentive. But in both settings much the same observation was made by those invited after the screening to step up to a microphone and pose a question or comment. A man in Saskatoon who introduced himself as a school survivor made the comparison most directly: "Indian residential school is no different from what happened to Jews. Part of the European conquest! ... We were physically and sexually abused in these residential schools. We were tortured for speaking our own language. A language that is so beautiful, so important, so expressive. So I don't see no difference."[6] And in both settings Waisman performed a delicate balancing act: "I've learned over the years not to compare pains. Everyone has a different way of dealing with it and I sympathize with everything that happened to you. I shall shy away from comparison. If the war had lasted another six months, I wouldn't be here. We were targeted for annihilation."[7]

Members of two communities brought together by the mandate of the TRC—the Oblates and the survivors—tend to express radically different views of the place of Indian residential schools in Canadian history, one representing the schools as a valid (in the conditions of the time) effort at education and improvement, the other arguing that the schools were a manifestation of genocide directed toward Canada's aboriginal peoples. Even though the lessons of genocide may not be so adamantly and narrowly interpreted by all who see themselves as survivors, the starkly expressed version of it exemplifies a perspective that seems to be widely shared. The distance between these interpretations of history could not be greater.

The message of resilience, of persistence and the possibility of happiness in the aftermath of traumatic experience, was overlooked by some survivors in favour of a conception of self as a surviving victim of genocide and a view of the Canadian state and the churches as the perpetrators of a mass crime. This genocide-as-our-experience response to depictions of the Holocaust illustrates the great conceptual success of genocide and of crimes against humanity. Since their elaboration by the great jurist Raphael Lemkin (who was unrecognized in his lifetime and whose funeral in New York in 1959 was attended by five people), the concept and terminology of genocide that he took a leading role in formulating and entering into international law have successfully taken hold, both in popular imaginations and in the newly minted criminal institutions of international law.

An outcome of the genocide concept's success can also now be found in the readiness with which it is possible to see oneself and one's people as victims of the worst of all collective crimes. Where the sense of injustice finds no outlet, where the indignities of daily life accumulate without resolution, one can easily arrive at a sense of hopelessness, at a conception of the self as subject to external forces beyond control, with the sense of injustice manifest in the idea of a basic struggle for survival against the will of a hostile, dominant state and society.

I-WITNESSING

As far apart as these perspectives are, they do still have one thing in common: they are not only expressing views about history but are also active agents in *producing* historical evidence and interpretation based on personal experience. Of course, for the Oblates the venue for it (the recorded interview with an anthropologist) differed radically from the hearings of the Commission, but there was still an element of historical witnessing that they brought to our conversations—a quality that they can be seen as sharing with the survivors who gave testimony to the Commission.

The way that both these kinds of narrators situated the self in the past corresponds with an ideal long sought after in the Occidental historical tradition: a close connection to reality based on the I-witnessing and I-heard-tell-of narrative tradition. This persistent feature of the Western intellectual heritage has clearly not been lost, though it is certainly undergoing change. Contemporary history, Jacques Le Goff observes, is in tension between, on the one hand, the methods of a critical approach that aims at eliminating mystification and falsification in knowledge of the past; and, on the other hand, the revival of narrative testimonial traditions, a trend attributable to historical journalism and new media.[8]

To this we can add that truth commissions have now become a central source of this latter approach to historical knowledge and interpretation, manifesting a new iteration of historical witnessing. It is in these commissions that public understanding is sought concerning the recent occurrence of state-sanctioned abuse of power, with, among other purposes, a view to providing the raw material for future historical interpretation. The knowledge they produce, in keeping with this central goal, ideally bypasses the interested, implicated assertions of the powerful and holds at arm's length those academic abstractions that seem distant from lived experience. They situate themselves squarely in the I-witnessing tradition of historical narration by privileging the testimony of sufferers of political abuse, whose personal stories are gathered into a counter-narrative, an interruption of the assertions and erasures of state-sanctioned history. Documents are also there in the commissions' reports, but secondarily, by way of accompaniment. Histories are to be amended with priority given to the testimonies of the victimized.

In Canada's TRC, some iteration of this goal was stated by one or another of the commissioners in an introductory statement before each meeting, as in Marie Wilson's introduction to the TRC Urban Inuit Community Hearing in Ottawa, which seems to have been directed in particular to the survivors about to give testimony: "We have a chance to put on the record all those things that did not have their day in court ... This is not ancient history; this is history in our midst ... No future generation will ever be able to say this never happened ... You are rewriting the history of Canada in a true way."[9] In truth commissions, history is re-narrativized by those whose suffering can be seen, heard, and poignantly felt in the immediacy of narrated experience, presented to public gatherings, and recorded for posterity.

EXHIBITING DIFFERENCES

In spite of their lofty goals, truth commissions, by their nature, make poor historians. This is so for a variety of reasons. The first and most obvious of these is the inherent limitations of their reliance on testimony as a foundation for historical narration and interpretation. In the last chapter we saw some of the ways that testimony is subject to the plasticity and constructive capacities of memory, while being shaped by performance and, by extension, by the presence of audiences, media representation, and (by further extension) the preferences and influences of wider publics. There is a tendency for testimony to focus on traumatic individual experience, without regard for the wider contexts of institutional structure and political responsibility. Testimony tends to be personal, motivated, and subject to the vagaries of memory—tending toward "relative truth," in Commissioner Sinclair's terms—and is for these reasons, if relied upon exclusively, an insecure foundation for the reappraisal of the history of the state and its marginalized peoples.

Historical interpretation and opinion were shaped by institutional action outside the reach of the Commission even before it began its work. The documentary record of the past was limited, and to some extent strategically controlled, by the way that records were (and are) managed or, in some cases, destroyed. A former student living in Inuvik remembered being faced with just such an erasure of the past: "When [in 1998] they tore down Grollier Hall [the Catholic school in Inuvik] everything went to the dump. All the photos, all the trophies, the records. All the student records. People [were] finding stuff at the dump ... Like, people were going to the dump and actually finding personal records, student records, health records, at the local dump when they tore down the hostel ... it's almost like that period of time, they're trying to erase it."[10]

At the same time, access to those records that do survive in some government and church archives is controlled by gatekeepers, empowered with rules that give them institutional authority to include or exclude and refuse access. In its approach to its obligations under the Settlement Agreement to provide the TRC with copies of documents that might inform the Indian residential schools' legacy, the Government of Canada elected to throw up barriers, maintaining that it had no obligation to furnish the documents, numbering in the millions, that the TRC required as part of its truth-seeking mission. This documentation included basic information on thirty-seven residential schools as well as files held by the Royal Canadian Mounted Police (RCMP) concerning criminal complaints about abuse in the schools.[11] Resistance to releasing these documents was based, in large part, on the federal government's interpretation of the word "relevant" in the formal mandate of the Commission, which calls on the government and churches to "provide all *relevant* documents in their possession or control" (emphasis added).[12]

With a federal definition seemingly indefinitely delayed in the inner workings of the Department of Justice, the TRC sought a clarification of its mandate from the courts, and on 30 January 2013 received a decision from the Ontario Superior Court of Justice that called on the federal government to provide the TRC with copies of those documents from Library and Archives Canada (including the much-coveted RCMP records), without which the TRC would have been limited in its efforts to provide a thorough report and historical record of the Indian residential school system and its legacy.[13] Such obstruction and foot dragging over the provision of archive material is consistent with the federal government's minimal presence in TRC events as discussed in chapter 4, except that historical records have more potential to connect the government with the schools' legacy of harm than would any possible "guilt-by-association" effect of official presence at TRC events.

The acceptable range of historical fact-gathering and interpretation is also limited by the basic structure and scope of the Commission. Legal efforts to keep their mandates within bounds prevent this and other truth commissions from considering wider contexts, including the kind of testimony that trespasses into alien territory, the "related experiences," the "while I have the microphone" moments of those who use their time before the audience to stray from the topic at hand, to talk about what is really bothering them, the injustices in their lives that rankle and fester and keep them awake at night.

The TRC's contest over history was occasionally evident in the speeches and witnessing activities of the main events, as in Brother Cavanaugh's testimony in Victoria and Bishop Gordon's testimony in Inuvik; but it is perhaps more clearly evident, though also more muted, in peripheral representations of ideas, notably the photographs and captions in exhibits hosted by the Commission. In Winnipeg and Inuvik,

"Learning Tents" presented a similar content to the Learning Places in Halifax, Victoria, and Saskatoon. Through these exhibits the Commission seemed to invite the churches and research organizations to present and represent their versions of the history of Indian residential schools. In contrast to the dominant themes of the testimony in the Commissioner's Sharing Panel, more space was given here—temporarily at least—for multiple perspectives. The most prominent display that toured with the major TRC venues was that of the Legacy of Hope, self-described as "a national Aboriginal charitable organization dedicated to raising awareness and understanding about the legacy of residential schools."[14] This display took great care to present a range of material, supported with photographic and documentary evidence, assembled into timelines, and presented with brief, plain-language summaries under clear captions. Prominent in the Legacy of Hope display were photographs and transcribed testimony from survivors, illustrating the connections between residential schools and territorial removal as well as the traumas associated with the school experience. In one section of the display, headings taken from statements from survivors like "I learned to feel shame ..." "I wanted to go home ..." "I died in this place ..." and "They cut my hair and burned my clothes ..." stood out prominently above explanations of the interruptions brought about by the schools. The poster describing the sense of shame felt by students, for example, explained that, "An Aboriginal child's education did not begin when they arrived at the residential schools. As young children they had been mentored and guided by their parents and Elders. Traditions and ceremonies passed down through generations provided knowledge, skills, and wisdom." Then came the child's experience with school—and the nature and consequences of these schools are elaborated with equal poignancy: "The residential schools taught Aboriginal children that the practices of their parents and Elders were 'uncivilized' and 'revolting.'"[15] The overall argument made in this display is that the essential goal and common quality of residential schools was to be found in their systematic efforts to eliminate the distinct identities of the students. "They were often separated from their siblings and were not allowed to speak their own language—even to their brothers or sisters. The process of stripping away Aboriginal identity began within minutes of arriving at the school."[16]

In contrast, an Anglican "Church Display" in Halifax—immediately adjacent to the Legacy of Hope display—featured photographs of children in the schools engaged in group activities: girls baking bread, boys tobogganing, skating, and canoeing, sometimes assembled together in formal poses, smiling next to the priests and nuns. Here the implicit argument is that the schools were places of life, learning, and joy.[17] Photographs of children engaged in archery or standing on the shore of a lake holding up an impressive fish make an implicit argument that the intention of the church was not to eliminate aboriginal distinctiveness, but to accommodate aboriginal peoples' core values. Even the formally posed photographs argue obliquely against narratives

FIGURE 7.1: Photographs in the Anglican Church display, Atlantic National Event, Halifax.

of suffering. After all, the implicit argument goes, if the children were in such deep pain, why all the smiles?

In another part of the Halifax Learning Place, a second display case sponsored by the Anglican Church featured a Mi'kmaq dictionary and two books of the bible, Genesis and Exodus, in Mi'kmaq translation. This seemed to be a material rebuttal of arguments, common in testimony, to the effect that one of the assimilationist goals of the churches was to eradicate native languages. And, as though to build on the argument made by the translations, this display case also featured examples of native beadwork and embroidery done by students in the school. Could there really be such a material production of culture where that culture was targeted for elimination?

(Much the same argument was made by a librarian at the archives in the Deschâtelets residence in Ottawa when, in a moment of leisure, he proudly showed me and a research assistant the collection of native-language dictionaries produced by Oblate missionaries, some bound in elaborately wrought leather, some meticulously hand-written. The point he made was: "Why would the priests have gone through all this effort if their goal was to destroy these languages?")

This was not an isolated effort. Similar exhibits were presented by local church groups at other National Events. At the Learning Place in Saskatoon, for example, the Anglican Fund for Healing and Reconciliation had arranged selected photographs from the General Synod Archives under the headings "Playing," "Eating," "Sleeping,"

"Learning," "Sports," "Sewing," and "Going Home," all depicting the students and staff in the pleasurable moments that one readily associates with these words. (Notably absent here is anything about "leaving home" or "arriving," two of the episodes most often associated with trauma in TRC testimony.)

Immediately adjacent to this display, the United Church had put a little more detail into their captions, with optimism coming through in both the photographs and descriptions that accompanied them: "Girls with their dress-up hats at the swings on their playground," "Mrs. G.H. Bennie, President of Saskatchewan Conference Branch, W.M.S. unveiling the cairn to commemorate 50 years of Christian service among the Indians at File Hills," "Mrs. F.W. Therrion heading the famous Round Lake Residential School Choir," and "Students going home to Fort Qu'Appelle from the File Hills Residential School." The common themes—impossible to miss—in these exhibits are play, disciplined experience, and homecoming (in one instance going so far as to describe a transfer from one school to another as "going home").

The church archivists who attended the events seemed to be blithely unaware that any of the material presented in these displays comprised a particular position in a contest of history. Their attitude was more one of pride at the quality of the items dredged up from the records and now made available to the public, and to survivors in particular. What is more, the contest of ideas inherent in the exhibited material also seemed to go unnoticed (or was ignored) by most of the event's participants. There was a certain permissiveness toward arguments made through photographs and objects, an indulgence that did not seem to apply to evidence presented through words. The reality depicted in a snapshot seemed incontrovertible, as though the image itself conveyed a simple, unimpeachable thought, something like, "Well, there they are, the girls with their hats on a swing." As though nothing more need be added.

By far the most popular features in the Learning Place venues in which all denominations participated were the archives of church photographs, gathered into thick ring binders with protective document sleeves, in which former students, usually for the first time in their lives, could situate themselves in the past and receive some tangible confirmation of their memories. This reminded me of the interest aroused by the photographs from St. Joseph's School that I brought to the Band office at Cross Lake. Former students visiting the Learning Place would tell the archivist what school they had been to during what years, and in most cases a photograph, usually a posed group photo of a class or sports team, could be found and a copy or two printed for them to take away.

In Halifax, photographs of groups of students mounted on the walls were soon supplied with names (or the word "unknown") written in the margins by former students. One former student had evidently taken an initiative, followed by others, of inscribing the photograph of anonymous students with the particulars of memory, giving them, to the extent possible, identities and individuality. The evident appeal of the photographic records and the practice by which survivors engaged with them—marking themselves and others in them, narrativizing and personalizing them—tells us something more general about the appeal for survivors of the events of the Commission: it frames this as a way toward self-inscription in history and as a way of creating a coherent sense of the self. Here the pervasiveness of loneliness and absence of place commonly reported by survivors can be seen in the enthusiasm with which it was symbolically overcome.

The National Event in Inuvik was a bit different from the others in the extent to which local organizers included community members in the process of self-representation. Almost everywhere one looked there was evidence of revival and rediscovery, sometimes in juxtaposition with representations of suffering and loss. Here among the displays set up in a high school gymnasium were metre-and-a-half square posters featuring larger-than-life photographs of notable former students, mostly of Inuit and Inuvialuit origin, all with serious, sad expressions, accompanied by text that emphasized the traumas of their school years, their struggles to overcome the legacy of these schools, and their subsequent leadership roles.

On the other side of the room were cultural displays, including one hosted by two Inuvialuit men in their twenties, who were there to explain to visitors the manufacture and use of the tools and hand-crafted kayaks featured in the display. A poster board propped against a divider announced its subject matter, the most prized catch in the traditional economy, in Inuvialuit and English: "*Qilalukkat!* Belugas!" The text that accompanied a photograph of a dead whale being carved up on a pebbly beach explained, "Inuvialuit have a right, under their 1984 land claim, to hunt beluga whales for subsistence purposes in the Inuvialuit Settlement Region. Hunters follow rules set by each community." Next to the poster board was a plastic bucket containing what looked like squares of feta cheese in water. Evidently (as I deduced by its proximity to the poster board), these were pieces of whale skin and blubber (*maktaaq*). One of the men confirmed this, and went on to recommend to me the beluga available at a popular lunch counter set up expressly for the TRC event that featured "country food" of all kinds, including ptarmigan or muskrat stir fry, caribou, arctic char chowder, and (this I did not know) beluga, raw or cooked—the raw version being especially highly recommended. (Later, by the time I got to the counter, it was sold out.) When I looked at the whale blubber beside the display more closely I noticed something odd about it, or rather something odd that was absent from it:

"It doesn't smell."
"No, it doesn't smell."

He explained to me that this particular *maktaaq* was not really from a beluga at all but was made out of rubber especially for the purpose of their display.

Contradictions abound: here we find an exercise in public representation of an essential self—rubberized whale blubber—depicting the significance and persistence of traditional hunting. It is an inventive, even artistic use of new materials to represent a practical product of ancient technologies of survival. And, perhaps most poignantly, it was a display making use of such creativity while surrounded by poster-board stories depicting the trauma of cultural interruption. If they had taken any notice of it, many visitors to the display might have considered this bucket of synthetic beluga blubber to be inauthentic, but from another perspective it was an illustration of the very kind of practical ingenuity called for in living from the land, the creativity involved in designing an object to meet a precise need. The former residential school students, whose images stared at the whaling display from across the room, had every reason to be proud.

STATUS DEGRADATION

The naturalization of a re-narrativized history of the state through the TRC calls for a clear perpetrator of systemic harm. Governments tend to be too abstract to serve as agents responsible for very personal harms. Clarity calls for someone, some category of person, to stand in as a malefactor, an instrument of the state with attributes of moral corruption. States may not be fully complicit in the construction of church representatives as offender-agents, but neither do they vigorously object to it. We can speculate that this is because attributing responsibility for harm to these agents is not only easy because they stand out in public view; it also takes attention away from policy and policy-makers.

Lori Ducharme and Gary Fine provide insight into this interpretive shift in a discussion of the ways that negative historical reputations are constructed. Biographies of historical agents are reconstructed "through selective emphasis on historical events" while the motives that underpin reputations are ascribed, assessed, and possibly challenged. "The construction of villainous reputations," they argue, "depends upon society's ability to negate positive actions and characteristics and to see only those deeds and qualities that confirm the malefactor's transformed identity."[18] The result of successful efforts to reassess and reassign historical reputations can be far-reaching. "Largely irreversible, successful status degradation processes relegate the offenders, and their reputations, to the area outside society's moral boundaries."[19]

Such historical reappraisal of the moral character of principal actors is not restricted to the influence of individuals. What we are seeing in the TRC, the status degradation at the origin of the priests' sense of grievance, is part of a wider phenomenon in which dominant institutions are subject to moral assessment and discontinuity. To see this as clearly as possible, it is useful to take as a starting point the legitimacy of human rights, through which state-sponsored agencies have taken on some of the attributes of persons, including the capacity for maturity and moral growth. Public opinion is empowered by an originary assumption: the expectation of ethical improvement in public ideas and institutions. Agencies are personalized in the sense that they are expected to change and grow in the manner of an experiencing and learning individual. This is a process that comes from a deeper source than policy. It is a reflection of basic public values.

This epiphenomenon of human rights can then be seen in the way that it lays waste to careers. Once-celebrated commitments and activism become—by slow accretions and seemingly out of the blue—subject to doubt and derision. Politicians find themselves unelectable and out of office. Academics who spent the better part of their working lives being rewarded for their commitments to human betterment find themselves at a place on the margins, representing ideas considered by emerging scholars as corrupt or naive, or both. And priests, brothers, and nuns who entered their professions not only with faith and idealism, but with respect and avenues to influence and power, find themselves in a declining profession, with full retirement homes and empty convents and seminaries. The missionary enterprises and the values of intervenient human improvement on which they based their lives have been cast to the margins, leaving those with persistent commitments to them now struggling with the sense of being forgotten, while possessing memories that are the potential foundation of a different and, in their view, more truthful history. If only they could be heard. If only people would listen.

LOVE AND HOCKEY

Bishop Douglas Crosby, who delivered the Oblate apology of 1991 on the occasion of the annual Lac Ste. Anne Pilgrimage north of Edmonton, Alberta, later expressed disappointment about the press response to the event:

> Toward the end of the session, a woman spoke up: "I want to say something," she announced. "I went to residential school." All the cameras turned toward her; all the tape recorders pointed in her direction ... The woman continued, "I want to thank the Oblates for the work they did at the schools." As she explained why she thought the Oblates deserved thanks, the cameras were turned off, the microphones put away ... It was not the story the media wanted to cover then—or now.[20]

This sense that coverage of residential schools was being skewed toward crude, popular inclinations was in the background to much that was said to me about the TRC by former members of the clergy and school workers. Much the same sense of exclusion applied to the Commission's hearings. It is true that high-ranking church officials regularly appeared before cameras, microphones, and spectators of the Commission to read prepared apologies, but the rank and file of the religious orders and clergy, particularly those who at some point in their careers worked in Indian residential schools, were notably absent from the proceedings. This applied in particular to the Oblates with experience working in the schools, who not only did not (aside from those of high rank) appear at the TRC proceedings, but who privately expressed deep resentment toward what they saw as the Commission's emerging history of their schools; they saw it as incompatible with their order's historical contributions to the survival and prosperity of aboriginal peoples in Canada, and above all with their memories of what it was like participating in (and making personal sacrifices for) this project of human welfare.

Because of this, there was nothing casual about my interviews with Oblate priests, brothers, and nuns. True, no one had dressed formally for the occasion. (Archbishop Weisgerber was the only exception, but even he, dressed smartly in black with his priest's collar, disarmingly removed his slip-on shoes and sat comfortably, ankles crossed, with his stocking feet on his chair.) In general, those with whom I spoke were almost stereotypes of church retirees, the priests and brothers with plaid shirts, roomy wool pants or chinos, and belts worn high on their waists; the nuns tightly coiffed, with long skirts and sensible shoes.

But there was a sense in which my interviews with them, despite my best efforts, became events. It was they, the priests, brothers, and nuns at the mission in St. Albert, at the Despins retirement facility in Winnipeg, at the Our Lady of the Assumption parish in Iqaluit, and at the Maison Deschâtelets in Ottawa, who had something important to say—who, given the opportunity of an interview, produced their own tribunal-like atmosphere. Some, with trembling hands, would offer documents, evidence, archive material, school records, newspaper clippings, written statements, sometimes for me to take away, at other times just to look at for a moment. In groups they tended toward caution—there was always at least one among them with superior rank ready to temper the reckless opinions of others. One-on-one with aggrieved priests (nuns did not meet with me alone), memory and experience were narrated almost in the manner of a confession, but one that emphasized the transgressions of others. This sense of correcting the record was sometimes said explicitly at the outset: "I'm going to orient you toward something. It will be important for someone to say it."[21] Or, "so I just put this out because I think you need to hear [it]."[22]

There were not only truths that had to be told; there were also uncomfortable truths that were avoided or approached with caution, even in the private context of my interviews. Not surprisingly, sexual abuse was not foremost among the topics they wanted to address. Most of their testimony to me (it was often my sense that they were giving testimony) was oriented toward correcting the record, setting things straight. As one priest testified:

Just a few days ago I was called to Assiniboia and meet former students. I had a very nice experience with them. There were very few but however we reminisced about the past and the general mood was so good, very good ... When I read the report about the schools I was shocked and very sad, deeply sad about [what] I had heard because it is something that I didn't know before except what I heard, but I had never seen in the school where I was. This is what I told them, my own experience about residential school is very positive. It is not all darkness. I know that there were abuses; I'm not denying that, but not all darkness. There were some very good people working there, very good. We need to provide some balance, I told them, in public perception. The residential school has such a bad reputation but this is not what I experienced in four schools. I like to mention that, [to give] the proper balance to public perceptions, some good relationships were developed among students and staff. I recall how staff were doing their best. Yes, they were doing their best, very, very dedicated staff to ensure the total well-being of all the students. I told them I remember how much friendship and care there was in the schools. So this has been my experience. For me it was a good place in which to live. This is why I am so shocked to hear such negative, of course there were, I'm not denying that, but lots of positive too and I think we don't mention enough the positive. Just my opinion.[23]

Where the origins of the Oblate involvement in residential education arose, they tended to take an exculpatory approach by invoking the historical necessity of the schools. "There was simply a changing North, a changing situation with all the influx of immigrants coming in and, you know, the Bishops and the priests would say, 'How are they going to live?'"[24]

To each of the reported sources of trauma stemming from institutional routine (the sorts of things prominent in the Legacy of Hope exhibit discussed above) there was an answer based on their own memories of the schools, one that pointed to necessity. To the reports of excessive discipline, the common response was that there was no other way the schools could have been run. This was simply an outcome of the challenge of housing and educating so many students with so few people employed. As one of the nuns who had formerly worked in the Lebret school remarked: "When you have seventy-eight [children] you, you had them all in groups and so it's time to [go to] supper; group A go, go B; and so that lacked family spirit, if, if anything."[25] There was also a sense among some of the priests that discipline was character forming in ways that were absent from the children's lives at home. One priest, proudly recalling the military drills given to students in the Qu'Appelle Indian Residential School in Saskatchewan, exclaimed, "We gave them personalities!"[26]

In response to the trauma of compulsory haircuts, there was an element of practical necessity: "They had nits so we had to do it. That first year was bad when we would have to fine-comb them and everything ... They were so generous amongst themselves, they would share combs and everything with each other, which was the worst thing to do, so they learned you don't do that."[27]

The loss of language as an outcome of assimilation efforts was, if anything, more strenuously contested. How else would one communicate with children from different origins if not through English, the language of instruction? Under circumstances of linguistic diversity, it was, according to one priest, the *students* who made English the preferred medium of communication: "We never stopped them from speaking their language. That they did together among themselves."[28] The priests, putting into words memories that ran counter to the narrative of assimilation, emphasized being closely involved in learning and teaching in aboriginal languages:

I was sent in 1954 when I was just a young priest ... Bishop D ... told me go talk to the children, they'll teach you the language. In chapel, the sisters would say to me, have the children [sing] Soto hymns and I recorded forty-three of those hymns so that was very much one positive thing. Because we had many of our priests there, I counted about nine, who knew the language, who learned the language. So the language was important. They told us you don't go to work with the native people unless you learned the language, so that was very positive. So when I heard that we were taking away the language, it bothered me again because one thing [that] was stressed was to learn the language....

And I noticed, I was in one of the reserves here, and the only children that could read the Soto hymns were those that had gone to the residential schools. Those that had gone to Sandy Bay and Camperville, they could read, they could sing, because they had learned it at school.[29]

More than this, some of the school workers themselves experienced language repression. The vast majority of Oblates who had once worked in some fifty-two residential schools across the country were French-speaking (mostly from Quebec), but were required to teach in English. As one retired priest remembered, there was even a sense of *French* being illicit and repressed: "I'm [from] a French background ... [but] I was forbidden to teach French in any of our schools. It had to be English. And when the inspector came, we hid our French books ... Am I mad at the government today because they forbid [sic] me to [teach] French?"[30]

The survivor statements that describe inadequate clothing and food in the schools were countered by recalling the inadequate funding from the federal government and descriptions of making do with what one had. Under circumstances of chronic under-funding, the school administrators had to make arrangements for hunters to bring in meat, and in southern regions with an agricultural season, for potatoes to be planted in early summer and harvested in the fall. "The students would take a half-day away from classes and we would go harvest potatoes; and that, that allowed us to go buy a televi-sion for one of their rooms. The government would never have given it to us."[31] The lack of funding applied even to the most basic of necessities. "They couldn't just have any-thing ... They had a lot of porridge and a lot of potatoes and things like that ... People were not demanding like they are today. They were satisfied with that."[32] A nun who had worked in a remote northern school remembered that even the students' cloth-ing had to be made with whatever was at hand: "[The school] was not rich and ... the senior girls had the air force colours, the air force clothes that they made into jumpers. That is what they wore every day. And they had a blouse or a little sweatshirt with that, and their shoes ... [were] supplied by school. They would come with clothes but it was never enough for the year."[33]

Not only did the people charged with the daily operation of the schools do their best with little resources, they did it with love and joy. The interviews with priests, brothers, and nuns emphasized the moments, and even routines, of happiness, in which "people were surrounded by respect and love."[34] Recreational activities were the most common source of positive memories. As one Grey Sister remembered, "We had a lot of fun too, going swimming. The lake was right there. We were at one end and the boys at the other."[35] And in winter, quintessentially Canadian (or at least northern) sports found their way into the routine: "I remember playing curling with them with jam cans. We'd put cement in a jam can and you had [a curling stone], and we'd play because there was no money, but we managed."[36]

The one activity that stood out from all others in terms of the passion it evoked was hockey: "And during [those] eleven years in schools I was happy with the kids. I was always involved in hockey with them, all of them ... I was always on the ice with them."[37] Games against teams from schools run by Protestant denominations were remembered particularly vividly by the Oblate priests; and several of my interviews included long digressions into training regimes, bad weather, poor funding (and hence equipment shortfalls), rigged games (the outcome determined in advance by church politics), and other obstacles overcome (or not overcome) in the school's engagement with the most beloved of Canadian sports.

All of this amounts to a sense of grievance, not just in terms of the accusations being levelled against them, but, perhaps more importantly, in terms of the leg-acy, the foundations for the history that is being formed by the accumulating mass of testimony from former students. Father L'Heureux expressed this sentiment in a letter to Commissioner Wilton Littlechild. Ever since the Report of the Royal Commission on Aboriginal Peoples, he declaimed, "Canada seized the opportunity to sideline the culture and language questions to sexual abuses committed by the churches. From then on [Indian residential schools] were presented to the general public and to the world as brothels and torture camps created for the benefit of maniac and sadistic church people."[38] The message from the Oblates with whom I spoke emphasized themes that ran counter to the usual narratives of the Commission. At no point in my conversations with them was there a direct, considered discussion of the sociopaths and predators who made use of (in the abuse of) their absolute power to exercise tyranny and sexual sadism. When this subject did arise, usually in passing, it was to argue that this was a rare exception that did not happen in their school or with their awareness. Instead, the former school workers emphasized their positive experience, usually without directly addressing the remembrances of survivors. Their interviews were counter-narratives to stories of abuse and trauma, without an opposing point of reference. To those Oblates who had once worked in the schools, there is another history to be constructed out of their very different memories, out of things not being said but that stand out to them: the good intentions, the making do with little, the care, the sacrifice, the love, and hockey.

NOTES

1   Interview with Camille Piché, St. Albert, Alberta, 10 September 2009.
2   Ibid.
3   Ibid.
4   Ibid.
5   Robbie Waisman, "The Resiliency of the Human Spirit," keynote address, Truth and Reconciliation Commission of Canada, Saskatoon, 23 June 2012.
6   Ibid.
7   Ibid.
8   Jacques Le Goff, *Histoire et Mémoire* (Paris: Editions Gallimard, 1988), 20.
9   Marie Wilson, "Commissioner's Welcome," TRC Urban Inuit Community Hearing, Ottawa, 16 August 2012.
10 Lucy Kuptana, Interview with Marie-Pierre Gadoua, Inuvik, 14 October 2011.
11 Unusually thorough media coverage of the dispute between the TRC and the federal government can be found in Jorge Barrera, "RCMP Files, Records of Missing Children, Graves May Never Surface if Ottawa Wins Battle with TRC," *APTN National News*, 3 December 2012, accessed 27 February 2013,

http://aptnnews.ca/2012/12/03/rcmp-files-records-of-missing-children-graves-may-never-surface-if-ottawa-wins-battle-with-trc.

12 Government of Canada, *Indian Residential Schools Settlement Agreement, Schedule "N"* (Ottawa: Government of Canada, 2007), article 11, accessed 26 February 2013, http://www.residentialschoolsettlement.ca/SCHEDULE_N.pdf.

13 *Fontaine v. Canada (Attorney General)*, 2013 ONSC 684, Court File No. CV-00–192059 and CV-12–447891, 30 January 2013.

14 Legacy of Hope, "Who Are We?" Panel presented in the Learning Place, TRC National Events.

15 Legacy of Hope, "I learned to feel shame ..." Panel presented in the Learning Place, TRC National Events.

16 Legacy of Hope, "They cut my hair and burned my clothes ..." Panel presented in the Learning Place, TRC National Events.

17 In the two pages that follow, including the photograph in figure 7.1, I draw from my contribution to Ronald Niezen and Marie Pierre Gadoua, "Témoignage et histoire dans la Commission de vérité et de reconciliation du Canada," *Canadian Journal of Law and Society/La Revue Canadienne Droit et Société* 29, no. 1 (2014): 21–42.

18 Lori Ducharme and Gary Fine, "The Construction of Nonpersonhood and Demonization: Commemorating the Traitorous Reputation of Benedict Arnold," *Social Forces* 73, no. 4 (1995): 1311–12.

19 Ibid., 1310.

20 Bishop Douglas Crosby, OMI, "A Reflection on the Oblate Apology," unpublished presentation to St. Joseph's Parish, Ottawa, 19 March 2009.

21 "Mais je vais tout de même t'orienter vers quelque chose, il serait important que quelqu'un le dise." Interview at Résidence Despins, Winnipeg, 20 June 2010.

22 Interview at Résidence Despins, Winnipeg, 21 June 2010.

23 Ibid.

24 Interview with Fr. Camille Piché, Résidence St. Albert, 11 September 2009.

25 Interview at Résidence Despins, Winnipeg, 21 June 2010.

26 Interview at Résidence St. Albert, 10 September 2009.

27 Ibid.

28 Ibid.

29 Ibid.

30 Interview at Résidence Despins, Winnipeg, 20 June 2010.

31 "Les étudiants prenaient une demi-journée des classes et on allait ramasser des patates pis ça, ça nous permettait d'aller acheter une télévision pour une de leurs salles. Le gouvernement ne nous l'aurait jamais donné." Interview at Résidence Despins, Winnipeg, 21 June 2010.

32 Ibid.

33 Ibid.

34 Ibid.

35 Ibid.

36 Ibid.

37 Ibid.

38 Jaques L'Heureux, unpublished letter from Les Missionnaires Oblats de Marie Immaculée, Ottawa, Ontario, to Chief Wilton Littlechild, Commissioner, Truth and Reconciliation Commission of Canada, 12 January 2011.

Chapter 8

SOLITUDES

PUBLICS REVISITED

My explicit goal in this book has been to explore the space that separates those who occupy (willingly or not) increasingly reified categories of sufferer and perpetrator, accuser and accused. This space is hedged about with zones of illegitimate, forbidden memories. It is situated in the aftermath of judgment, in efforts to construct a record of the range of experience that characterizes a wrong of the state. The question with which I began concerned the bulwarks erected on either side of that forbidden space, the ways and means by which institutions and individuals could be at such wide variance in their views of past events, of the legitimate reach of government, and of the pathways to human betterment. I am also concerned with how there could come to be such a considerable disjuncture between communities with privately held opinions and views expressed publicly by spokespeople representing institutions. Throughout addressing these issues, I have tried to show the untidy emotions and behaviour at work in the erection and patrol of boundaries of belonging. The logic behind these boundaries, if indeed there ever was any, fades fully from view as soon as we begin to consider the involvement of audiences and more distant publics in their construction. How do publics involve themselves in the consumption and mediation of ideas about injustice and remarkable or compelling experience? And how does this involvement impact the oppositions of history and the emphases and exclusions of legal remedy?

With reference to the non-aboriginal Canadian public, there are indications from its occasional appearance, when its most forthright members send out messages to others, that the Commission communicated broadly—at least during and surrounding the occasions of the National Events. The online threads that followed media coverage of TRC events offer glimmers of emerging opinion; and it is sad to say that where the Commission did manage to garner attention, public views were not always consistent with reconciliation. Much of this, of course, has to do with the extent to which moderators filtered out (or failed to do so) views intended to be hurtful. The online edition of the *National Post* left many of these intact, but this tells us more about the general human proclivity toward violence (including textual aggression) than about anything related to the legacy of residential schools. The discussions pursuant to stories by the CBC have tended to be more informative, and it is here that we can find a greater overlap with the visible compassion of live audiences at TRC events: "My direct descendants were not involved, but as a white person, I do apologize sincerely. It makes me sick to my stomach, to think that anyone could be so 'screwed up.' Please know, that not all 'white' people, are like that ... I'm so sorry ..."[1] Of course, just because the story gets "out there" does not mean it will be persuasive and change opinion, and in online threads there is some indication of skepticism in response to stories related to the TRC:

I wonder how things would be today if we did not have residential schools. Would we be paying money for not providing education in the past? There are a lot of [First Nation] people who benefited from the residential schools, why don't we get to hear their stories in the media?[2]

And then there are those occasional expressions of opinion that, seemingly without intending to be destructive, blur the boundaries inherent in the category of Indian residential school survivor: "While I am part Aboriginal, ironically the 'white' side of my family experienced the residential school type treatment for several generations ... Our Acadian family members were also sent to boarding schools run by the church and subject to abuse which closely resembles some of the stories you hear from Aboriginal survivors."[3] Once outside the relatively cohesive communities of accuser and accused, opinion seems to fan out, giving us little indication of the direction, if any, it might choose in response to the Commission's long-term efforts at education and persuasion.

Much of what Canada's Truth and Reconciliation Commission did can be attributed to the incomplete tasks of public persuasion and group affirmation. In the aftermath of court judgments and a major restitution agreement, residential school policies and their widely ramifying consequences were still unknown to many Canadians; so an explicit goal of the Commission was to increase awareness of this national-historical truth. It pursued this goal with little help from the government or churches, particularly in the investigative aspects of its project. Add to this the limited judicial powers of its mandate—above all its inability to overcome the unwillingness of former educators and officials to provide statements—and what remained was a near-exclusive focus on language and persuasion as an instrument of justice, on the affirmation of survivor experience.[4] Where the perpetrators of injustices being addressed by a truth commission continue to be socially dominant, we can expect just such a victim-centred approach to knowledge and a symbolic approach to reparations.[5]

Consistent with these limitations, the TRC's activities emphasized honouring and affirming the experiences of survivors. The Commission embarked on a mission of public education and persuasion, of gathering evidence for future use in research, and informing the unenlightened along the way, mostly through the survivor-centred events it sponsored and the media activity surrounding them.

This was a project that involved a certain cultivation of opinion. The "survivors" and "intergenerational survivors" who offered their testimony were often people who had experienced not only the worst things that can be done to children, but later in their lives the worst abuse of opinion that can be perpetrated on a fellow human being: imposing the stigma of victimization. Those who experienced abuse in the schools and shame in their adult lives had need of the restoration of their dignity. So it was perfectly reasonable that the Commission would also set itself the goal of making suffering acceptable or even noble, with a complementary emphasis on self-improvement through cultural rediscovery.

What can we say about those who were the targets of this persuasion, those before whom the survivors expressed their anguish and affirmed the accomplishment of their healing? Judging by the audiences that appeared at the Commission's National Events, they consisted in good measure of those who saw themselves as survivors and the friends and relatives of survivors. From here the circle widened to include church-goers who heard about the meetings from someone on the pulpit or from activities organized by the churches. The greatest prize of the Commission's publicity efforts, however, was to reach the uninformed, undecided, and uncommitted—the wider public—to provoke its members' sense of injustice and engage their willingness to immerse themselves in a reappraisal of history and public policy. And let us not omit from consideration that remote, abstract public that only exists somewhere on the other side of a lens or microphone cable, and from there back to the imagination of the witness, including a futurity that also (or especially) stands in need of persuasion.

This is the point at which the targets of persuasion become more nebulous and difficult to reach. The trouble with these more distant publics is that they're not all that they're cracked up to be. As I discussed in chapter 1, they are persuaded more by emotion than by the historian's sense of complex interconnections or the reason of dispassionate justice. They are more like the people who slow traffic to a crawl at the scene of an accident, even when there is no consideration of safety, just to get a glimpse of the carnage. They are both drawn to and repulsed by the experience of horror and revulsion, the closer the better. But where life itself does not provide this experience, they consume it second-hand, in images presented through media. It is as though in the dull zone of safety in front of their screens they need something to awaken their human senses. They are readily captivated and possibly persuaded by many of the same kinds of emotion that fill cinemas. They seek the most stimulating, imagination-inspiring, evocative, extraordinary things that make life interesting, even if vicariously and only for a moment.

But they are also driven by curiosity and compassion. Once the disgust and horror responses are over, many want to know more. How did it happen? Who was responsible? And from here one can make an appeal to the indignant response that says, "That should *not* have happened!" The asymmetries in moral order call for correction, with some members of the public more than others obsessively drawn to engagement, like fixing a picture that is hanging crooked, but with more consequence. The publics that respond to justice claims also experience the urge to reach and straighten, to make things right, and maybe to learn something in the process, by *looking* at the image they are straightening.

Knowing that there is an audience outside the meeting room, how and with what do speakers choose to represent themselves and their experience? Recall the Commission's efforts in the hearings to be welcoming to survivors and permissive toward what they have to say. It was made clear to survivors who gave statements that their listeners were there to hear them without judgment, that they were free to express themselves almost any way they choose, at least within certain thematic preferences and within loosely, informally enforced limits of time. More than this, the Commission provided various models for their statements by offering examples of witnessing done by others or displaying powerful symbols of suffering, making it easier for inexperienced speakers to narrate painful experiences.

The Commission itself made representations to the abstract publics of present and future with its own selection and interpretation of survivor statements. It is instructive to compare the choices it made against the great variety of narratives available to it. The "highlight reels" emphasized those poignant fragments that provoke compassion, things like children sleeping on toilets, not wanting to wet their beds; like victimization at the hands of sexual predators; like loss of language, suddenly realized in a flood of loneliness and isolation, in a moment of being unable to communicate with elders. The highlights, in other words, conveyed an argument that adhered fairly closely to the complementary conceptual paradigms of genocide and historical trauma, and the antidote to them to be found in cultural renewal.

But when we consider the entire spectrum of testimony presented to the Commission, we cannot fail to come away with a different impression of the compelling ideas that motivate people to sit before the microphone. We can start with narratives given by those who were categorically excluded from the highlight reels, the stroke victim, the schizophrenic, the mute-from-grief, those who appeared only to make noises in a struggle to communicate. We might be tempted to dismiss this testimony as inconsequential, certainly not worth noting in preference to others. Yet, through their mere appearance, these witnesses had something to say. Their testimony spoke to the power of the urge to connect with those in the room and on the other side of the cameras and microphones, to mark their existence, above all to make it known that in some way they are troubled. If nothing else, they communicated the sounds of life in the throes of grief and grievance. The person before the microphone was sometimes able, through his or her presence alone, to represent a new category or community of rights claimants, and to embody the moral gravity of the social world.

Others came more prepared to speak on the record and off the topic. The TRC was not just a venue for restitution of a past wrong; it was a pathway for putting unresolved claims on the table. Taken together, the statements presented to the Commission were far broader in their identification of trauma-inducing institutions than the narrow scope of the Settlement Agreement's terms of reference. Those who sat before the microphone at Commission events tended to be inclusive in their approach to the conditions that fostered such things as pedophilia, racism, and cultural loss. They liberally mentioned institutions like Indian day schools, orphanages, schools for the deaf, convents, TB wards, and prisons as sources of their oppression.

Statement providers also came to the microphone with more personal expressions of their sense of injustice. If one were to collect the entire range of causes put forward by survivors in the Commission's public hearings, one would no doubt be impressed by their number and variety. In this limited sense, the Commission had an unrestricted mandate and acted on it with an open mike. Besides testifying about their experience in residential schools, survivors gave voice to every conceivable injustice, every nagging feeling of being wronged, from the usurpation of their people's political autonomy in centuries past to the personal indignities and insecurity experienced in the criminal justice system in the present. There was always a sense in which these while-I-have-the-microphone moments could relate in some way to Indian residential schools, as though the schools might serve as the axis through which all other harms and injustices narrated in survivor statements were connected. But often what we heard was inspired by an *active*, unrequited sense of wrong, not just childhood experience intended to inform the past. This kind of narrative was really about legal and political lobbying, involving an effort to bring public attention to something that rankled, in the hope that those who hear might share a sense of the wrongness of it.

But if people listening to these accounts of active injustices did feel sympathy, it was usually shallow and fleeting. It takes a great deal to attract a public's attention, and even more to move it (or the most activist parts of it) to action. When every media venue is replete with images and descriptions of horror and atrocity, what makes one cause stand out against others? How does one attract the easily distracted and impel the apathetic to involvement?

With reference to this problem, the TRC began with the advantage of the attention-getting nature of the violence and the innocence of its victims; it began with an astonishing repertoire of all the poignant indignities suffered by many of the children incarcerated in residential schools and their aftershocks in families and communities. Part of this follows from the nature of child abuse and in particular the sexual abuse of children as a moral wrong. In the dominant themes that emerged in the hearings, we have what is quite possibly the worst crime in private life, the sexual abuse of children, applied in the context of one of the worst wrongs in public life, the purposeful, policy-driven elimination of a people. And while it is true that only a relatively small number of individuals were responsible for sexual predation in the schools, the effects of their acts have ramified broadly, in more ways than the immediate suffering they caused. They have also influenced ideas of trauma and the limits of compassionate understanding. In the public mind, it is easy for one compelling instance to stand for the many. There is a kind of symbolic generalization that occurs in popular opinion when attention is fixed on an especially forceful image or idea. But there is a major drawback to giving the public the dishes it desires (in Gabriel Tarde's terms).[6] The goal of expressing affirmation toward survivors is fundamentally at odds with cultivating a historical truth to serve as a foundation for a new narrative of the state.

Seeking historical truth in conditions in which testimony often has heightened qualities of public performance, or in which approval is garnered for emotional poignancy, moral clarity, and narrative continuity, is inimical to "historical truth." Under such circumstances, as Donald Spence puts it, "the memory becomes a bribe; the more it sparkles, the more it seems to fill a narrative niche, the more likely it is made of fool's gold."[7]

By constant exposure to things that appeal, including (sadly) those that disgust and horrify, publics more readily lose touch with the banality of evil (to use Hannah Arendt's term).[8] They are unattracted to things like treaty violations, or assimilation policies in legislative form, even though these may be consequential for peoples' lives. Evidence of the ultimate source of residential school experience—the federal government's misguided policies and broken regimes of implementation—are filed away in archives, beyond the public's attentions and imaginations. Consistent with the dynamics of witnessing before audiences, attentions are fixed on the compassion-inducing remembrances of violated bodies and broken spirits.

SOLITUDE

There is a tremendous gulf between the occurrence of a traumatic event and the ability of victims to narrate that experience publicly. Of course, there have long been models available for the public revelation of personal failings in the Western intellectual and religious traditions, at least since Augustus. But while Christian notions (and their accompanying institutions) of confession as a pathway to self-knowledge and atonement of sin have long been present and available, there is still something new about the readiness with which confession, in the form of intimately narrating the suffering of the self as a consequence of the sins of others, is being taken up as a pathway of rights claims and remedies. Perhaps the voluntary lack of privacy in various forms of new media is part of a movement toward self-revelation or self-exposure to anonymous others, a kind of taken-for-granted confessional of self-representation.

Through this ethic of self-revelation in the context of human rights discourse, we can also see dramatic changes in the normative foundations of belonging. In this book I have described a situation in which survivors are increasingly honoured and publicly visible, while the priests, brothers, and nuns who once worked in the schools are implicitly or explicitly categorized as "perpetrators" and called upon to reject and atone for their former values and life commitments. This divide can be seen as an example of a more general phenomenon, the institutional production of *solitudes*. I am taking this term from Hugh MacLennan's 1945 novel *Two Solitudes*, where it referred to the solidarities and separation of English and French Canadians, and am applying it more generally to those forms of knowledge and belonging within particular regimes of law that speak past one another while creating conditions for internal conformity of behaviour and uniformity of belief. I am generalizing the idea of a solitude to include new and emerging communities of affirmation and exclusion.

One of the most significant qualities of Canada's TRC is the extent to which it has been able to shape a coherent world view out of the range of possible experiences arising out of childhood memory. Considering the immense variety of grievances and sources of trauma invoked in statements to the Commission, the affirmation and naturalization of the concept of the Indian residential school survivor was that much more of an accomplishment. The Commission not only managed to make the most repellent forms of abuse and the most intense, protracted forms of suffering "sayable," but it also made these the dominant themes of a distinctive, powerful kind of public testimony. Ideas about suffering, trauma, victimhood, and school experience (predominantly defined as survivor experience); ideas about the clergy, the priests and nuns, of Christianity, of discipline; these ideas emerge when people speak. And one senses that their memories are real, starkly present, and emotionally evocative, both to the narrators in their summoning of memories and to their audiences in their listening.

The connections between people brought together within this coherence of common experience were sometimes evident in testimonial activity, with survivors appearing together at the microphone, supporting one another—sometimes with gestures of consolation—through the ordeal of bearing witness. As one survivor, Gus Joshua, pointed out in his statement to the Commission, "It's like a secret bond, because we all have the pain."[9] Another speaker, Rose-Marie Prosper, described it as a kind of kinship: "I consider all school survivors my family ... I call them brother and sister, even though we're not related."[10] In the high-profile Commissioner's Sharing Panels, those who were connected in this way supported each other through their testimony, sometimes appearing together at the table and in sequence on the speaker's list.

Another kind of solitude, a more literal form of loneliness, is a condition of those who reject this conformity, who choose to be out of step with others: the former residential school students who refuse to speak publicly or to meet the expectations of testimony, whose sense of shame is too great or who feel they have nothing to offer; it also includes the priests and nuns struggling to come to terms with rejection of the institutional values to which they once unquestioningly adhered. Their experiences as they see them are not being remembered, not entered into the archive intended to make up Canadians' new sense of themselves, as citizens of a state seeking absolution. In part, this exclusion was an outcome of the Settlement Agreement's stark portrayal of the residential school experience, that is to say, a straightforward result of the structure of restitution out of which much of the testimony given to the Commission developed. Here, the world consisted of claimants and Persons of Interest, translated crudely as victims and perpetrators.

The act of bearing witness to the Commission can be seen as a venue for a personal struggle with traumatic memory, while simultaneously being considered by organizers and participants as a remedy for trauma through personal affirmation and self-expression. This means that, more than in other truth commissions, the act or process of speaking involved the challenge of breaking down the barriers of childhood memory, adding a sense of poignancy and personal urgency to the resulting narratives. It also means that giving statements involved a process by which trauma was shaped and represented, while providing an opportunity to observe the unfolding of new paradigms of history, suffering, and selfhood.

If the concept of trauma or post-traumatic stress can become a guidepost for personal identity, the concept of historical trauma can accomplish much the same for a group or community. Even without direct use of the term "historical trauma," the ideas on which it is based—ideas of intergenerational transmission of suffering in consequence of mass crime—are present, if not pervasive, in the work of the Commission and in the experiential reference points of those who call themselves survivors.

Here we have a category of belonging with a foundation in the names contained in school registries, extended to include key markers of experience. And as part of the healing process, survivors and their supporters constructed a sense of supportive belonging. At the same time, they formed an ontological niche protected from, and at times actively defending itself against, competing opinions—a solitude.

This is to say, the sense of injustice is more than a symptom of the accumulation of grievances; it can be at the same time a foundation for group membership. For one thing, collective claims are necessarily a source of common belonging among those who are claimants and who are therefore potential beneficiaries of restitution. Those whose grievances are without avenues of redress or persuasion are no different, except insofar as they also have a moral boundary of being unjustly excluded, misunderstood, and alone (in company with others) against the world. These are favourable conditions for a community of affirmation that exists—usually online—in a closed, self-reinforcing ontological space, protecting itself from contrary opinion even as it draws energy from the possibility of encounter with it.[11]

Didier Fassin and Richard Rechtman make the important observation that the concept of trauma has developed a broad application, to the point that not only the sufferers of violence count among the traumatized, but also witnesses and those who committed violence.[12] In the aftermaths of the Algerian and Vietnam wars, trauma was considered to have burdened not only the immediate sufferers of violence, but also those who colluded with or participated in atrocities. Recognizing the humanity of even these participants in violence was an essential step toward more completely understanding and recovering from the burden of the past.

One of the notable qualities of the Truth and Reconciliation Commission on Indian Residential Schools in Canada is the absence of a similar effort to include the priests, brothers, nuns, and laypeople who worked in the schools among those who might be suffering guilt, nightmares, "flashbacks," or "triggers" resulting from their experience. The concept of reconciliation simply does not extend that far. For Morley Googoo, addressing a gathering of the Outreach Residential School Atlantic Committee, the solution to the challenge of reconciliation was to be found within: "We have to reconcile among ourselves."[13] This view was consistent with a consensus in this meeting, to the effect that "Reconciliation starts at home," and "We've always had knowledge about how to reconcile," at least in the sense of restoring peace among those in conflict in the community.[14] In some of the statements given in Commission hearings, this understanding of reconciliation was extended only as far as the idea that the state has reconciliatory obligations, as in Myrna Whiteduck's sense that "reconciliation means reparation."[15] And in Montreal, Alvin Tolley was among those for whom hope lay in international criminal law: "To have a true reconciliation we are asking justice from the International Court to resolve Canada's genocide."[16] But the inclusion of former school workers in the category of survivors as a possibility for establishing a point of compassion and reconciliation between them was, to my knowledge, never discussed or acted on.

It is not that the raw material for such an extension of empathy wasn't there. A nun once told me in vivid detail about the arrival of five- and six-year-old girls from small northern settlements to their rendezvous point in front of the imposing edifice of the new school, emphasizing her overwhelming mixed feelings of sympathy and sorrow and daunting sense of responsibility. She described how the newly arrived girls, terrified by the size of the building, the long stairway, and the open door through which they had to pass, sat on the stairs with their back to the entrance, moving up each step one at a time until they reached the top and were close enough to stand, turn, and enter in one motion.

To extend this point further, there are very likely priests and survivors who could find points of common experience in their wrongful (or wrongfully enacted) identification by the Indian Residential Schools Adjudication Secretariat as "Persons of Interest," probably the furthest extension one could make of the collective harm wrought by the schools. Yet the broad, almost forgiving application of trauma that occurred in the aftermath of recent wars does not seem to apply broadly to those who once worked in Indian residential schools and who are therefore commonly seen as complicit in their operation. Acceptance and inclusion does not extend to those whose memories and moral commitments might run counter to a conventionalized survivor experience.

The energy of a sympathetic audience does not negate the filtering, excluding effects of the Commission's mandate or of journalistic/public interest. The focus in both is really on the past, on the residential schools, and more narrowly on the open wounds, which consist of the awful events being narrated and the visible suffering of the narrator. At the same time the public venues of the Commission, through the emotional power of survivor testimony, applied conditions of moral insecurity to unwanted narratives, to those who offered perspectives that in significant ways contradicted or challenged the dominant themes of history and experience, of cultural genocide, systemic childhood trauma, and the durable intergenerational consequences of multifaceted oppression.

We can speculate that there is a wider context to this enclosure, that it is an outcome of the successful dynamics of justice lobbying by aboriginal peoples in the Americas, and more broadly in the international movement of indigenous peoples.[17] In both domestic and international rights claims, aboriginal peoples have had historically recent political success through their engagements with new processes of justice lobbying, of making claims through public audiences as a way to gain leverage with judiciaries, legislatures, and governments. This is a process that calls for a selective focus on the worst abuses of states and the most colourful and picturesque qualities of the claimants to be emphasized. Rights claims are "pitched" in this way to impersonal, abstract public consumers of suffering and injustice; and the qualities of injustice, trauma, and, in a contrary direction, cultural vitality and spiritualism—qualities to which public audiences are likely to respond—are refined and reformulated largely in accordance with their supposed, obliquely indicated, preferences. The statements of residential school survivors in TRC hearings can be seen as consistent with these lobbying dynamics. If this background to the TRC's claim assertions and lobbying holds true, it is part of a much more generalized condition in which nation-states recognize a commensurable field of "soft law," and in which there is growing professionalization and specialization in the competition for public support and influence in a market of moral activism.[18]

The potential connections between claimants and their publics are facilitated by new media and the extended reach of collaboratively constructed imaginings and images of injustice. The need to repeat messages and to present them in simple form means that interest groups sponsoring justice campaigns are themselves persuaded of the ideas they are trying to communicate. At the same time, the dynamics of the production of knowledge through new conceptions and institutions of rights and humanitarianism are constitutive not just of political and legal resources and avenues of redress, but of new ways of being and belonging in the world.

With these dynamics of public justice in mind, it becomes easier to see the source of ideas that reify the categories of survivor and perpetrator and place them beyond the reach of reconciliation. It is not (or not only) the influence of the regime of restitution, with its own guiding incentives, categories, and preferences; it is also an outcome of the goal of national-scale persuasion, which defines and clarifies for public consumption an essential self of spectacular suffering, caused by a personalized (in the sense of not being abstract) offender, offset by the pageantry of ceremonial healing.

As a consequence of this, two fundamentally contrary paradigms of the history and experience of residential schools are being fixed in place, with one virtually excluded (and/or self-excluded) by the structure of the proceedings of the TRC. The focus on perpetrators and victims through the prism of childhood memories and life histories of suffering and healing distracts public attention from ongoing forms of neglect and active sources of indignation for which the state is responsible. The views encouraged and cultivated in the course of the Commission's work were influenced by the emotional and persuasive power of survivor testimony, which follows quite simply from the repulsion and indignation evoked by the idea of child abuse. But there is a point at which such testimony fills the space needed to understand the actual dynamics of residential institutions, the motives behind their establishment, the causes behind the corruption of their goals, and the qualities they might have in common with other, more contemporary forms of misguided power and opinion.

NOTES

1   "Electrified Chair Used to Punish Children, Commission Hears," *CBC News, Canada*, 29 January 2013, accessed 26 February 2013, http://www.cbc.ca/news/

canada/thunder-bay/story/2013/01/29/sby-truth-reconciliation-fort-albany.
html.

2 "Truth Commission Begins Saskatchewan Hearings," *CBC News, Saskatchewan,*
16 January 2012, accessed February 2013, http://www.cbc.ca/news/canada/sas-
katchewan/story/2012/01/16/sk-truth-reconciliation-regina.html.

3 "Residential School Survivor Says Compensation Process Failed Him," *CBC
News, North,* 11 February 2013, accessed 26 February 2013, http://www.cbc.ca/
news/canada/north/story/2013/02/11/north-iap-fails-survivor.html.

4 I have borrowed language here from Teresa Phelps, who writes: "If one of the
significant things that victims lose in oppression is the ability to use language,
then language as retribution begins to make sense." Theresa Phelps, *Shattered
Voices: Language, Violence, and the Work of Truth Commissions* (Philadelphia, PA:
University of Pennsylvania Press, 2004), 39.

5 Matt James, "A Carnival of Truth? Knowledge, Ignorance, and the Canadian
Truth and Reconciliation Commission," *International Journal of Transitional Justice* 6 (2012): 183.

6 "We must deplore the inventive genius expended on clever lies, specious fables, all
continually contradicted, continually revived, for the simple pleasure of serving
each public the dishes it desires, of expressing what they think to be true, or what
they wish to be true." Gabriel Tarde, *On Communication and Social Influence,* ed.
and trans. Terry Clark (Chicago, IL: University of Chicago Press, 1969), 293.

7 Donald Spence, *Narrative Truth and Historical Truth: Meaning and Interpretation
in Psychoanalysis* (New York: Norton, 1982), 97. Spence is writing of the relationship between analyst and patient in psychoanalysis, but his observations nevertheless apply to the "transference" between witness and audience in testimony to
truth commissions.

8 Hannah Arendt, *Eichmann in Jerusalem: A Report on the Banality of Evil* (New
York: Penguin, 2006).

9 Gus Joshua, TRC Atlantic National Event, Halifax, 28 October 2011.

10 Rose-Marie Prosper, TRC Atlantic National Event, Halifax, 28 October 2011.

11 See Cass Sunstein, *Infotopia: How Many Minds Produce Knowledge* (Oxford, UK:
Oxford University Press, 2006).

12 Didier Fassin and Richard Rechtman, *The Empire of Trauma: An Inquiry into the
Condition of Victimhood,* trans. Rachel Gomme (Princeton, NJ: Princeton University Press, 2009), 20–21.

13 Chief Morley Googoo, statement to the Outreach Residential School Atlantic
Committee, meeting under the auspices of the Atlantic Policy Congress of First
Nations Chiefs Secretariat, Glooscap Heritage Centre, Millbrook, Nova Scotia,
6 March 2012.

14 Interview with Andrea Colfer, Millbrook, Nova Scotia, 7 March 2012.

15 Myrna Whiteduck, Commissioner's Sharing Panel, TRC Saskatoon National Event, 22 June 2012.

16 Alvin Tolley, Commissioner's Sharing Panel, TRC Montreal National Event, 26 April 2013.

17 I further discuss the international realm of indigenous rights and identity in *The Origins of Indigenism: Human Rights and the Politics of Identity* (Berkeley and Los Angeles: University of California Press, 2003).

18 See Paul Rabinow's observations on human rights and humanitarianism in *Anthropos Today: Reflections on Modern Equipment* (Princeton, NJ: Princeton University Press, 2003), 25.

EPILOGUE

RECEPTION

Wilton Littlechild, with his long experience as an indigenous expert in the UN (I first met him in meetings of the Working Group on Indigenous Populations in Geneva in the 1990s), was the ideal person to present the work of the Commission to a standing-room-only audience at a side event in the 2016 Session of the Permanent Forum on Indigenous Issues. He carried the authority of someone who not only had served as commissioner for Canada's TRC as it gathered nearly 7,000 statements from residential school survivors, but also as someone who was himself taken to a residential school at age six and who had spent fourteen years of his life in several of these institutions. Speaking without notes, Littlechild began describing the work of the Commission with an emphasis on the experience of survivors and their families: "This is about children and what happens to children when you take them away from their parents. And about parents and what happens when you take their children away from them." Explaining how the commissioners approached the "sacred trust" of their leading role in the work of the Commission, Littlechild pointed out straightforwardly, "We thought we should get guidance from the survivors themselves." Based on this guidance, the Commission emphasized hearing from and supporting the survivors, while recognizing how difficult it was for them to give expression to painful memories. "Some said 'it hurts too much to tell my story,'" Littlechild recalled, "but I will sing you a song or do a painting"; these forms of truth telling, along with documents, transcripts, and audio and video recordings of statements, will be housed in the National Centre for Truth and Reconciliation hosted by the University of Manitoba.

Littlechild spoke about how the Commission, through its investigative work, now had the names of at least 4,300 students who died in the schools. (On hearing this, there was a moan of sympathy from the audience.) This figure was arrived at through the ongoing work of a National Residential School Student Death Register. In some cases, the Commission sponsored funerary rituals for those family members who did not have a chance to grieve the loss of their loved ones. He recalled some of the grim evidence he had seen in the course of his work as a commissioner: a photo of four children, huddled together, frozen to death after they had run away from their school; testimony from survivors who, as four-year-old girls, had pins stuck in their tongues for speaking their language. Such information on the schools was to be a foundation not only for understanding the past, but also for reforming aboriginal policy more broadly, with the *United Nations Declaration on the Rights of Indigenous Peoples* serving as a reference point for recognizing treaty and constitutional rights and a framework for reconciliation. "We take that truth," Littlechild said, "and try to shape reconciliation."

Completing the work of the Commission and presenting it to an international audience at the UN had by no means been easy. As I have discussed at several points in this book, some of the limitations of the Commission were built into its mandate, while others spilled over from weaknesses in the *Indian Residential School Settlement Act* (IRSSA), in which the mandate of the Commission was defined and regimes of compensation for survivors of the schools elaborated.

As part of the tasks set out in the IRSSA, for example, the government contracted seventeen private investigation firms to locate those people who were accused of physically and sexually abusing students in federal Indian residential schools. The full extent of this effort came to light only after the TRC had completed its work. This process eventually resulted in a list of 5,315 alleged abusers, including both employees and students in the schools. On the surface, this list may seem to have offered a solid foundation for the kind of justice that many school survivors were hoping would be an outcome of the Settlement Agreement. The purpose of identifying these individuals, however, was not to investigate the accusations with a view to possibly pressing criminal charges against them, but to invite them to participate in Independent Assessment Process (IAP) hearings to determine compensation for residential school survivors. Investigators were responsible merely for locating the accused, not inquiring into the accusations against them. There was no amnesty for those who came forward and agreed to participate (as there was under some conditions in South Africa's TRC) but neither was any of the information compiled in the investigation released to law enforcement.

The results of the investigations therefore remained as "allegations" against "alleged" abusers, a circumstance that resulted in the disaffection of the priests, brothers, and nuns who were subjected to unsubstantiated allegations and the accompanying "rebranding" of their vocation, and an equally strong sense of injustice among many survivors, who wanted to publicly identify their abusers and see justice done. Only 708 alleged abusers, of the more than 5,300 located by investigators, agreed to participate in the IAP hearings. Far from feeling reconciled with the survivors, those who were collectively viewed as alleged "perpetrators" were indignant, and felt that they were themselves the victims of an injustice; far from feeling reconciled toward those who ran the schools, those who came to be seen (and considered themselves) survivors of the schools felt that perpetrators had escaped a criminal reckoning and that, despite (or because of) the work of the TRC, justice had not been done.

The prohibition on identifying perpetrators of abuse sometimes found its way into the work of the Commission, expressed in the form of frustration among those survivors who came to the hearings to report abuse. Some ignored the Commission's guidelines for avoiding the names of perpetrators in giving statements. Sylvester Green, recalling his statement about the Edmonton Residential School to one of the Survivor Committee's Sharing Circles in a YouTube video, offers an example: "I said, this is all bullshit. Here's the names of the people that abused me, three white assholes that abused me in Edmonton. [Gives the names.] These bastards, they are the ones that abused me when I was a little kid." The Settlement Agreement and mandate of the Commission reified the categories of "survivor" and "perpetrator" and, rather than bring them into meaningful encounter, pulled them further apart.

Beyond the limitations of its mandate, however, the federal government proved to be another significant obstacle to the work of the Commission. There was, in particular, an ongoing battle between the Commission and the Harper government concerning access to archival records, which was coming to a head around the time that the first edition of this book went to press, and which took on greater importance since. As I discuss briefly in chapter 7, the government had refused to provide the Commission with access to millions of documents in Library and Archives Canada. A January 2013 decision by the Ontario Superior Court of Justice forced the Government of Canada to compile and organize all the documents that the Commission said it needed to fulfill its mandate. The documents were not released until more than a year after this decision, requiring the mandate of the Commission to be similarly extended by a year. Some 60,000 boxes of material in four Library and Archives Canada locations were released to the Commission in the summer of 2014, forcing the Commission to rush its research to produce its final report within a time frame that would still benefit from the momentum of the Commission hearings. Documents released to the Commission late in its mandate included, for example, death certificates of aboriginal children who had died in British Columbia, which the Commission needed to cross-reference with residential school records to determine how many children had died in the schools.[1]

The need for recourse to the courts to gain access to documents was combined with desultory participation by federal government officials in Commission events. A pattern continued throughout the work of the Commission in which officials from

Aboriginal Affairs and Northern Development would attend for a few hours on the first day of a National Event, offer a brief statement supporting the work of the Commission, and then leave, without even a low-level representative present during the remainder of the hearings. The federal government approached the TRC almost as a form of political pollution, with exposure and the risk of infection to be kept to a strict minimum.

This pattern of government refusal and foot-dragging was to continue throughout the mandate of the Commission. Then a newly elected Liberal government under Justin Trudeau was sworn into office on 4 November 2015, just a month before the Commission was to present its final report. The election was too late to influence the pattern of government non-cooperation during the hearings, but was to have important implications for subsequent reception of the Commission's work, above all its recommendations or "Calls to Action," oriented toward sweeping reforms of indigenous peoples' relationships with Canadian society and its institutions.

When I attended the fifteenth Session of the UN Permanent Forum on Indigenous Issues in May 2016, this change had already been made manifest. Canadian Justice Minister and Attorney General Jody Wilson-Raybould opened the Session in the meeting room of the General Assembly with a statement on the new direction to be taken in Canada's relationship with indigenous peoples, first by introducing herself as an indigenous person, "My traditional name is Puglass. I come from the Musgamagw Tsawatineuk and Laich-Kwil-Tach people from the westcoast of Canada. I am part of the Eagle clan and my father, Hemas Kla-Lee-Lee-Kla, is our hereditary chief." The fact that she, as an indigenous person, stood as the holder of this powerful office, she said, "speaks volumes to how far our country has come but also how far we intend to go." Conveying the intention of the new prime minister to renew the federal government's relationship with indigenous peoples, Wilson-Raybould went on to outline her own approach to this challenge, in which she began with the observation that "we need to find long-term solutions to decades old problems as we seek to deconstruct our colonial legacy. Important to this work will be implementing the Calls to Action set out in the recent report of the Truth and Reconciliation Commission which considered the legacy of the Indian residential schools."[2] At the conclusion of her statement, the justice minister was given a standing ovation. Indigenous delegates and UN officials attending the meeting were impressed and hopeful that Canada was now in a position to provide a new model to the international community for how a government should treat its indigenous peoples.

After this rousing beginning, the "honeymoon," not surprisingly, did not last long. The extent to which the government of a country with a national economy based largely on extractive industries could rapidly and thoroughly overhaul its policies toward indigenous peoples should probably have been in doubt from the outset. One of the most significant disappointments for indigenous activists was Prime Minister Trudeau's approval in November 2016 of the Kinder Morgan Trans Mountain Pipeline expansion project, building on an existing 1,150 km pipeline from Edmonton to the Pacific coast. Protesters vowed to engage in a long battle. This is likely to be one of many decisions that indigenous leaders will find objectionable as the government seeks to balance opportunities for revenue from extractive industries against the environmental and justice concerns of indigenous peoples and their allies.

Yet the transition of governments that marked the end of 2015, and that accompanied the completion of the TRC's mandate, still signalled a significant reorientation of policy toward indigenous peoples, arguably one of the most important to have occurred within any state government on the international scene. The TRC was front and centre in this transition. From being considered a pariah institution, to which the government gave public lip service and behind-the-scenes sabotage, the Truth and Reconciliation Commission was given new standing, with its final report and its Calls to Action serving as a reference point for policy reform across a broad spectrum of Canadian society.

THE CALLS TO ACTION

The focus of the Commission's efforts up to and including its closing ceremonies and the public unveiling of its five-volume final report in December 2015 involved media outreach to conventional media outlets, local newspapers, journals, and televised news outlets that covered each of the National Events, as well as the use of the TRC's web page, sponsored videos, Facebook page, and Twitter feed. This was the "consciousness-raising" aspect of the Commission's work, the effort to overcome what the organizers saw as widespread ignorance and apathy among non-indigenous Canadians concerning a dark chapter of their nation's history. There was a limited window of opportunity to engage in public outreach that drew directly from the statements and physical presence of survivors at the Commission's events. As the TRC moved toward the completion of its mandate, this aspect of its work developed into a veritable campaign to convey information about the history of residential schools and the work of the Commission.

Truth commissions do not always produce the results of their inquiries with timeliness or proficiency. South Africa's hearings ran for fifteen months during 1996 and 1997, but it was not until 2003 that the final two volumes of the report were presented to President Thabo Mbeki, who only then decided which of the recommendations to endorse and implement.[3] Canada's truth commission, by contrast, was extraordinarily efficient. The report was in fact being produced through most of the period in which it was conducting hearings, with the result that there was a very short delay between its closing events on 3 June 2015 and the submission of its completed final report on 15 December that year. And when its work was completed and the report submitted, the influence of the Commission took quite a different direction.

One of the TRC's proudest accomplishments are its 94 recommendations, or "Calls to Action," released together with its final report. These Calls have galvanized officials, activists, and academics alike in a process of policy reform, largely under the impetus of the change in direction announced by the new Liberal government. Unlike the Royal Commission on Aboriginal Peoples, which in 1996 laid out an ambitious set of guidelines for policy reform in a 4,000 page report that basically collected dust, Canada's TRC has produced a set of recommendations that are being recognized and acted on, probably to an extent that is exceeding their authors' expectations. The TRC went far beyond a restrictive interpretation of its mandate to address the experience and wider consequences of Indian residential schools, broadening its conclusions to include essentially every conceivable aspect of indigenous peoples' relationships with the dominant society.

The recommendation with arguably the farthest-reaching implications is number 43, which calls on the federal government, provinces, territories, and municipalities of Canada "to fully adopt and implement the *United Nations Declaration on the Rights of Indigenous Peoples* as the framework for reconciliation."[4] The Trudeau government announced its intention to implement the Declaration at the 2016 Session of the Permanent Forum on Indigenous Issues as part of the policy reform that is closely interconnected with its promise to implement the TRC's recommendations. This would include the Declaration's call for recognition of indigenous peoples' rights to self-determination (Article 3) and free, prior, and informed consent (FPIC) (Articles 10, 11, 19, 28, 29, and 32). FPIC calls for a much higher threshold of discussion and approval by indigenous peoples on all developments (including extractive and legislative projects) affecting their interests.[5] Because of this, it has arguably surpassed self-determination as a source of leverage in international law employed by indigenous activists and their supporters. The TRC's Calls to Action are a reference point for this shift in Canada's legal relationship with indigenous peoples.

The influence of the Commission has already gone far beyond the domains of international law and state governance to include a wide range of institutions and actors. The TRC's Calls to Action have been taken up by corporations, philanthropic organizations and other NGOs, and institutions of higher learning, all engaged in efforts to bring their policies and practices more in line with the ideals of "reconciliation" (however that might be understood).

The Faculty of Law at McGill University, where I am employed as a professor, is a case in point. As soon as the TRC released its summary report and Calls to Action in June 2015, the Faculty's attention was drawn to Call to Action number 28, which calls upon "law schools in Canada to require all law students to take a course in Aboriginal people and the law, which includes the history and legacy of residential schools, the *United Nations Declaration on the Rights of Indigenous Peoples*, Treaties and Aboriginal rights, Indigenous law, and Aboriginal–Crown relations. This will require skills-based training in intercultural competency, conflict resolution, human rights, and antiracism."[6] This prompted the Faculty of Law to develop a response to the Call to Action, first by investigating and reporting on the initiatives that were already in place, which would then highlight the gaps and weaknesses in the Faculty's approaches to faculty recruitment, admissions, and legal education relative to the goals identified by the TRC.[7] The next steps in this reform will involve implementing further curricular reforms and other measures intended to give indigenous people a central place in the life of the Faculty. Law schools and faculties elsewhere in Canada have adopted similar measures. As a result, it will likely soon be virtually impossible to obtain a legal education in Canada without having some knowledge of the emerging field known as "indigenous legal traditions."

Another aspect of the Commission's influence has to do with the phenomenon of "travelling models," an apparatus or protocol for intervention inscribed with particular ideas about reality that "transfer as blueprints to new sites."[8] Canada's TRC has taken an active role in translating its institutional and ideological model of human rights intervention for application in other locations. The most direct example of this is the recent work of the Native American Boarding School Healing Coalition (NABS), which is petitioning the US government "to acknowledge the true history of the US Policy to forcibly assimilate Native Americans through boarding schools which resulted in cultural genocide and legacies of inter-generational trauma." Inspired directly by Canada's truth commission, NABS is "creating a national campaign using multi-media as a means to educate and unite around the inter-generational trauma caused by boarding schools in the U.S."[9] The connections between Indian residential schools in Canada and boarding schools for Native Americans in the United States make this effort a logical extension of the model of Canada's truth commission. Given the globally widespread nature of the residential school model as a tool of assimilation, there are many other places where Canada's model could potentially also apply.

The influence of Canada's TRC on domestic policy and international models of transitional justice is, of course, a complex work in progress. There is ongoing resistance to its insights and calls for reform, as exemplified by Senator Lynn Beyak's lengthy discourse on the floor of the Senate, which revisited Canadian history and emphasized the willing participation of aboriginal peoples in the civilizing efforts initiated on their behalf.[10] In response to this discourse, she was removed from her position on the Senate's Committee on Aboriginal Peoples. Very likely Beyak represents a constituency that is disaffected by the reassessment of Canadian colonial history through such initiatives as the TRC. In light of this episode, it remains to be seen how far the Commission's influence will go in terms of meeting its more ambitious goals of reforming Canadians' sense of their history and creating a favourable climate for policy reform for the primary benefit of indigenous peoples. My sense is that the Commission has accomplished (and is accomplishing) a great deal, in ways that are inseparable from wider changes in federal politics, but that obstacles remain in the form of entrenched conservative ideas and political identities.

The substance of my concerns about this and other truth commissions does not have much to do with their capacity to raise awareness or influence policy, which can of course vary greatly from one social and political context to another. It has to do more with the regimes of knowledge that are built into the commissions' mandates and that are constructed through victim-centric approaches to "statement sharing" or "bearing witness." Although I have framed these concerns in the form of an ethnographic inquiry, my intention is wider, having to do with an effort to understand a contemporary phenomenon that has become a central quality of human rights claims-making. I will therefore conclude this epilogue by revisiting the phenomenon of victim centrism in collective justice claims, informed by what I observed during the conclusion of Canada's TRC.

VICTIM CENTRISM

The "victim centrism" of truth commissions involves the production of regimes of truth that ideally reflect the values, experiences, and identities of those who have been historically subjected to systemic, mass-scale human rights abuses by their own states. As Gerhard Anders and Olaf Zenker point out in their overview of recent truth and reconciliation commissions in Africa, the aftermath of violence is usually one in which the terms of new beginnings are negotiated, in which "former combatants and their leaders, politicians, civil society activists, village elders and ordinary people advance their views on how to realize justice or seek to secure a place in the new political system."[11] That no such inclusive negotiation took place in Canada's TRC is largely an outcome of its victim-centred mandate and its educational, publicity-oriented goals, which had the effect of reifying survivor experience, with a focus on sexual abuse and crises of cultural loss.

In its orientation toward victim affirmation, Canada's TRC is not alone. Nneoma Nwogu emphasizes the consequences of victim centrism in her discussion of truth commissions that aspired to overcome the harms of ethnicity-based violence in Africa. These include a tendency for the categories of "victim" and "perpetrator" to be essentialized and for the commissions to shy away from exploration of the complex motivations behind violent actions. Instead, the classifications of grand narratives become "entrenched in the truth-telling space and unwittingly restrain victims' and perpetrators' voices within imposed categories."[12] The victim centrism in Canada's truth commission can thus be seen as an example of a much wider phenomenon that has accompanied the global human rights movement during the past several decades, in which the emphasis on survivor testimony is gaining in prominence over judicial powers as a central feature of collective justice claims and of human rights inquiry.

I am thus led to return briefly to the central questions of the book, which, if anything, are already more relevant than they were three years ago: What is gained and what is lost when truth commissions focus on survivor testimony? Are victim narratives a substitute for "actionable" commission powers (including the power to compel witnesses) and state accountability? And, finally, what do such truth commissions produce in terms of the sense of self, how people understand the essence of who they are as individuals and collectivities?

Truth commissions are now generally less concerned with the exercise of judicial powers and the quest for justice and more concerned with affirming the experience of victims or "survivors" in a quest for knowledge. The Nuremberg trials offer a point of reference for this issue, even though they were not part of a truth commission as we know it, in that the prosecutors explicitly wanted to *avoid* testimony from victims of the Holocaust and to prosecute Nazi officials solely on the basis of the material evidence, which they had in abundance. Several decades later, a completely different approach was taken in the prosecution of a high-ranking Nazi official: the chief prosecutor of Adolf Eichmann, Gideon Hausner, in the first internationally televised event of its kind, made the emotionally-laden oral testimony of victims central to his case, which became as much about documenting the experience of the Holocaust as about establishing Eichmann's part in it.[13] Another turning point in the reliance on survivor narratives was South Africa's Truth and Reconciliation Commission, which explicitly avoided the use of juridical powers, but chose instead a reconciliatory path in dealing with past atrocities that emphasized victim testimony.[14]

This shift from a juridical focus to an emphasis on emotion-laden experiential narrative has more recently accompanied an increase in the deployment of survivor testimony in "leverage politics." This is a genre of witness reporting that Winnifred Tate observed, for example, in encounters between Colombian activists and US policymakers to whom the activists were appealing for changes to US programs in their country. The practice of *testimonio* by the Colombian villagers, Tate observed, involved "particular forms of emotional expression as well as the presumed implication of the listener in political commitments through the newly acquired comprehension of suffering."[15] Accounts of devastating personal tragedies, of villages burned, crops destroyed, family members and friends disappeared and brutally killed, constituted an unfamiliar form of discourse in Washington and a new strategy toward fostering solidarity between rights claimants and policy-makers.

Giving such testimony is not a normal or natural process. South Africa's TRC, for example, faced difficulty in encouraging witnesses to reveal "unspeakable truths," with many deponents unwilling to publicly revisit the violence and loss they experienced under Apartheid.[16] Presenting credible and sympathizable testimony thus involves cultivating knowledge of a particular kind, from particular sorts of witnesses. For example, in 2016, when talks were taking place in Havana between FARC rebels and the government of Colombia, the Catholic Church under Archbishop Luis Augusto Castro Quiroga took an active role in selecting witnesses from among some 8 million victims of Colombia's civil war and accompanying them in groups of 12 to the talks in Havana. Archbishop Castro told the Catholic News Service that the victims "went with their hearts filled with bitterness, yet they were able to express all that they had lived and felt, and they asked for an explanation of what happened in their situation. At the same time, each victim had the possibility to hear 11 other victims and to realise that they weren't the only ones in the world who suffered."[17] This is another instance of the way that victim identities are institutionally constructed, in this case by selecting from the mass of victims those who most poignantly represented loss, suffering, resilience, and forgiveness in accordance with the values of the Church.

Truth commissions and those engaged in leverage politics appear to be more commonly acting on the insight that, in the process of affirming human rights claims, a central place is occupied by public opinion and access to public information. This lends an insidious kind of market logic to claiming recognition of human rights violations, with sympathy as a limited currency in competition with other claimants. Victims are called upon to present themselves as worthy subjects of compassion and engagement appealing to the consumers of justice causes. In the process, they are called upon to be perfect, sometimes even more than perfect, to be models of dignity and worth, in competition with others who are also claiming rights and sympathy following from *their* victimhood. Under these circumstances a collective rights claim does not gain the requisite degree of attention (and therefore does not ultimately affect the conditions of oppression) if the public perceives a failure of the claimants in incarnating an ideal of victimhood. There is a fundamental dilemma at work in collective human rights claims: victims of state-sanctioned violence become invisible to public perception and indignation (and are therefore excluded from possibilities of remedy) if they fail to achieve impossible standards of innocence and dignity, standards which are compromised by the actual and inherent effects of violence.

One of the results of victim centrism, in the TRC and similarly oriented truth commissions, is that we hear a great deal about the pain, struggle, and redemption that characterize a particular kind of survivor experience, while our knowledge of the "perpetrators," their motives, and the institutions that harboured them are left obscured. Yet this is precisely the knowledge on which truth commissions should concentrate if the harms of state policies and of the institutions they create are to be properly understood—and avoided. Because of its mandate and its survivor centrism, Canada's truth commission was not only de-judicialized, it was also unable to effectively function with reference to the actual causes of warped disciplinarity, the sources of misguided policies that were the immediate source of the collective harm it sought to address. Under these circumstances, evil becomes a moustache-twisting caricature that stands in the way of complexity, shades of grey, and durable forms of remedy.

That is to say, the survivor affirmation that I have described in this book, and that is now a widespread quality of collective justice claims, comes with a cost. The affirmation and ennoblement of survivor identity obscures the complete range of the consequences of violence and suffering. And the exclusion or discouragement of "perpetrator" narratives keeps out of view a central dimension of institutional harm. There are technologies of knowledge at work in the TRC and other truth commissions that make it all but impossible to reconcile divided societies, that instead cultivate enclosures of indignation as foundations for identity, and that make use of the discomforts of testimony to reinforce the comforts of ontologically invulnerable belonging.

NOTES

1 Connie Walker, "New Documents May Shed Light on Residential School Deaths," *CBC News*, 7 January 2014, accessed 14 April 2017, http://www.cbc.ca/news/indigenous/new-documents-may-shed-light-on-residential-school-deaths-1.2487015.

2 Jody Wilson-Raybould, "Justice Minister Jody Wilson-Raybould's Opening Address at UN Permanent Forum on Indigenous Issues," *Northern Public Affairs*, 9 May 2016, accessed 16 April 2017, http://www.northernpublicaffairs.ca/index/justice-minister-jody-wilson-rayboulds-opening-address-at-un-permanent-forum-on-indigenous-issues.

3 Rita Kesselring, *Bodies of Truth: Law, Memory, and Emancipation in Post-Apartheid South Africa* (Stanford, CA: Stanford University Press, 2017), 25.

4 Truth and Reconciliation Commission of Canada, *TRC Findings*, 2015, accessed 17 April 2017, http://www.trc.ca/websites/trcinstitution/index.php?p=890.

5 For a discussion of FPIC in the Canadian context see Sasha Boutilier, "Free, Prior, and Informed Consent and Reconciliation in Canada: Proposals to Implement Articles 19 and 32 of the UN Declaration on the Rights of Indigenous Peoples." *Western Journal of Legal Studies* 7, no. 1, art. 4 (2017): http://ir.lib.uwo.ca/cgi/viewcontent.cgi?article=1219&context=uwojls.

6   Truth and Reconciliation Commission of Canada, *Truth and Reconciliation Commission of Canada: Calls to Action*, 2015, accessed 17 April 2017, http://www.trc.ca/websites/trcinstitution/File/2015/Findings/Calls_to_Action_English2.pdf.

7   Molly Churchill, "Final Report on McGill Faculty of Law Initiatives Relevant to the Truth & Reconciliation Commission's Report and Calls to Action: Phase 1 of the Faculty's Response," unpublished report (Faculty of Law, McGill University, 2015).

8   Andrea Behrends, Sung-Joon Park, and Richard Rottenburg, "Travelling Models: Introducing an Analytical Concept to Globalisation Studies," in *Travelling Models in African Conflict Management: Translating Technologies of Social Ordering*, ed. Andrea Behrends, Sung-Joon Park, and Richard Rottenburg (Leiden and Boston: Brill, 2014), 1–42. See also Richard Rottenburg, *Far-Fetched Facts: A Parable of Development Aid*, trans. Allison Brown and Tom Lampert (Cambridge, MA: MIT Press, 2009).

9   NABS (Native American Boarding School Healing Coalition), "Moving Forward: NABS Expands Staff and Board: The National Native American Boarding School Healing Coalition (NABS) Hires First Staff Member and Adds Four New Board Members to Help Jumpstart Truth and Reconciliation Process," press release, 2 December 2015, accessed 16 April 2017, http://www.boardingschoolhealing.org/wp-content/uploads/NABS-hires-staff-and-increases-board-of-directors-_12-2-15-Press-Release2.pdf.

10 Senate of Canada. "Latest Debates of the Senate (Hansard)," 7 March 2017, accessed 17 April 2017, https://sencanada.ca/en/content/sen/chamber/421/debates/102db_2017-03-07-e.

11 Gerhard Anders and Olaf Zenker, "Transition and Justice: An Introduction," *Development and Change* 45 (2014): 396.

12 Nneoma Nwogu, "When and Why It Started: Deconstructing Victim-Centered Truth Commissions in the Context of Ethnicity-Based Conflict," *International Journal of Transitional Justice* 4, no. 2 (2010): 276.

13 Sonali Chakravarti, "More than 'Cheap Sentimantality': Victim Testimony at Nuremberg, the Eichmann Trial and Truth Commissions," *Constellations* 15, no. 2 (2008): 223.

14 Richard A. Wilson, *The Politics of Truth and Reconciliation in South Africa* (Cambridge, UK: Cambridge University Press, 2001).

15 Winnifred Tate, "Proxy Citizenship and Transnational Advocacy: Colombian Activists from Putumayo to Washington, DC," *American Ethnologist* 40, no. 1 (2013): 58.

16 Fiona Ross, *Bearing Witness: Women and the Truth and Reconciliation Commission in South Africa* (London: Pluto, 2003).

17 Catholic News Service, "Priests Stand Up for Victims during Colombia Peace Talks," *Catholic Herald*, 22 June 2016, accessed 14 April 2017, http://www.catholicherald.co.uk/news/2016/06/22/priests-stand-up-for-victims-during-colombia-peace-talks.

REFERENCES

Aboriginal Healing Foundation. *1999 Annual Report.* Ottawa: Aboriginal Healing Foundation, 1999. http://www.ahf.ca/downloads/annual-report-99.pdf.

Anders, Gerhard, and Olaf Zenker. "Transition and Justice: An Introduction." *Development and Change* 45, no. 3 (2014): 395–414. https://doi.org/10.1111/dech.12096.

Angeconeb, Garnet. "Speaking My Truth: The Journey to Reconciliation." In *Speaking My Truth: Reflections on Reconciliation and Residential School,* ed. Shelagh Rogers, Mike Degagne, and Jonathan Dewar. Ottawa: Aboriginal Healing Foundation, 2012.

Arendt, Hannah. *Eichmann in Jerusalem: A Report on the Banality of Evil.* New York: Penguin, 2006.

Avruch, Kevin. "Truth and Reconciliation Commissions: Problems in Transitional Justice and the Reconstruction of Identity." *Transcultural Psychiatry* 47, no. 1 (February 2010): 33–49. https://doi.org/10.1177/1363461510362043.

Bartlett, Frederic Charles. *Remembering.* Cambridge, UK: Cambridge University Press, 1932.

Behrends, Andrea, Sung-Joon Park, and Richard Rottenburg. "Travelling Models: Introducing an Analytical Concept to Globalisation Studies." In *Travelling Models in African Conflict Management: Translating Technologies of Social Ordering,* ed. Andrea Behrends, Sung-Joon Park, and Richard Rottenburg, 1–42. Leiden, Boston: Brill, 2014. https://doi.org/10.1163/9789004274099_002.

Bettelheim, Bruno. *Surviving and Other Essays.* London: Thames and Hudson, 1979.

Bieling, Peter, Randi McCabe, and Martin Antony. *Cognitive Behavioral Therapy in Groups.* New York: Guilford, 2006.

Bisset, Alison. *Truth Commissions and Criminal Courts.* Cambridge, UK: Cambridge University Press, 2012. https://doi.org/10.1017/CBO9781139026406.

Borneman, John. *Political Crime and the Memory of Loss*. Bloomington, IN: Indiana University Press, 2011.

Boutilier, Sasha. "Free, Prior, and Informed Consent and Reconciliation in Canada: Proposals to Implement Articles 19 and 32 of the UN Declaration on the Rights of Indigenous Peoples." *Western Journal of Legal Studies* 7, no. 1, art. 4 (2017). http://ir.lib.uwo.ca/cgi/viewcontent.cgi?article=1219&context=uwojls.

Catholic News Service. "Priests Stand Up for Victims during Colombia Peace Talks. *Catholic Herald*. 22 June 2016. Accessed 14 April 2017, http://www.catholicherald.co.uk/news/2016/06/22/priests-stand-up-for-victims-during-colombia-peace-talks.

Chakravarti, Sonali. "More than 'Cheap Sentimantality': Victim Testimony at Nuremberg, the Eichmann Trial and Truth Commissions." *Constellations* 15, no. 2 (2008): 223–35. https://doi.org/10.1111/j.1467-8675.2008.00486.x.

Churchill, Molly. "Final Report on McGill Faculty of Law Initiatives Relevant to the Truth & Reconciliation Commission's Report and Calls to Action: Phase 1 of the Faculty's Response." Unpublished Report, Faculty of Law, McGill University, 2015.

Clifford, James. "Power and Dialogue in Ethnography: Marcel Griaule's Initiation." In *Observers Observed: Essays on Ethnographic Fieldwork*, ed. George Stocking, 121–56. Madison, WI: University of Wisconsin Press, 1983.

Cox, Christy. "Abuse in the Catholic Church." *Dart Center for Journalism and Trauma*, 7 April 2003, accessed 12 September 2013, http://dartcenter.org/content/abuse-in-catholic-church.

Daly, Erin. "Truth Skepticism: An Inquiry into the Value of Truth in Times of Transition." *International Journal of Transitional Justice* 2, no. 1 (2008): 23–41. https://doi.org/10.1093/ijtj/ijn004.

Ducharme, Lori, and Gary Fine. "The Construction of Nonpersonhood and Demonization: Commemorating the Traitorous Reputation of Benedict Arnold." *Social Forces* 73, no. 4 (1995): 1309–31. https://doi.org/10.2307/2580449.

Evans-Campbell, Teresa. "Historical Trauma in American Indian/Native Alaska Communities: A Multilevel Framework for Exploring Impacts on Individuals, Families, and Communities." *Journal of Interpersonal Violence* 23, no. 3 (March 2008): 316–38. https://doi.org/10.1177/0886260507312290.

Fassin, Didier, and Richard Rechtman. *The Empire of Trauma: An Inquiry into the Condition of Victimhood*. Trans. Rachel Gomme. Princeton, NJ: Princeton University Press, 2009.

Fiemeyer, Isabelle. *Marcel Griaule: Citoyen Dogon*. Arles: Actes Sud, 2004.

Fischer, Michael. "Emergent Forms of Life: Anthropologies of Late or Postmodernities." *Annual Review of Anthropology* 28, no. 1 (1999): 455–78. https://doi.org/10.1146/annurev.anthro.28.1.455.

Gadoua, Marie-Pierre. "The Inuit Presence at the First Canadian Truth and Reconciliation National Event." *Études/Inuit/Studies* 34, no. 2 (2010): 167–84. https://doi.org/10.7202/1004096ar.

Goldstein, Daniel. *Outlawed: Between Security and Rights in a Bolivian City*. Durham, NC: Duke University Press, 2012. https://doi.org/10.1215/9780822395607.

Government of Canada. *Indian Residential Schools Settlement Agreement, Schedule "D," Independent Assessment Process (IAP) for Continuing Indian Residential School Abuse Claims*. Ottawa: Government of Canada, 2006. Accessed 29 July 2012, www.residentialschoolsettlement.ca/schedule_d-iap.pdf.

———. *Indian Residential Schools Settlement Agreement, Schedule "N," Mandate for the Truth and Reconciliation Commission*. Ottawa: Government of Canada, 2007. Accessed 20 May 2013, http://www.residentialschoolsettlement.ca/SCHEDULE_N.pdf.

———. *School Decisions*. Ottawa: Government of Canada, 2012. Accessed 16 July 2012, http://www.residentialschoolsettlement.ca/SchoolDecisions.pdf.

Greensboro Truth and Reconciliation Commission Report, Executive Summary, 2006, accessed 9 November 2012, http://www.greensborotrc.org/exec_summary.pdf.

Griaule, Marcel. *Méthode de l'ethnographie*. Ed. Geneviève Calame-Griaule. Paris: Presses universitaires de France, 1957.

Hacking, Ian. *Rewriting the Soul: Multiple Personality and the Sciences of Memory*. Princeton, NJ: Princeton University Press, 1995.

———. *The Social Construction of What?* Cambridge, MA: Harvard University Press, 1999.

Hayner, Priscilla. *Unspeakable Truths: Transitional Justice and the Challenge of Truth Commissions*. New York: Routledge, 2011.

Indian and Northern Affairs Canada. Notes for an Address by the Honourable Jane Stewart, Minister of Indian Affairs and Northern Development, on the occasion of the unveiling of *Gathering Strength—Canada's Aboriginal Action Plan*. Ottawa: Indian and Northern Affairs Canada, 1998. http://www.aadnc-aandc.gc.ca/eng/1100100015725/1100100015726.

James, Matt. "Uncomfortable Comparisons: Canada's Truth and Reconciliation Commission in International Context." *Les ateliers de l'éthique/The Ethics Forum* 5, no. 2 (2010): 24–35.

James, M. "A Carnival of Truth? Knowledge, Ignorance, and the Canadian Truth and Reconciliation Commission." *International Journal of Transitional Justice* 6, no. 2 (2012): 182–204. https://doi.org/10.1093/ijtj/ijs010.

Jung, Courtney. "Canada and the Legacy of the Indian Residential Schools." In *Identities in Transition: Challenges for Transitional Justice in Divided Societies*, ed. Paige Arthur, 217–50. Cambridge, UK: Cambridge University Press, 2011., .

Kesselring, Rita. *Bodies of Truth: Law, Memory, and Emancipation in Post-Apartheid South Africa*. Stanford, CA: Stanford University Press, 2017.

Krystal, Henry, ed. *Massive Psychic Trauma*. Madison, CT: International Universities Press, 1968.

Law Commission of Canada. "Restoring Dignity: Responding to Child Abuse in Canadian Institutions." Ottawa: Minister of Public Works and Government Services, 2000.

Leader-Williams, Nigel, and Holly T. Dublin. "Charismatic Megafauna as 'Flagship Species.'" In *Priorities for the Conservation of Mammalian Biodiversity: Has the Panda Had Its Day?* ed. Abigail Entwistle and Nigel Dunstone, 53–81. Cambridge, UK: Cambridge University Press, 2010.

Le Goff, Jacques. *Histoire et Mémoire*. Paris: Gallimard, 1988.

Levi, Primo. *The Drowned and the Saved*. Trans. Raymond Rosenthal. New York: Vintage, 1988.

L'Heureux, Jacques. Unpublished letter from Les Missionnaires Oblats de Marie Immaculée, Ottawa, Ontario, to Chief Wilton Littlechild, Commissioner, Truth and Reconciliation Canada, 12 January 2011.

———. "The only politically acceptable speech about the Indian Residential Schools." Unpublished open letter, 29 June 2011.

———. Unpublished letter from Les Missionnaires Oblats de Marie Immaculée, Ottawa, Ontario, to Dan Ish, Chief Adjudicator, Regina, Saskatchewan, 1 February 2012.

Lindholm, Charles. "An Anthropology of Emotion." In *A Companion to Psychological Anthropology*, ed. Conerly Casey and Robert Edgerton, 30–47. Malden, MA: Blackwell, 2007.

Manovich, L. *The Language of New Media*. Cambridge, MA: The MIT Press, 2001.

Marcus, George. *Ethnography through Thick and Thin*. Princeton, NJ: Princeton University Press, 1998.

Mattingly, Cheryl, and Linda Garro, eds. *Narrative and the Cultural Construction of Illness and Healing*. Berkeley, Los Angeles: University of California Press, 2000.

McNally, Richard. *Remembering Trauma*. Cambridge, MA: Harvard University Press, 2003.

Milloy, John. *A National Crime: The Canadian Government and the Residential School System, 1879 to 1986*. Winnipeg, MB: University of Manitoba Press, 1999.

Minow, Martha. *Between Vengeance and Forgiveness: Facing History after Genocide and Mass Violence.* Boston, MA: Beacon, 1999.

———. "Institutions and Emotions: Redressing Mass Violence." In *The Passions of Law,* ed. Susan Bandes, 265–81. New York, London: New York University Press, 1999.

Moyn, Samuel. *The Last Utopia: Human Rights in History.* Cambridge, MA: Harvard University Press, 2010.

NABS (Native American Boarding School Healing Coalition). "Moving Forward: NABS Expands Staff and Board: The National Native American Boarding School Healing Coalition (NABS) Hires First Staff Member and Adds Four New Board Members to Help Jumpstart Truth and Reconciliation Process." Press release, 2 December 2015. Accessed 16 April 2017, http://www.boardingschoolhealing.org/wp-content/uploads/NABS-hires-staff-and-increases-board-of-directors-_12-2-15-Press-Release2.pdf.

Nagy, Rosemary. "The Scope and Bounds of Transitional Justice and the Canadian Truth and Reconciliation Commission." *International Journal of Transitional Justice* 7, no. 1 (2013): 52–73. https://doi.org/10.1093/ijtj/ijs034.

Niezen, Ronald. *The Origins of Indigenism: Human Rights and the Politics of Identity.* Berkeley and Los Angeles: The University of California Press, 2003.

———. *Public Justice and the Anthropology of Law.* Cambridge, UK: Cambridge University Press, 2010.

———. "The Law's Legal Anthropology." In *Human Rights at the Crossroads,* ed. Mark Goodale. Oxford, UK: Oxford University Press, 2012.

———. "Internet Suicide: Communities of Affirmation and the Lethality of Communication." *Transcultural Psychiatry* 50, no. 2 (2013): 303–22. https://doi.org/10.1177/1363461512473733.

———. "Templates and Exclusions: Victim Centrism in Canada's Truth and Reconciliation Commission on Indian Residential Schools." *Journal of the Royal Anthropological Institute* 22, no. 4 (2016): 920–38. https://doi.org/10.1111/1467-9655.12497.

———, and Marie Pierre Gadoua. ""Témoignage et histoire dans la Commission de vérité et de reconciliation du Canada." *Canadian Journal of Law and Society/ La Revue Canadienne* 29, no. 1 (2014): 21–42.

———, and Maria Sapignoli, eds. *Palaces of Hope: The Anthropology of Global Organizations.* Cambridge, UK: Cambridge University Press, 2017. https://doi.org/10.1017/9781316412190.

Nussbaum, Martha. "'Secret Sewers of Vice': Disgust, Bodies, and the Law." In *The Passions of Law,* ed. Susan Bandes, 19–62. New York, London: New York University Press, 1999.

Nwogu, Nneoma. "When and Why It Started: Deconstructing Victim-Centered Truth Commissions in the Context of Ethnicity-Based Conflict." *International*

Journal of Transitional Justice 4, no. 2 (2010): 275–89. https://doi.org/10.1093/ijtj/ijq010.

Paulson, Michael. "World Doesn't Share US View of Scandal: Clergy Sexual Abuse Reaches Far, Receives an Uneven Focus." *The Boston Globe*, 4 August 2002, A1. Accessed 11 September 2013, http://www.boston.com/globe/spotlight/abuse/stories/040802_world.htm.

Phelps, Theresa. *Shattered Voices: Language, Violence, and the Work of Truth Commissions.* Philadelphia, PA: University of Pennsylvania Press, 2004. https://doi.org/10.9783/9780812203271.

Popic, Linda. "Compensating Canada's 'Stolen Generations.'" *Indigenous Law Bulletin* 14, no. 7, issue 2 (2008). Accessed 31 July 2012, http://www.austlii.edu.au/au/journals/ILB/2008/4.html.

Pottage, Alain. "Introduction: The Fabrication of Persons and Things." In *Law, Anthropology, and the Constitution of the Social: Making Persons and Things*, ed. Alain Pottage and Martha Mundy, 1–39. Cambridge, UK: Cambridge University Press, 2004., . https://doi.org/10.1017/CBO9780511493751.001.

Quinn, Joanna. "The Politics of Acknowledgment: An Analysis of Uganda's Truth Commission." YCISS Working Paper no. 19, March 2003, York University. Accessed 26 September 2012, http://yciss.info.yorku.ca/files/2012/06/WP19-Quinn.pdf.

Rabinow, Paul. *Anthropos Today: Reflections on Modern Equipment.* Princeton, NJ: Princeton University Press, 2003.

Regan, Paulette. *Unsettling the Settler Within: Indian Residential Schools, Truth Telling, and Reconciliation in Canada.* Vancouver: University of British Columbia Press, 2010.

Ricoeur, Paul. "The Question of Proof in Freud's Psychoanalytic Writings." *Journal of the American Psychoanalytic Association* 25, no. 4 (1977): 835–72. https://doi.org/10.1177/000306517702500404.

Riles, Annelise. *Collateral Knowledge: Legal Reasoning in the Global Financial Markets.* Chicago, IL: University of Chicago Press, 2011. https://doi.org/10.7208/chicago/9780226719344.001.0001.

Robins, Simon. "Challenging the Therapeutic Ethic: A Victim-Centred Evaluation of Transitional Justice Process in Timor-Leste." *International Journal of Transitional Justice* 6, no. 1 (2012): 83–105. https://doi.org/10.1093/ijtj/ijr034.

Ross, Fiona. *Bearing Witness: Women and the Truth and Reconciliation Commission in South Africa.* London: Pluto, 2003.

Rotberg, Robert, and Dennis Thompson. "Truth Commissions and the Provision of Truth, Justice, and Reconciliation." In *Truth v. Justice: The Morality of Truth*

Commissions, ed. Robert Rotberg and Dennis Thompson, 3–21. Princeton, NJ: Princeton University Press, 2000. https://doi.org/10.1515/9781400832033-002.

Rottenburg, Richard. *Far-Fetched Facts: A Parable of Development Aid*. Trans. Allison Brown and Tom Lampert. Cambridge, MA: MIT Press, 2009. https://doi.org/10.7551/mitpress/9780262182645.001.0001.

Royal Commission on Aboriginal Peoples. *Report of the Royal Commission on Aboriginal Peoples, Volume 1: Looking Forward, Looking Back*. Ottawa, ON: Minister of Supply and Services Canada, 1996.

Sarfaty, Galit. *Values in Translation: Human Rights and the Culture of the World Bank*. Stanford, CA: Stanford University Press, 2012.

Senate of Canada. "Latest Debates of the Senate (Hansard)." 7 March 2017. Accessed 17 April 2017, https://sencanada.ca/en/content/sen/chamber/421/debates/102db_2017-03-07-e.

Sherwin, Richard. *Visualizing Law in the Age of the Digital Baroque: Arabesques and Entanglements*. New York: Routledge, 2011.

Shore, Megan. *Religion and Conflict Resolution: Christianity and South Africa's Truth and Reconciliation Commission*. Surrey, UK, and Burlington, VT: Ashgate, 2009.

Soosaar, David. "Bernard's Lawsuit Helped Natives Nationwide." *The Daily News (Halifax)*, 30 December 2007. Accessed 17 June 2017, http://archives.algomau.ca/main/sites/default/files/2010-061_014_008.pdf.

Spence, Donald. *Narrative Truth and Historical Truth: Meaning and Interpretation in Psychoanalysis*. New York: Norton, 1982.

Stout, Madeleine Dion, and Rick Harp. *Lump Sum Compensation Payments Research Project: The Circle Rechecks Itself*. Ottawa: Aboriginal Healing Foundation, 2007.

Sunstein, Cass. *Infotopia: How Many Minds Produce Knowledge*. Oxford, UK: Oxford University Press, 2006.

Tarde, Gabriel. *Les Transformations du Droit: Étude Sociologique*. Paris: Félix Alcan, 1893.

———. *On Communication and Social Influence*. Ed. Terry Clark. Chicago, IL: University of Chicago Press, 1969.

Tate, Winnifred. *Counting the Dead: The Culture and Politics of Human Rights Activism in Colombia*. Berkeley, Los Angeles: University of California Press, 2007.

———. "Proxy Citizenship and Transnational Advocacy: Colombian Activists from Putumayo to Washington, DC." *American Ethnologist* 40, no. 1 (2013): 55–70. https://doi.org/10.1111/amet.12005.

Tolley, Alvin. "Federal Rules of Engagement: The Government's War against Survivors and the Churches." Accessed 21 May 2013, http://www.turtleisland.org/news/ours.pdf.

Truth and Reconciliation Commission of Canada. *Missing Children and Unmarked Burials: Research Recommendations. Report of the Working Group on Missing Children and Unmarked Burials.* Accessed 27 January 2013, http://www.trc.ca/websites/trcinstitution/File/pdfs/Working_group_on_Mis_7456E0.pdf.

———. *They Came for the Children: Canada, Aboriginal Peoples, and Residential Schools.* Winnipeg, MB: Author, 2012.

———. *TRC Findings.* 2015. Accessed 17 April 2017, http://www.trc.ca/websites/trcinstitution/index.php?p=890.

———. *Truth and Reconciliation Commission of Canada: Calls to Action.* 2015. Accessed 17 April 2017, http://www.trc.ca/websites/trcinstitution/File/2015/Findings/Calls_to_Action_English2.pdf.

Truth and Reconciliation Commission, Sierra Leone. *Witness to Truth: Report of the Sierra Leone Truth and Reconciliation Commission.* Accessed 26 September 2012, http://www.sierra-leone.org/TRCDocuments.html.

Walker, Connie. "New Documents May Shed Light on Residential School Deaths." *CBC News,* 7 January 2014. Accessed 14 April 2017, http://www.cbc.ca/news/indigenous/new-documents-may-shed-light-on-residential-school-deaths-1.2487015.

Wassermann, Jakob. *Der Fall Maurizius. 1928.* Munich: Langen/Müller, 2008.

Waugh, Thomas, Michael Brendan Baker, and Ezra Winton, eds. *Challenge for Change: Activist Documentary at the National Film Board of Canada.* Montreal, Kingston: McGill-Queen's University Press, 2010.

Weber, Max. *From Max Weber, Essays in Sociology. 1948.* Ed. Hans Gerth and C. Wright Mills. New York: Routledge, 2007.

Wesley-Esquimaux, Cynthia, and Magdalena Smolewski. *Historic Trauma and Aboriginal Healing.* Ottawa: Aboriginal Healing Foundation, 2004.

Wilson-Raybould, Jody. "Justice Minister Jody Wilson-Raybould's Opening Address at UN Permanent Forum on Indigenous Issues." *Northern Public Affairs,* 9 May 2016. Accessed 16 April 2017, http://www.northernpublicaffairs.ca/index/justice-minister-jody-wilson-rayboulds-opening-address-at-un-permanent-forum-on-indigenous-issues.

Wilson, Richard A. *The Politics of Truth and Reconciliation in South Africa.* Cambridge, UK: Cambridge University Press, 2001. https://doi.org/10.1017/CBO9780511522291.

Yalom, Irvin, and Molyn Leszcz. *The Theory and Practice of Group Psychotherapy.* 5th ed. New York: Basic Books, 2005.

Yellow Horse Brave Heart, Maria. "The Historical Trauma Response among Natives and Its Relationship with Substance Abuse: A Lakota Illustration." *Journal of Psychoactive Drugs* 35, no. 1 (January–March 2003): 7–13. https://doi.org/10.1080/02791072.2003.10399988.

Yellow Horse Brave Heart, Maria. "The Return to the Sacred Path: Healing the Historical Trauma and Historical Unresolved Grief Response among the Lakota through a Psychoeducational Group Intervention." *Smith College Studies in Social Work* 68, no. 3 (1998): 287–305. https://doi.org/10.1080/00377319809517532.

Yellow Horse Brave Heart, Maria, and L.M. DeBruyn. "The American Indian Holocaust: Healing Historical Unresolved Grief." *American Indian and Alaska Native Mental Health Research* 8, no. 2 (1998): 56–78.

Young, Allan. *The Harmony of Illusions: Inventing Post-Traumatic Stress Disorder.* Princeton, NJ: Princeton University Press, 1995.

INDEX

tangents and digressions in, 99–102
and truth, 83–84
tissues at events, 64–65
Tolley, Alvin, 153
To Tell the Story (movie), 127–28
trauma
and compensation, 48–49
historical trauma, 113–16, 152
inclusion in, 153
and memory, 107–10, 111–12, 152
and survival, 18–19
and TRC, 5, 152
triggering and flashbacks, 105–6, 107–8, 112
triggering
definition, 105
health support, 106–7, 112
and trauma, 105–6, 107–8, 112
warnings about, 105, 107
trolls and trolling (online), 119–20
Trudeau government, 162–63, 164
truth, as quality of TRC, 83–84
Truth and Reconciliation Commission (TRC) of Canada
accusations in, 54
achievements, 151, 163–65
activities and role, 146–47
and apology of federal government, 37
audiences (*See* audience of TRC events)
Calls to Action, 162, 164–66
as civil litigation case, 3–4, 8–9
digital technologies, 10–11, 88
documentary records and archives, 131, 161
emotions in hearings, 61, 85–86, 91–92, 109
emphasis on survivors, 147, 159
"ethnos" in, 6–7
events descriptions and locations, 7–8
exclusion and inclusion, 79, 152, 153–54, 155
exhibits and displays at events, 132–35
experience of events and narration, 5
Facebook page, 117, 123n40
federal participation, 78–79, 161–62
films at start of events, 68–71, 148
French name of, 83
good stories in, 61–62

guidelines and ideas, 112–13, 115–16
and historical trauma, 115–16, 152
history and historical witnessing, 130, 131–32, 150
and human rights, 113
inaugural opening ceremony, 62–63
issue of "naming names," 3, 4–5
judicial powers, 4–5, 146–47
mandate, 4, 72, 74, 75, 76, 102, 131, 146, 159, 160, 161
and mental health, 5
non-aboriginal children, 74–75
permissiveness in hearings, 59, 109–10, 148
persuasion of public audiences, 4, 6, 15–16, 60, 146–48, 150
preferred narratives and themes, 68–70, 102, 148, 150
presentation of work to UN, 159–60
public exposure and dissemination, 10, 11–13
qualities of, 3–6, 151, 153
registration form, 79
and reorientation of federal policy, 163
reports and results, 163–64
sacredness and rituals, 61–67
secrecy in, 8–9
statements collected, 7
templates in (*See* templates)
testimony by clergy, 52–53, 138, 152
and trauma, 5, 152
truth and testimony, 83–84
the unsayable, 58–59, 151
victim centrism, 166–67, 169
victimization of children, 5
witnesses (*See* witnesses in TRC)
See also specific events and topics
Truth and Reconciliation Commission of South Africa (1995–2002)
issue of "naming names," 2
public exposure, 10–11
reports and results, 163–65
victim centrism, 167, 168
truth and reconciliation commissions
children's victimization, 5
chronology and description, 2